SHATTERED GRIEF

SHATTERED GRIEF

HOW THE PANDEMIC TRANSFORMED THE SPIRITUALITY OF DEATH IN AMERICA

NATASHA L. MIKLES

Columbia University Press   *New York*

Columbia University Press
Publishers Since 1893
New York   Chichester, West Sussex
cup.columbia.edu

Copyright © 2024 Columbia University Press
All rights reserved

Library of Congress Cataloging-in-Publication Data
Names: Mikles, Natasha L., 1986– author.
Title: Shattered grief : how the pandemic transformed the spirituality of death in America / Natasha L. Mikles.
Description: New York : Columbia University Press, [2024] | Includes bibliographical references and index.
Identifiers: LCCN 2023055034 (print) | LCCN 2023055035 (ebook) | ISBN 9780231211468 (hardback) | ISBN 9780231211475 (trade paperback) | ISBN 9780231558921 (ebook)
Subjects: LCSH: Death—Religious aspects—United States. | COVID-19 (Disease)—Religious aspects—United States. | Pandemics—Religious aspects—United States. | Grief—Religious aspects—United States. | Funeral rites and ceremonies—United States.
Classification: LCC BT162.D57 M55 2024 (print) | LCC BT162.D57 (ebook) | DDC 202/.3—dc23/eng/20240126
LC record available at https://lccn.loc.gov/2023055034
LC ebook record available at https://lccn.loc.gov/2023055035

Cover design: Elliott S. Cairns

*For my parents,
who survived the pandemic;
and Arun,
who did not.*

CONTENTS

Acknowledgments ix
List of Research Interlocutors and Conversation Partners xi

Introduction: In a Barbecue Parking Lot   1

1 Ritual   17

2 Community   59

3 Narrative   105

4 Trauma   151

Conclusion: Taking the Book of Job Seriously   195

Appendix: Notes on Methodology   203
Notes   209
Bibliography   227
Index   237

ACKNOWLEDGMENTS

The COVID-19 pandemic taught all of us that no one is an island and that we are far more interconnected than anyone previously realized. It is impossible, therefore, to thank everyone ultimately responsible for this work coming to be. To some extent, without the vast web of colleagues, students, baristas, nail artists, and grocery store employees who keep my life whole, *Shattered Grief* would not have happened. I highlight a few people below but am grateful for everyone who populated my universe during the pandemic and beyond.

I want to thank Lisa Haegele, who provided the earliest seeds for this project and Erin Burke, who brainstormed nurturing them into their fullest form. Stephen Prothero read early chapters and gave invaluable guidance at the project's birth, for which I have the utmost gratitude. Many colleagues at Texas State also gave me the opportunity to share my work in its initial stages, including Josh Paddison, Justin Randolph, and Jo Ann Carson; I similarly thank Kalpana Jain for giving me feedback on my ideas in their infancy.

I am eternally grateful to Wendy Lochner, Lowell Frye, Kathryn Jorge, and all the editorial staff at Columbia University Press. Their encouragement helped me find my voice in discussing a difficult topic far afield from my academic training and gave me the courage to write the type of academic book I always wanted to read. Early reviewers of this work, both those known and unknown to me, have also been critical in correcting errors, developing my insights to their furthest extent, and creating a work that I can be proud of. I hope one day to be as generous and kind a colleague as such reviewers were to me.

Shattered Grief would not have been possible without my husband Joe, who is my tireless cheerleader, in-house editor, intellectual partner, whiskey sommelier, pirate-crusader, and all-around adventuring companion. Perhaps it would have been written a little more quickly if we did not have so much fun together, but I would not trade even the tiniest moment spent with you for a timelier release. My family, spread from coast-to-coast across the United States, were also important sources of support. I am particularly grateful, however, for my parents who have always encouraged me in my academic and professional pursuits, even if they did not always understand them.

Above all, I owe my perpetual gratitude to my research interlocutors and conversation partners, who allowed me into their lives during what was one of the darkest and most painful periods. Their voices form the heart of *Shattered Grief*, and I am humbled by their trust. Without their generosity of spirit and faith in me as a researcher, this project would never have come to fruition.

RESEARCH INTERLOCUTORS AND CONVERSATION PARTNERS

Shattered Grief would have been impossible without the generosity, benevolence, and vulnerability of those who agreed to be interviewed. As a guide for readers, I have listed them here, along with a few contextual details. To protect the privacy and emotional intimacy of grief, those who lost loved ones to COVID-19 are referred to by their first name only, or by pseudonyms when requested. The names of religious, medical, and funerary professionals are provided in full, along with their institutional affiliation at time of interview. Because of their role as civic leaders, such contextualizing information is necessary and may aid readers' interpretation of their words. Some of the conversation partners who described encountering death in a professional setting, however, still requested to give anonymous interviews and be referenced only by a pseudonym or first name alone. I have indicated such individuals with an asterisk.

LOST LOVED ONES TO COVID-19

Arla, Southern California
Arla is a multicultural educator and high school administrator with Chinese, Peruvian Quechuan Indian, and Scandinavian backgrounds.
She identifies as Evangelical Christian and lost her father to COVID-19 in December 2020.

Amanda, Southern California
Amanda is a registered member of the Apache Nation and identifies as Christian.
She lost her mother to COVID-19 in January 2021.

Bianca, north Texas
Bianca is a Hispanic Italian educator who lost her grandmother to COVID-19 in February 2021.

Carmen, south Florida
Carmen is a Hispanic nursing student originally from New York City.
She lost her mother to COVID-19 in May 2020.

Dan, central Texas
Raised Roman Catholic, Dan now identifies as an atheist.
He lost his grandmother to COVID-19 in March 2020.

Gurpreet, New York metropolitan area
Gurpreet is a second-generation, Indian American Sikh living in New York City.
He lost his father to COVID-19 in March 2020.

RESEARCH INTERLOCUTORS AND CONVERSATION PARTNERS ⌘ xiii

Jennifer, central Texas
A nurse by training, Jennifer lost her mother to COVID-19 in March 2021.
She and her mother were converts to the Church of Jesus Christ of Latter-day Saints.

Julia, Maryland
An insurance professional, Julia is a second-generation, Filipino American woman who identifies as Roman Catholic.
She lost her brother with developmental disabilities to COVID-19 in January 2021.

Kay, Chicagoland
Of Puerto Rican descent, Kay lost both her father and grandfather to COVID-19 in summer and fall 2020.

Manpreet, New York metropolitan area
Manpreet is an Indian American woman living in the New York metropolitan area who was raised in the Sikh religious tradition.
She lost her father to COVID-19 in March 2020.

Olivia, northern Virginia
Olivia is an African American veteran who lost her father to COVID-19 in late summer 2020.

Paul, New York City
A Roman Catholic man in his seventies, Paul lost his Jewish wife to COVID-19 in December 2020.

Sabila, New Jersey
A second-generation, Pakistani American woman, Sabila lost her father to COVID-19 in March 2020. She is the founder of the COVID-19 Loss Support for Family & Friends Facebook group.

Sofia, south Texas
Sofia is a Hispanic college student who lost her grandfather to COVID-19.

Yoon Tae, north Georgia
A second-generation, Korean American man, Yoon Tae lost his father to COVID-19 in January 2021.

RELIGIOUS PROFESSIONALS, WITH AFFILIATION AT TIME OF INTERVIEW

Reverend Richard R. Andre, C. S. P., Austin, Texas
Associate pastor, St. Austin Catholic Parish

Bishop Bruce Baillio, San Antonio, Texas
San Pedro Ward, San Antonio Texas North Stake, Church of Jesus Christ of Latter-day Saints

Ērvad Khursheed Dastur (Barjor), Houston, Texas
Zoroastrian Association of Houston

Rabbi Neil Blumofe, Austin, Texas
Senior rabbi, Congregation Agudas Achim

Reverend Kristel Clayville, PhD, Chicago, Illinois
Disciples of Christ, medical chaplain

Ajit Giani, Austin, Texas
Bahá'í of Austin, secretary of Interfaith Action of Central Texas

Venerable Doctor Jue Ji, Austin, Texas
Fo Guang Shan Xiang Yun Buddhist Temple

Reverend Charles R. Kuhlman, C.S.P., Austin, Texas
Pastor, St. Austin Catholic Parish

Pastor Lou McElroy, Houston, Texas
Senior pastor, Antioch Missionary Baptist Church

President Greg Neuberger, San Antonio, Texas
San Antonio Texas North Stake, Church of Jesus Christ of Latter-day Saints

Swami Nikhilanand, Driftwood, Texas
Radha Madhav Dham Hindu Temple

Imam Sheikh Attia Omara, Austin, Texas
Islamic Center of Lake Travis

Bishop Suffragan Kathryn M. Ryan, Austin, Texas
Episcopal Diocese of Texas

Pastor Craig Taylor, Houston, Texas
Senior pastor, Willow Meadows Baptist Church

Reverend Chuck Treadwell, Austin, Texas
Rector, St. David's Episcopal Church

President Jason Tveten, San Antonio, Texas
Texas San Antonio Mission, Church of Jesus Christ of Latter-day Saints

MEDICAL PROFESSIONALS, WITH AFFILIATION AT TIME OF INTERVIEW

Mary Barton, central Texas
Nurse, Ascension Seton Medical Center
Mary worked extensively during the pandemic as a travel nurse in hardest hit areas.

*Dr. Black, east Texas
Semi-retired primary care doctor

Christine Celio, central Texas
Clinical nurse specialist, Ascension Seton Medical Center
Christine specialized in supportive and palliative care.

*Kevin, Houston, Texas
Emergency nurse, Houston Methodist Hospital

Dr. Jack Kravitz, north Florida
Hospice and palliative care doctor, HCA Florida Northwest Hospital

Dr. Larry C. Kravitz, central Texas
Primary care physician, Austin Regional Clinic

Dr. Paul E. Tatum III, central Texas
Hospice and palliative care doctor, Ascension Seton Medical Center

FUNERARY PROFESSIONALS, WITH AFFILIATION AT TIME OF INTERVIEW

Richard Davis, Pflugerville, Texas
General manager, Cook-Walden Funeral Home & Cemetery

Mitzi Chafetz, Austin, Texas
Funeral director, Austin Natural Funerals

Eric Neuhaus, Austin, Texas
Founder, Green Cremation Texas

*Sophie, Houston, Texas
Funeral director, Winfred Funeral Home

MISCELLANEOUS OTHER PROFESSIONALS, WITH AFFILIATION AT TIME OF INTERVIEW

*Carla, New York metropolitan area
Spirit medium

Scott van Camp, LMFT, Austin, Texas
Grief counselor, Yellow Chair Counseling

Susan, Southern California
Spirit medium and intuitive

Maria, New England
Spirit medium

Martha B. Heymann, Corpus Christi, Texas
INELDA certified end-of-life doula and grief coach
Founder, Together Forward

INTRODUCTION

In a Barbecue Parking Lot

On January 12, 2021, I was sitting in the parking lot of Franklin Barbecue in Austin, Texas, waiting for takeout and watching my friend's funeral on my phone. It was a strange and horrible juxtaposition, to say the least. In times before the COVID-19 pandemic, Franklin Barbecue would have had a line, hundreds of people long, snaking through the parking lot, some customers arriving as early as 6 a.m. to wait hours for slabs of brisket, ribs, and smoked turkey. Franklin had shifted to "takeout only" during the pandemic, and my husband and I had guests in town who wanted to experience the famous barbecue joint. My friend Arun had died of COVID-19 only a few days earlier, so while we waited for our barbecue to be delivered to the car's trunk and my friends commented on the vibrant tattoos of passersby, I watched his funeral on my phone.

Arun and I had not been close, but we were part of the same social circle—a group of professors who met weekly at the little bar across the street from Texas State University to drink beer and swap stories about our foibles while teaching students at one of the largest public universities in Texas. Arun's death hit all of us hard. He was young and healthy, not the anonymous statistic of elderly death we had all seen on the news; he left behind an almost-finished dissertation and two little girls who were not even teenagers yet. His daughters lived with his ex-wife and his parents were thousands of miles away in New Jersey, so, another professor from our little group was asked to clean out Arun's apartment. She remembered walking in and finding evidence of a life halted in medias res—leftovers in the fridge that were still good and half-folded laundry on the dining room table. "He had just done a big run to Costco, Natasha," she told me, "There were bags and bags of unopened nuts, crackers, and dried fruit. Do I eat them? Do I throw them away? What do I do?"

Death, funerary traditions, and the afterlife were central components of my scholarly research in Asian religious traditions, and I was familiar with the complex rituals surrounding a traditional Hindu funeral. The body would be draped in flowers and blessed by a Hindu priest chanting mantras from the ancient Vedic texts that are the foundation of Hindu ritual practice. Auspicious spices would be smeared along the body, then it would be cremated to allow the spirit to escape and go on to its next rebirth—ideally in a large, outdoor funeral pyre. In America, Hindu immigrants have elected for a traditional crematorium, although many British Hindu groups have championed changing the legal code to allow for open-air cremation. Despite this academic knowledge, I was unprepared for experiencing such a funeral personally. I watched as a Hindu pandit chanted around my friend's flower-covered body, maintaining a significant distance for safety, before anointing Arun with turmeric, smeared on a Q-tip to ensure as little touching of the body as possible. Arun's body was later transported to a crematorium and his father pressed the button to start the machine. Usually, the eldest son lights his father's funerary pyre, but in tragic cases like these a father must take on that responsibility.

There were so many things that made this funeral feel wrong and even perverse. From our conversations over beer, I knew that Arun had a complicated relationship with his Hindu heritage, and I sensed he would have been uncomfortable having a traditional Hindu funeral like this. However, during his illness, Arun had been swiftly transferred from San Marcos to a larger hospital in Houston after his mother's relentless calling located an open ventilator. After his death, the body was quickly removed from the hospital to allow for the next wave of COVID-19 patients and his funeral had to be planned in haste, from across the country, by family left unable to confirm his postmortem desires. Beyond what I knew would have been Arun's personal discomfort with the funeral, all of the rituals I might expect at a Hindu funeral had to be modified to protect the health and safety of the priest and family present, introducing the exotic presence of Q-tips and plastic gloves into rituals that had been performed largely without change for centuries. And there was, unforgettably, the digital interface. Watching his funeral from a camera, rockily positioned over a door in a distant east Texas funeral home, only added to the sense that this was somehow not real, like a scene from a Netflix series or a newsreel of a far-off land.

My experience is not unique. Millions of Americans underwent an ordeal similar to my own as they watched the funerals of colleagues, friends, and family members from afar. At the time of writing in December 2023, the Centers for Disease Control (CDC) reports that over a million Americans have died of COVID-19,[1] but the World Health Organization's calculation of excess deaths—deaths that occur at a greater than expected pace and may be a better indicator of COVID's impact—put America's death toll from the pandemic closer to two million.[2]

The reported global death toll at the time of writing is over six million deaths with close to fifteen million excess deaths.[3]

However, it was not only our funerals that were isolated, but our grief as well. The pandemic meant that our mourning took place separated from loved ones—privately at home, hidden behind digital screens, in small outdoor groups of ten or less, and during masked moments, rushed in passing. Such isolated mourning represented a marked transformation from times before the pandemic, when grief was, at least in part, attended to communally—in mosques praying together the Salat al-Janazah (the customary Islamic funerary prayer), in Baptist prayer groups meditating on Psalm 34, in Sikh gurdwaras singing the traditional funerary hymn of the Kirtan Sohila. Beyond these religious institutions, pre-pandemic grief had a place in other community spaces that form the bedrock of American society at large—at wakes and parties with family and friends, in coffee shops with office colleagues, or in public rituals of memorial acknowledging those we have lost. In light of the pandemic, however, these public spaces, religious institutions, and spiritual communities were largely unavailable or radically transformed.

It was with Arun's death that this research project commenced, and I began seeking to understand how the way we "do death" in America has changed in the wake of COVID-19. I reached out to dozens of individuals to hear about their experiences during the pandemic, and by the end of my research I had collected close to one hundred hours of interviews with a variety of stakeholders involved with death in America. These included funerary professionals and those working in the medical sector, as well as ordained clergy and other religious leaders seeking to guide their communities through the crisis. I also spoke with grief counselors, death doulas, spirit mediums, community organizers, and others working one-on-one with those who were grieving. The largest and most important group that I interviewed were those who lost loved ones to COVID-19, the majority of whom I connected with through social media and other virtual communities. The ethnic, cultural, and religious range of those I spoke with is noteworthy. COVID-19 affected absolutely everyone living in America, which is among the most religiously and ethnically diverse countries in the world. My conversation partners included Indian American Sikhs, Native American Christians, Egyptian and Pakistani American Muslims, Texan Jews, African American veterans, Catholic widowers mourning Jewish wives, Chinese immigrant Buddhists, converts to the Church of Jesus Christ of Latter-day Saints, Bahá'í community organizers, Episcopal bishops, Chinese American Evangelicals, Hindu meditation leaders, Parsi Zoroastrian ritual specialists, and a whole host of individuals expressing other religious and ethnic identities. During an early presentation of this research, an audience member commented on the diversity of voices, wondering if I had gone out of my way to find interview subjects outside the boundaries of "traditional America." The truth is that Americans are simply much more diverse than the image that many people hold in their minds, and this book reflects that diversity.

Academics are notorious for deflecting any engagement with issues of true emotion or vulnerability via the shield of research, and perhaps my project is no different. However, as a scholar of religion, the ways in which we as a human society deal with death have long fascinated me. For most of recorded human history, death and its associated rituals have largely been the purview of religious institutions. This changed, in some part, for Americans in the nineteenth and twentieth centuries with the rise of public hospitals and funeral homes.[4] However, at a foundational level, death is still generally understood as a profound experience of transition that must be marked with rituals, spiritual support, and the participation of a collective community in mourning. While these can, of course, happen outside the confines of a specific religious tradition, religious institutions are most commonly the places where Americans engage with these practices. It is important, therefore, to document and consider how COVID-19 has transformed our deathways in tandem with religious identities, beliefs, and practices, for these are where many Americans seek comfort from their grief.

A LITURGY OF DEATH

COVID-19 has brought about incredible transformations to American religious life and deathways, especially to what I call the "liturgy of death." Originally a Greek term meaning "work done on behalf of the people," *liturgy* today refers to the specific and appropriate way to do a religious practice or ritual. While it is most often associated with Christianity, other religious traditions like Buddhism have begun adopting the term to label their own orchestrated rituals and reoccurring observances. Indeed, the term reflects an expectation for how an event is going to go, although few Masses, services, or rituals ever follow such a script perfectly. We can imagine that there are liturgies all throughout our lives—ways that we expect certain life events and life transitions to happen.

Thus, there is a liturgy of death—a way that we, as Americans, roughly expect a loved one's passing to transpire. Throughout history and across cultures, human societies have developed liturgies of death. In the fifteenth century, Latin texts known as *Ars Moriendi* (The Art of Dying) provided Christian readers with guidance on how to have "a good death";[5] Muslims have generally looked to hadith and other stories about Muhammad as a primer on the best way to die;[6] and medieval Japanese Buddhists read manuals detailing how to orient the body and chant during one's final moments to ensure rebirth in Amida's glorious Pure Land.[7] In our own context, one particularly prevalent (if unwritten) liturgy that many Americans have come to expect goes something like this:

- A sudden event requires a rushed visit to the emergency room, or a mysterious symptom requires further testing.
- Test results bring bad news.
- Extensive medical treatment to battle the illness follows.
- An acknowledgment by the medical team that all that can has been done.
- A quiet transition to hospice.
- Family members travel to see the dying.
- Stories, expressions of emotion, and final words are shared with the dying.
- Friends and family come over to make food, clean house, and help grieving families cope.
- A funeral where the deceased's legacy and impact can be publicly appreciated takes place.
- There is repeated checking in and assistance from friends and family in the days, weeks, and months after the death.

Such a liturgy reflects one expectation for how death will proceed—a social script and a mental map for what death might look like in twenty-first-century American society. The liturgies we hold are, of course, as diverse as America itself, and it is impossible to detail the attributes of a liturgy shared by every American. I would maintain that all liturgies feature certain expectations and hopes: that family and friends will be able to be at the death bed, a desire to know that one's wishes for medical care will be observed, to have the opportunity to begin processing grief through shared last words, as well as to mourn and celebrate a life together with friends and family.

However diverse, the liturgies of death as Americans understand them were fundamentally fractured by COVID-19. Funerals could not be held, loved ones could not be visited in the hospital, and public grieving was denied by a nation (at least in part) unsure whether the pandemic was really happening or not. Obviously, before the COVID-19 pandemic, not every death followed this liturgy—there were sudden deaths from car accidents, children dying before parents, and an uneven distribution of medical treatments resulting in deplorable and unnecessary deaths. However, such deaths are understood as *especially* tragic specifically *because* they do not follow our established liturgy of death—they are the exception which proves the rule. Additionally, while such deaths may not have followed our expectations, the second half of the liturgy—the funerals and commemorations—could follow apace, allowing for public grieving, mourning, and the support of a larger social network rushing to the bereaved's aid.

Shattered Grief examines how COVID-19's fracturing of our liturgies of death impacted—and continues to impact—American grief, spirituality, and religious practice. Grief and religion are not necessarily bedfellows, but oftentimes religious traditions are called upon to address and provide meaning to emotional anguish.[8] Hospital chaplain Kristel Clayville identified this inclination through her own work in medical settings, explaining that "Hospitals are big boxes of grief and everyone in them is grieving something. In that context, religion becomes the solution to the problem of grief—at least that is how the hospital administration and the medical team see religion working. While sometimes medical teams think of religion as a problem or barrier to care, in situations of public grief—be that anger, vocal displays of emotion, or unsettling and heartbroken demonstrations—they see grief as the problem and religion as the solution."[9] This conception of religion as a potential antidote to grief is found outside the medical world as well. Scholar of religion Thomas Tweed affirms the idea that a central function of religion is confronting, contextualizing, and addressing emotional suffering and grief.[10]

When the cultural models through which we encounter death and grief change, our relationship with the religious tools by which we interpret and process that grief will change as well. For many individuals, religion has served as a source of great comfort during their experience of losing a loved one to COVID-19. But for others, the pandemic fundamentally transformed the ways in which they understood their spiritual and religious identities. *Shattered Grief* not only documents this period, but also seeks to begin analyzing where we see religion serving as a comfort, as an arena for innovation, or as a hindrance to overcoming the grief and trauma of COVID-19.

As a result, this is not a book that simply details stories of Americans finding solace in their religious communities and their belief in seeing their loved ones again. Some people took great comfort in their faith, but others left their churches entirely, questioned the leadership of priests and pastors, or explored alternative forms of spirituality unthinkable to them before the pandemic. The pandemic's confusion became the fertile ground out of which new spiritual traditions and rituals emerged. Nurses on the COVID-19 floor created rituals, performed for them alone, to commemorate the seemingly endless stream of death, while those grieving built transnational, virtual communities that became havens of sympathy and refuge from a vocal minority who refused to accept the pandemic's truth. The pandemic also fundamentally undermined the religious beliefs and identities of many, causing rifts within religious communities that, to this day, have not healed. What emerges is a snapshot of an American people grappling with their grief, their religion, and their spirituality, as the liturgy of death changes around them. One thing this study reveals is that sometimes religion changes the experience of grief, and sometimes grief changes the experience of religion.

WHAT ARE WE TALKING ABOUT WHEN WE TALK ABOUT "RELIGION"?

Shattered Grief is about religion and spirituality, but these frequently used terms have a long and convoluted history that often makes scholars like me hesitant to use them. In the past, scholars spent inordinate amounts of time debating the exact boundaries of "religion." An early definition was a belief in gods and similarly divine figures that inspired feelings of absolute dependence in believers.[11] Theorists like Émile Durkheim focused their definitions on religion's social effects, arguing that religion serves to produce a unified moral community with coordinated goals, interests, and identities.[12] Others emphasized religion's political aspects as a means to control society and pacify marginalized groups.[13] Psychologist William James famously highlighted the transcendent experiences of individuals as the key to understanding religion.[14]

It is hard to define religion, because at some fundamental level, religion does not really *exist*—at least not in the way that rocks and trees and puppy dogs do. Far from being a term with intrinsic meaning that identifies something tangible in the world, the category of religion is at least, in part, a construct of the early modern European milieu.[15] Most cultures do not have a word that easily translates to religion in the generic, categorical sense of the word. Arabic refers to the way of life taken on by followers of Islam as *dīn*; Chinese refers to what we call Buddhism, Taoism, and Confucianism as simply the teachings (*jiao*) of the various communities (*fo*, *dao*, and *ru* respectively); many other languages similarly have a word to identify their own unique way of doing offerings, prayers, contemplations, and other rituals. There is, however, a lack of the transcultural and transnational categorical designator of religion. This is not to say that individuals outside of Europe were not praying, making offerings, or telling stories about gods and goddesses before European intervention, only that it was a European impulse to first gather these things together in a single category and call them religion. The word religion, therefore, is a way that the speaker organizes the world, grouping together certain things they see as having similarities and putting to the side ones they perceive as not belonging. This is why people can have boisterous debates about what groups in America deserve tax-exempt status as religions and whether certain activities or groups should be labeled as "superstitions" or "cults" (all categorical terms that entail the same vested interests and messiness as religion).

"Spirituality" is an even trickier word because the way that it is used in contemporary America is generally to define what it is not, rather than what it is—to emphasize one's freedom from institutional and communal identity markers. For these reasons, spirituality is sometimes understood in opposition to religion— something personal and individual, while religion involves rules and communities. However, just as there is no single, accepted definition for religion, there is no single, accepted definition for spirituality. Whenever this word is invoked, the individual is not only defining the term but is communicating something significant about why they used it rather than religion. It is the job of listeners—scholars and friends alike—to suss out what they mean. Here, I use spirituality largely in deference to the way that my conversation partners did; as a term reflecting the feelings of, and practices related to, personal fulfillment and understanding of a transcendent significance to the universe.

While these caveats on religion and spirituality are important to note, they should not halt our conversation entirely. Religion and spirituality are categories used today by Americans to make sense of their personal beliefs and practices, so they are words which scholars like me must continue to use. I am not particularly concerned with attempting to develop final and accurate definitions of these words. Rather, I am interested in those attributes or features that tend to cluster around these categories and how individual speakers understand or designate them as religious or as spiritual.

Instead of defining religion by any one criterion, historian Catherine Albanese has proposed framing our discussion in terms of four criteria: Creed (i.e., beliefs), Code (i.e., rules), Cultus (i.e., rituals), and Communities (i.e., those things bound together by the other three).[16] These dimensions not only provide the foundation for a comparison, but also help to tease apart the various components that combine to produce something as rich and complex as a religious tradition. Adopting a similar approach, *Shattered Grief* is organized along four broad facets that inform religious or spiritual life: *ritual*, *community*, *narrative*, and *trauma*. These are most certainly not the totality of what makes a religion, or even the essential qualifications for something to be a religion. Instead, these are the four sites of religious identity, practice, and belief where the most dramatic transformations have occurred in the wake of COVID-19. As will become apparent, each of these four facets harbors its own web of complexity that I will attempt to gently disentangle and reweave in each chapter.

With the exception of trauma, each element has long been considered necessary for, or foundational to, a religion. While the human experience of trauma has always existed, our vocabulary for acknowledging and thinking about trauma and its effects is relatively new. As a result, the relationship of trauma and religion is rather understudied and undertheorized. However, during my interviews, over and over, people used the words "trauma" and "traumatic" to describe their experiences. So, while trauma is not necessarily an objectively measurable reality, this term was meaningful for my research subjects and helped them describe their experiences in ways that conveyed the profound significance of those events in their lives. Much as people turn to religious traditions in the face of death, religion is often called upon to help heal individuals after experiences that we would call traumatic. As will be discussed in chapter 4, sometimes religion and spirituality have a great deal to say to someone suffering from a traumatic experience, but sometimes they do not.

LIMITATIONS AND RESOURCES

Shattered Grief is a snapshot of a specific moment in American life. In that way, it is the beginning of a conversation and not the final word on how COVID-19 affected Americans' grief and religious life. As previously noted, the foundation of this research is a collection of interviews conducted between January and August 2021. In terms of the pandemic's timeline, this situates the majority of research in the middle of the second wave of

COVID-19, but largely before the rise of the Delta and Omicron variants and the post-vaccination waves. While I aspired to include some reflection on the pandemic in its Delta, Omicron, and post-vaccination realities, readers should note that this book is largely a product of the pre-vaccination, early 2021 milieu. The two sets of individuals who made up the largest group of my interviewees were religious professionals and those who lost loved ones to COVID-19; however, every interview was an important moment in documenting a distinctive voice working to understand and make sense of the death, chaos, and religious change brought about by the pandemic.

While I tried to gather as many diverse interlocutors and conversation partners as possible to reflect the wide-ranging American experience, I was fundamentally limited by who was willing to talk to me. Understandably, in the middle of a pandemic, many religious leaders, medical staff, and grieving families were not in a place to reply to a researcher's email, often sent with little prior introduction. The geographic spread became somewhat skewed as well; virtually all of the religious and funerary leaders were located in central Texas, while those grieving the death of a loved one from COVID-19 often emailed me from across the country. Despite these difficulties, I managed to collect a racially, religiously, and culturally diverse sampling from a wide swath of American life over eight months during the pandemic. When appropriate to the discussion, I will highlight these diverse cultural and religious elements. These are also related in my glossary of research interlocutors and conversation partners. Further reflections on the methodological component of this book are highlighted in the Appendix.

Due to the public facing nature of their work, religious, medical, and funerary professionals will be referred to by their given names, titles, and institutional affiliations at the time of our

INTRODUCTION ☙ 15

conversation unless specifically requested otherwise. Because their positions as civic and spiritual leaders gain authority and context in part from their professional institutions, I strove to provide that information whenever possible. A small percentage of these professional interview subjects, however, wished to be referred to only by their first name or remain anonymous to protect their privacy when speaking about sensitive subjects. In the glossary, I have indicated which professional conversation partners have had their full name redacted or have elected to use a pseudonym by an asterisk. Those who lost loved ones to COVID-19 will be referenced by a first name or pseudonym alone. Many of these interview subjects would speak to me only if they were completely anonymized with a pseudonym and transformed identifying information, as they were not accustomed to publicly sharing sensitive information. My choice to use a first name or selected pseudonym respects their intimate grief.

In addition to my interviews, I conducted virtual participant observation of a variety of digital communities and spaces related to COVID-19. This includes public platforms like YouTube, TikTok, and most prominently, Facebook, Instagram, and Reddit groups supporting those who lost loved ones to COVID-19. Among these, the largest community was the COVID-19 Loss Support for Family & Friends Facebook group. While this research captures only a small moment in what was, and still is, a years-long crisis, listening to the voices of individuals working through their conflicting and contradictory feelings is a valuable enterprise to begin understanding how COVID-19 transformed, challenged, and complicated Americans' religious life and spirituality.

One final note. Readers will notice that the structure of *Shattered Grief* is based around questions rather than answers. One reason for this choice is that the pandemic was an incredibly complicated and largely unprecedented event, and we are all still making sense of its impact. But the pandemic also created an opportunity for religion scholars to reassess our assumptions about the nature and function of religion. The ways in which people and communities responded to COVID-19 has implications for understanding how religious leaders, communities, and traditions have functioned throughout history. So, instead of grandstanding with an air of authority and pretending to know exactly why people dealt with their grief in the ways that they did, I invite the reader to explore these questions with me. Along the way, I will hopefully equip the reader with some new tools to think about the stories presented here and how human beings construct meaning in the face of death and impermanence.

1

RITUAL

If there is one thing consistently understood as at the heart of religion, it is "ritual."[1] Indeed, Sigmund Freud equated the two so much that he argued religion resembled a form of obsessive-compulsive disorder—an affliction marked by the performance of repeated rituals—played out on a society-wide scale. In the essay "Obsessive Actions and Religious Practices," Freud wrote that compulsive rituals represented "an individual religiosity," while religion served as a "universal obsessional neurosis."[2] Although perhaps not extending their claims quite so far as to identify *all* religious ritual as mental illness, many early interpreters of culture echoed what we might call the "functionalist" sentiment of Freud's claims, arguing that religious ritual served an important function to ease anxiety and achieve a sense of control over the world.[3]

While scholars today generally do not equate religion with mental illness so readily, the perspectives of Freud and other early thinkers demonstrate how intimately religion and ritual are intertwined. Perhaps this is because ritual is a part of religion that we can see. Beliefs are generally private, personal affairs, invisible to anyone except those who hold them. Religious narratives often require knowledge of other languages or a guide to relate them to you; but ritual is action that can, theoretically, be observed or viewed by anyone, regardless of whether it is understood or joined. There are certainly rituals that exist outside the boundaries of what is traditionally identified with religion—the clinking of glasses after a toast, shaking hands with a new acquaintance, saluting veterans in a parade—but in large part our most prominent, most apparent, and most significant rituals are tied to our religious identities.

Ritual, however, represents something of a puzzle; in many ways, it is a form of magic—turning the mundane and ordinary into something distinguished and extraordinary. Religion scholar and YouTube commentator Andrew Mark Henry highlights the significance of ritual succinctly: "Why is taking a sip of wine at Thanksgiving dinner different than taking a sip of wine on Sunday at a church? Why is abstaining from food to lose weight called 'dieting,' but when you abstain from food for religious reasons, it's called 'fasting'?"[4] The answer is that doing such actions in a ritual context changes their significance and marks the action as set apart or "special," to use the terminology of religion scholar Ann Taves.[5]

Despite its centrality to our conceptions of religion, however, ritual is a loaded term, without a single definition. Some scholars emphasize the formal routinization of a set of behavioral practices.[6] Others highlight ritual as a technology to enact a structural change on the world.[7] Some scholars have even elected to drop the term entirely in favor of words like "performance" that allow a greater emphasis on individual agency within the boundaries of a specific liturgy.[8] Perhaps, as Supreme Court Justice Potter Stewart famously quipped when asked about the difference between the obscene and the erotic: "I'll know it when I see it."[9]

Definitional issues aside, people seem to call upon the magic of ritual especially in times of crisis. Both laboratory and observational studies have found that individuals engage in increasingly ritualized behavior during times of heightened stress and social instability.[10] In addition to the protection, comfort, and other benefits that religious traditions might claim these rituals can provide, they also give a sense of control over an uncontrollable world. Rituals, likewise, can serve an important role in defining identity. Marriages, baptisms, and various coming-of-age ceremonies work to move individuals from one identity to the next, often within the recognition of a wider social context. In this way, rituals can have dual purposes—working privately for individual comfort and working collectively for social organization and cohesion.

The crisis of the COVID-19 pandemic created a need for ritual and simultaneously rendered many traditional religious rituals impossible. Funerals, Masses, communal chanting, group prayer meetings, and a whole host of other publicly oriented rituals were quickly identified as potential super-spreader events because they involved close, intimate contact between individuals not in the same household. While religious communities utilized technology to recreate these rituals in the virtual space, for many Americans, something was missing. This was, perhaps, felt most keenly around those rituals commemorating death; in the early months of the pandemic, at a time when many Americans needed rituals and community support to make sense of the loss of their loved ones to COVID-19, these resources were often not available to them.

To understand how individuals reacted to, utilized, or rejected the ritual element of religious practice as they confronted death and grieved in the early COVID-19 pandemic, this chapter asks three questions:

1. What is ritual, and why do religion scholars care?
2. When does ritual work? (And when does it fail?)
3. Where does ritual come from?

These questions will act as guideposts in exploring the transformations to ritual in the early months of the pandemic. Importantly, these transformations were enacted not only among those who lost loved ones to COVID-19, but also those working in medical settings, funeral homes, and therapeutic roles. Ritual served as a diverse, multifaceted, and, at times, inadequate tool to confront the overwhelming death, dying, and grief during the early months of the pandemic.

WHAT IS RITUAL, AND WHY DO RELIGION SCHOLARS CARE?

Scholars other than myself have provided detailed histories tracing the various definitions and functions of "ritual," so I will make no efforts to engage such an exhaustive history here.[11] Rather, I hope to provide some context on how people have thought about ritual analytically as a means to frame, understand, and evaluate religious responses to the early COVID-19 pandemic. While this may seem to be sidestepping the question that opens this section—"What is ritual?"—I would argue that it helps us dive directly into the heart of the issue: Why do religion scholars, or anyone really, care about ritual?

Funerals as Ritual

Ritual has historically had an important place in helping communities understand death and move through grief. Every documented human culture has produced some sort of ritual to frame the death of loved ones. Perhaps it is for this reason that funerary rituals are often a great source of judgment and disparagement between cultures. Some of our earliest narratives of the encounter between Europeans and the Indigenous peoples living in Central and North America are vitriolic critiques of their death rituals.[12] British prime minister William Gladstone is famously quoted as linking particular care for the dead with a respect for law and morality. He is reported to have said: "Show me the manner in which a nation cares for its dead, and I will measure with mathematical exactness the tender sympathies of the people, their respect for the law of the land, and their loyalties to high morals."[13] For many peoples, death rituals become the touchstone by which they evaluate a given civilization's development and cultural advancement.

In the seventeenth and eighteenth centuries, most Americans would prepare the body for burial themselves and host the funeral at their homes. However, by the end of the nineteenth century, widespread social changes had nurtured the rise of the contemporary funeral home. First, an increasing number of people began dying not at home, but in hospitals while receiving medical treatment. Second, the industrial revolution propelled migration to cities, where most families lacked the necessary space to host a large gathering like a funeral. Finally, an increasing number of nineteenth-century Americans expressed belief in the polluting nature of vapors from the corpse that might spread disease and infection. This idea, known as miasma theory, spurred the development of trained funerary professionals who claimed to handle the body hygienically and scientifically.

In this way, funerary professionals became the public face of death and post life body care. As explored by Gary Laderman, funerary directors crystallized a variety of rituals that came to define the modern American funeral, including embalming, viewings, casket lowering, and so forth.[14] These invented rituals, and the American funerary industry as a whole, were famously criticized in Jessica Mitford's scathing *The American Way of Death* (1963) for what, in her estimation, was an obsession with unnecessary, constructed traditions that cost grieving families money. Funerary professionals have since maintained that these traditions have roots in the distant past and represent an important way for families to say goodbye that supports healthy grief and closure. Regardless of the origin of these rituals, they provide a framework for many Americans when imagining what a funeral should look like.

Funerals are also some of the most enduring of rituals, changing slowly in response to new situations and environments. This is especially true in the various immigrant communities who have come to call America home. As Venerable Jue Ji, Buddhist nun at the Fo Guang Shan Xiang Yun Buddhist Temple in Austin, Texas explained to me, "In my experience, Buddhist families want to have services that are the style they are familiar with. When they are grieving, it is important that the content is familiar to them. It is important for funeral homes to understand this; many local funeral homes allow us to come in and lead the funeral in the way we like, and some even have built special facilities for our rituals."[15] In response to the need for funerals that reflect personal cultures and customs, many funerary businesses specialize their offerings and spaces to specific local clientele. My interviews demonstrated that people selected a funeral home for their loved one based almost entirely on that business's familiarity with their community's cultural or religious traditions.

Indeed, social crisis is one of the few things that can inspire a widespread transformation to funerary rituals. Embalming, a form of preservation that replaces bodily fluids with chemicals to dramatically halt decomposition, became the norm in

America only after the American Civil War. The Civil War spurred a crisis to preserve the bodies of soldiers while they made the long trip home. Some embalmers even followed military troops to the site of a battle and accepted payment in advance for the procedure. After his assassination, President Abraham Lincoln's remains toured the United States for nineteen days, during which he was re-embalmed in each new city to ensure preservation. More recently, Shannon Lee Dawdy has argued that the public tragedy of 9/11 inspired Americans to radically reinvent death rituals in ways that popularized cremation, green burial, and other forms of body disposition previously unthinkable.[16]

The crisis of COVID-19 caused disagreement among funeral directors concerning the best way to handle a COVID-positive body. A funerary director at the Winford Funeral Home in Houston, Texas, explained that, in their practice, every COVID-positive body was embalmed as a matter of course to ensure sanitation and prevent the spread of infection.[17] In contrast, both Mitzi Chafetz of Austin Natural Funerals and Eric Neuhaus of Green Cremation Texas expressed suspicion of this practice. As Mitzi explained, "To say that you are embalming because of the virus makes no sense at all; embalming is an incredibly invasive procedure and you are just stirring up all the things that spread the virus!"[18] This disagreement reflected the confusion that many funerary directors faced in the early months of the pandemic as to how best protect employees and staff while providing services requested by families. While the Centers for Disease Control (CDC) initially stated in April 2020 that embalming was safe with the necessary Personal Protective Equipment (PPE) and precautions, the World Health Organization (only a few weeks earlier) recommended against embalming a COVID-positive body due to the excessive manipulation of tissue required.[19] The

National Funeral Directors Association offered webinars and continuing education opportunities, but most American funeral homes were largely left to determine their own safety limits. Richard Davis, director at the Cook-Walden Funeral Home in Pflugerville, Texas, compared the confusion to the early years of the HIV/AIDS epidemic, when funeral homes wrestled with similar confusions and contradictory information about how to handle a body infected with a virus about which little was known. Describing the early months of the COVID-19 pandemic, Richard explained, "It was an incredibly stressful time. Our funerary staff didn't know if they could adjust the deceased in the casket, if they could straighten their tie, this and that. It caused a lot of nerves. Everyone who works here has a server's heart, they are here to help. To have doubt about something as simple as adjusting the body to make the family happy caused them immense pain."[20]

But the crisis of COVID-19 inspired other transformations to American funerals as well, most notably a shift to online or Zoom funerals. Public health guidelines dramatically limited funeral size, often to only five to ten people, and virtual funerals provided the only option for large commemorations. Kay, a Christian living in Chicago, described the difficulty of having a large Puerto Rican family when only a small number were allowed in the funeral home:

> Only ten people could be in the funeral home building at a time, but my grandfather had raised his siblings and six children beyond that. Needless to say, when he died, there were more than ten people in our family. Every time a grandkid or cousin or sibling would arrive to see my grandfather, one of us had to step out into the cold. It was like some bizarre puzzle: how to let all our family see my grandfather one last time, while ensuring only ten people

were in the building and also none of the elderly were waiting outside in the cold.[21]

While some funeral homes experimented with using radio or Bluetooth technology to broadcast eulogies to isolated mourners sitting in their cars in the parking lot, Zoom funerals quickly became the solution to the problem that Kay described. Many funeral directors partnered directly with videographers, whose business filming weddings and other celebratory occasions had suddenly dried up overnight. These videographers found that their high-quality equipment could just as easily be put to use broadcasting Zoom funerals. Although virtual funerals had existed prior to the pandemic, COVID-19 accelerated their social acceptance and funerals could remain the primary ritual of remembrance in the American liturgy of death.[22]

Looking at Ritual Analytically

Returning to our initial question—What is ritual, and why do religion scholars care?—there are two lenses we can use to analyze funerals and other death-associated rituals: one that considers (1) the effects of ritual within a specific social situation (i.e., *what* it does) and one that considers (2) the means and mechanisms by which ritual accomplishes those goals (i.e., *how* it does it). While these are fundamentally intertwined, examining them separately gives us more tools and insight into understanding the functions of ritual.

Turning to our first lens, we can say that ritual *does* certain things and that these things have significant social impact. As evident in the earlier quote from Andrew Mark Henry, ritual transforms ordinary interactions into events that are special and set apart. This setting apart effectively communicates that *this* is special, *this* is important, *this* is different, and, in this way, creates a new reality. We see evidence of such a newly created social reality in the far-reaching and extensive social consequences that may continue long after the ritual has ended. For example, a man cheating on his wife causes very different reactions in his community, very different forms of subsequent legal proceedings, and very different financial repercussions than if the same man were to cheat on a girlfriend, even a long-term girlfriend. The ritual of marriage has transformed the relationship between the man and the woman in such a way that its reverberations were felt far into the future. It has also invited a variety of social and political organizations to confirm the relationship and become involved with its upkeep, including religious leadership, tax assessors, and government employees. Presumably, the ritual was also a public statement on the emotional states of the individuals involved—that they love each other and are committed to being together, though perhaps the fate of our fictional couple puts some of those claims into question.

As is evident in our example of marriage, it is common to assume that rituals are a reflection of an internal state—"I was in love, so I married him"; "I was grateful, so I bowed my head to pray"; "I was anxious, so I made offerings to a deity." However, sociologists like Adam Seligman have challenged this assumption. Such a claim presumes that rituals are fundamentally about something other than they are; it assumes that they exist to communicate an emotive or intellectual disposition, rather than being fundamentally about the *doing* itself. Seligman argues that emphasizing only ritual's communicative properties necessarily de-emphasizes the importance of ritual's embodied actions. If ritual can be reduced to communicating one's inner dispositions and beliefs, surely simply publicly declaring those dispositions and beliefs would have a similar effect to performing the ritual. However, anecdotally, we know that not to be true. There is a world of difference between the couple that says, "We are married. This is my spouse," and the ritual utterance of an officiant pronouncing them married. The ritual utterance bestows full legal and social recognition, whereas simply communicating a claim does not. As Seligman points out in a recent book, ritual "is more about *doing* something than saying something."[23]

So, when we think about *what* it does, ritual is fundamentally creating reality. While this reality may express internal feelings, ritual more often has a role in giving shape to, framing, and sometimes even producing those feelings. This is especially true when we consider rituals related to grief and mourning. In our interview together, Venerable Jue Ji spoke about the importance of performing various Buddhist rituals after someone dies. To illustrate her point, she used an example from her temple community:

> There is a woman in my community. When her husband passed away a few years ago, she said she felt no grief, which I thought was strange because they had been married a very long time. But she would come to the temple, sit in a single spot, and stare too long at the wall. I was worried she felt lost, so I gave her a key and told her to take the temple as her home. I told her she should come every day to do prostrations in front of the Buddha and visit her husband's tablet in the memorial room. She came to the temple and every time she went to the memorial room, she would bow to the Buddha and pray for her husband. Things began getting better after that, and she has since been able to feel grief for her husband.[24]

This case demonstrates ritual functioning opposite to the way we often imagine it. We cannot say that these mourning practices were about expressing an internal state of affairs—the widow was troubled exactly because she felt no internal grief to express. Rather, participating in the embodied ritual traditions of her community helped to create a new reality where her unfamiliar status as a widow was rendered meaningful and understandable. Venerable Jue Ji's example revealed how internal feelings followed the act of ritual, not the other way around. In this, the construction of a new identity through a ritual supported by a religious community is what allowed the widow to fully experience grief.

A similar insight was discussed by Rev. Chuck Treadwell of St. David's Episcopal Church in Austin, Texas. While discussing the disruptions that COVID-19 caused to funerary rituals more generally, he explained how the ritual of Last Rites—a sacrament where a priest prays together with a dying individual and their family—provides language and speech at a time when finding words can be difficult:

> When you witness a Last Rites ritual, you realize the incredible gift you have been given. To be with someone near their death and to ritualize that experience with them is a beautiful thing. This is exactly when the Episcopal prayer book really comes to our rescue, because the liturgies of the church are established exactly for this: at the hardest, most difficult times of your life, you don't have to be articulate. You can just come and read the words that are already beautifully written and encapsulate our belief. The Last Rites ritual becomes a cadence at the time of death, recited together, and moving you through this tremendous experience together.[25]

During and after the death of a loved one, most people presume that both the loved one and the surviving family are sorrowful; the function of a ritual of grieving, therefore, is not just to reveal these feelings of despondency to the world. Rather, as seen in the examples laid out by Venerable Jue Ji and Rev. Chuck Treadwell, rituals do important work in giving shape to grief and sorrow—ultimately mediating the emotional response of those soon to die and those in mourning. Rituals speak the words that those who are grieving are unable to say.

However, these rituals were often unable to happen during the pandemic—a fact that fundamentally altered the ways in which those who lost loved ones to COVID-19 understood their grief. This truth is especially evident in an excerpt from my conversation with Amanda. Amanda is a practicing Christian and a registered member of the Apache tribe. After she lost her mother to COVID-19, public health guidelines prevented her from returning to the reservation to perform traditional Apache mourning customs. As a result, Amanda was unable to participate in important rituals of grief, and this fundamentally hindered her ability to heal:

> My grief feels visceral. In my Apache Indian culture, you are supposed to mourn by cutting your arms and hair with an ancestral knife. The blood flowing down is meant to symbolize your loss and grief and how important this person was to you. I spoke with my elders, and they said I shouldn't do that unless I was living on the reservation, as people might misunderstand it and react to it poorly. What I ended up doing was getting a very large tattoo; if I can't cut myself, I can at least bleed somewhere else. It stretches across my shoulder. But it doesn't really feel like enough; it doesn't atone.[26]

Amanda's experience reveals how ritual mediates and shapes grief, as well as the significance of community involvement with rituals. Her attempts to replace the traditional Apache bloodletting ritual with a large tattoo were ineffective, and her grief remained unaddressed and unaltered. If ritual serves to move people through identities, then those mourning during the period of COVID-19 were fundamentally stuck in the transitional phase—neither recognized as a mourner, nor absolved of the responsibility to be one. Without the public acknowledgment of their grief through rituals, they were unable to move into new identities and roles.

Turning now to our second lens—*how* ritual functions. Jonathan Z. Smith famously stated, "ritual is, above all, an assertion of difference ... it is concerned with quite ordinary activities placed within an extraordinary setting."[27] He identifies, here, the engine of ritual as a creation of difference between one thing and the other—one period of time, one place, one person, and something generally identified as "normal." In other words, ritual takes elements from the ordinary world—words, gestures, symbols, etc.—and imbues them with extraordinary meaning. We might cry or wear black clothing every day for any number of reasons, but in funerary rituals these activities have special significance and can bring a sense of closure. For Smith, it is this repurposing of ordinary things that makes rituals satisfying. Psychological studies have supported Smith's claim. A 2012 study by Cristine Legare and André Souza has shown that the greater the difference between what happens in a given ritual and one's normal life—the greater the number of steps, the greater the repetition of certain phrases, and so forth—the more effective the ritual is believed to be.[28]

The COVID-19 pandemic has forced the question, however: what happens to ritual when no activities seem ordinary, when our sense of normal is shattered and remains shattered for years? Throughout COVID-19, Americans were unable to plan events as major as a wedding or as minor as a dinner out; there was the constant anxiety of office and business closure; children were attending school in virtual classrooms that often did not function; and adults were isolated from friends and family. People's sense of the daily rhythms and resonances of life had been completely destroyed—how could they recognize the difference of ritual when the reality of life looked so unlike anything they had experienced before? As Smith notes, rituals work by framing the ordinary as extraordinary, but if nothing feels ordinary, then nothing can feel extraordinary, either.

WHEN DOES RITUAL WORK? (AND WHEN DOES IT FAIL?)

If we analyze ritual along the two perspectives of (1) *what* ritual does and (2) *how* ritual does it, success in grieving and death rituals would mean that the ritual is able to remove the individual from ordinary time and bring about a transformation in feeling that provides comfort to the afflicted. As noted earlier, creating a sense of difference from the ordinary was often impossible due to the very nature of the COVID-19 pandemic, which fundamentally altered our shared sense of normal time. In fact, the *how* of ritual requires that two aspects be coordinated to successfully bring about the *what* of ritual: (1) a sense of continuity with a religious tradition and (2) a connection to a larger community. The role that these aspects play in supporting ritual success is evident in the comfort that many found in performing regular religious rituals in the middle of what had become a very irregular time.

Ritual Working: Comfort Through Connection and Community

As my own interests have been in examining the issues of death and grief, my conversations primarily concerned funerary rituals and the role of religious practice in providing comfort to those who are bereaved. However, several of my interviews touched on how the collective grief faced by spiritual communities during the early COVID-19 pandemic encompassed all whose lives had become upended. During this time, the rituals that seemed to provide the most comfort to those suffering were those ordinary rituals performed in extraordinary times—weekly or daily rituals performed during the unprecedented early lockdown. Reverend Richard R. Andre, C.S.P. of St. Austin Catholic Parish, explained:

> I'll always remember the first Sunday Mass after the lockdown—March 22nd, 8:45 in the morning. It was one of the most powerful experiences of my whole priesthood. I have been a priest nine years now, but it was just shockingly powerful. There were only nine of us in the church, but hundreds of people joining us on the digital feed. I felt the presence of Christ with all of us throughout, guiding us, and comforting us in that moment. There was something powerful going on.[29]

Rabbi Neil Blumofe of the Congregation Agudas Achim in Austin, Texas, experienced something similar. During the initial lockdown, he began to broadcast daily prayers via his Facebook account. The response he got was overwhelmingly positive:

> I have actually had lots of people contact me to say how uplifting it was to see my prayers—some are people who aren't Jewish or

associated with Judaism in any way, but many are Jews from across America who found my prayers on Facebook Live. People have made a practice of watching it because it gives them comfort. It comforted me too, to continue these daily prayers despite the lockdown.[30]

The experiences of Rev. Andre and Rabbi Blumofe provide interesting case studies in ritual at work: by performing traditional rituals in a time of crisis, both individuals were comforted through connection to a larger religious or spiritual community. Indeed, their experiences function as something of a ritual-within-a-ritual and reveal its necessarily contextual element—something is not objectively a ritual, but only becomes a ritual in comparison to the things around it. The ritual of the Catholic Mass happens every week in churches around the world and Jews are called to pray daily at morning, afternoon, and nightfall. While these rituals certainly elevate the ordinary into the extraordinary, they can also, in themselves, come to feel like ordinary obligations. The entirely novel situation of COVID-19 and the beginning of an unprecedented lockdown heightened the experience of these religious leaders because the new situation during COVID-19 was entirely different from other times. The reoccurring ritual that might have felt ordinary in normal times was transformed in those first moments of the pandemic to an extraordinary experience.

In a similar vein, some of those who lost loved ones to COVID-19 described ritual as the guide that helped them move through the initial uncertainty and confusion after death. Kay, who lost her father and grandfather, explained: "Even though there was a lot of ritual that couldn't happen, it made me grateful for the ritual that could happen." She described feeling appreciative of the funeral home that allowed her brother to come in and cut her father's hair in preparation for the viewing; in Puerto Rican families like her own, personally caring for the body is common and being able to connect to this cultural tradition in a time of crisis provided the family immense comfort. Gurpreet, a young Sikh American who lost his father to COVID-19, explained how in the days after his father's death, nothing felt normal. After the death of a loved one, Sikhs traditionally chant through the entirety of the Sikh holy scripture, the Guru Granth Sahib. This recitation is done as a family and concludes with a Bhog ceremony that is intended to mark the end of mourning. Gurpreet explained that performing this ritual gave structure to a scary time, connected him and his family, and helped him move forward in the immediate aftermath of his father's death:

> After someone passes away, Sikhs pray for ten full days and on the last day there is a large closing prayer with the whole family. You do this to pray that the soul of the person passing away is safe, happy, and in a good place. That was actually a good time for me and my family. We were all just lost, and it was something to do, something to follow. If we get through these ten days together, we can get through the rest of it.[31]

Such sentiments were echoed by other religious leaders about their work with grieving family members. Venerable Jue Ji explained how families in her Buddhist community found comfort in the virtual rituals that reflected the rituals that would have been performed before the pandemic:

> Before COVID-19, we monastics would go to their house for chanting when a person was near death or right after they passed away. We would chant the Buddhist scriptures and the holy name

of the Buddha so that they would get good karma and have a good rebirth. Normally, these moments are very touching, as the whole community can share their condolences. But during COVID, we couldn't do that when a community member passed away. I told the daughter of one person who died that I would do the chanting for her father via Zoom and give Dharma blessings directly to the dying person. Even though I was not there in person, he was able to put his palms together in front of the screen and receive the blessing at the end, which made his family feel better.[32]

Although significantly different than rituals in the "before times," the death-related rituals during the pandemic continued to provide comfort and support to many grieving family members through connection to their community and tradition.

These examples speak to the strength and vitality of grieving individuals as they find meaning in an unprecedented time. Performing a funerary ritual, even in a virtual, limited, or otherwise transformed format, provided a blueprint that helped to structure their grief in an uncertain time. As noted by Craig Taylor, head pastor at the Willow Meadows Baptist Church in Houston, Texas, these modified rituals were primarily successful when they most closely resembled pre-pandemic rituals:

> All the things that we have done for funerals and grief in the past, we can still do. However, it is going to look a little different—maybe there will be virtual receiving lines, maybe the sermon will be given outside, maybe the reception after the funeral will be individual bags to take home. The whole time, we just have to call it out, admit that it looks different, weird, and uncomfortable, but keep moving forward.[33]

For many, performing the normal daily and weekly rituals of their religion in the extraordinary time of the early pandemic brought incredible comfort through fostering connections with the historical continuity of their tradition.

Despite these efforts at fostering both connection and community in the time of the early pandemic, for the majority of individuals that I spoke with the change was simply too great. The shared sense of normal, upon which so much of ritual relies, was too shattered and traditional grieving rituals proved largely ineffective during the COVID-19 period. Families struggled with reconciling the rituals envisioned in their heads with the reality of what was possible due to the continuing pandemic. Because the *how* of ritual could not function, it could not complete the *what* of ritual.

Ritual Failing: Grieving in Isolation

The greatest challenge faced by those who lost loved ones during the pandemic was that they were grieving alone. Due to health and safety guidelines, most traditional funerary rituals had to be limited to only a handful of people; for many individuals, these small gatherings did not even register as a funeral. Rev. Rich Andre described assisting those losing loved ones in his own spiritual community: "The funeral helps you start a process of closure. But without the funerals they envisioned, people are just getting stuck and are unable to grieve. One of the most important things about a funeral is that it lets people know they are supported by a larger community, but without that, grieving has become this very isolated thing for a lot of people."[34] Rev. Chuck Treadwell echoed these sentiments—not only in his pastoral work, but in his own process of grieving as well. For him, an important component of grief was missing in the Zoom funeral:

> A friend of mine who was also a priest died during the pandemic; he was this larger-than-life guy, and I would have traveled to his funeral in a heartbeat. His family ended up doing the funeral on Zoom and there was this song performed. I knew it was a song he hated, but I guess his kids didn't know that. Maybe it's the training as a priest, but if a hymn starts playing, you just start singing it along with the congregation. So, I am sitting in my office singing this terrible song to myself, and my wife comes in crying. It wasn't a comment on my singing ability, but she said, me singing by myself, watching my friend's funeral on Zoom was the saddest thing she had ever heard. This is just not how it is supposed to be. We're supposed to be together in times of sorrow—to cling to each other and pray and cry and sing together.[35]

In the experiences of Rev. Andre and Rev. Treadwell, removing the element of in-person community involvement fundamentally undermined ritual's power to comfort.

Sometimes, this necessary isolation from larger communities denied individuals the opportunity to engage with specific cultural expectations. Amanda, who earlier described her frustrations at the inability to practice traditional Apache mourning practices, explained how the fear of COVID-19 kept her family separated after her mother's sudden passing in January 2020: "Because my family has been so terrified of COVID, we have not been able to gather together to process my mother's death. That has been really hard for me culturally – especially in Indigenous families like my own, you always grieve together."[36] This isolation was not simply a domestic issue, but an international one as well. The funerals of American immigrants are often global affairs, strengthening ties between the emigrated community in America and family abroad.[37] Manpreet, an Indian American Sikh woman, described holding on to her father's cremated remains, hoping that international travel regulations would relax and allow her family to return his ashes to India. Like Hindus, Sikhs practice cremation and the remains must be spread in flowing water. Many Sikhs elect to return to the Punjab region of India, where the religion began and where many Sikhs still have family, to spread the ashes. However, as the one-year anniversary of his death approached in the spring of 2021, and international travel seemed further away than ever, Manpreet's mother made the decision to scatter his ashes in Jamaica Bay in Queens, New York. Manpreet described this experience: "I was so upset that my family in India—my uncles, aunts, cousins—could not be there. I don't even know if it is the best decision. My father loved America, and a piece of him will always be here now, but I know he wanted his final resting place to be India, so it just hurts."[38]

Returning to our two dimensions of ritual, the *what* of ritual could not be accomplished because the *how* of ritual was not there. The how of ritual requires asserting that certain statements, actions, and symbols have a different meaning than in their normal, everyday context. But it also entails a sense of connection with the community and continuity with tradition. While we can have personal rituals or ad hoc rituals (as will be discussed below) such rituals become most powerful when affirmed within a larger community. The real magic of ritual lies in its ability to create new social realities, and to do this it needs the collective strength of a community that connects an individual with historic precedent. This is one reason why the conditions of the pandemic impaired the power of ritual to grieve.

Ritual Failing: "A Parody of a Funeral"

In response to the necessary social isolation, funeral homes were quick to offer virtual options that allowed for wider participation and many businesses shared ideas via trade magazines and online forums. Rick Davis of the Cook-Walden Funeral Home was praised in both mediums for his flexible response to the novel pandemic situation and his cultivation of relationships with local videographers to develop high-quality video funerals for Zoom, Skype, and Facebook Live. At the time of our conversation in February 2021, Davis said his primary videographer's funerary business was booming, and it was uncertain whether he would ever go back to producing wedding videos as he had before. While Davis acknowledged that nothing replaced the in-person experience, he was happy to offer this option in times like the pandemic, when families could not gather. Indeed, he said virtual funerals would remain a part of the American funerary experience in the future, a sentiment echoed by all the funerary professionals that I spoke with.

However, the majority of the individuals who lost loved ones to COVID-19 identified the virtual funeral as a largely unsatisfying experience. Dan, a conversation partner in San Antonio, Texas who lost his grandmother to COVID-19 explained, "I knew my grandmother would pass away sometime, but I always imagined I would be there; I never imagined I would be watching it virtually on Facebook. It felt like a parody of a funeral." Later he went on, "I just became upset—upset that I couldn't be there, upset that I couldn't recognize my uncles from the grainy camera footage, upset that my grandmother deserved so much better. I just began crying like a little child and pounding on the couch. My wife who was sitting next to me knew what I was feeling, but she was powerless. There was nothing she could do to help me in that moment."³⁹ For Dan and many others, missing the in-person component fundamentally altered the funeral into an entirely dissatisfying experience.

Indeed, my conversation partners often seemed haunted by the funerals that could have been. In describing the funeral that she had envisioned for her mother, Florida nursing student Carmen emphasized to me that "We would need Central Park to have the celebration of life my mom deserved! So many lives she touched, she was such an angel."⁴⁰ Yoon Tae echoed these beliefs. A Korean American Christian living in the South, his father had been deeply involved with the local Evangelical Korean church. After his father's death from COVID-19, Yoon Tae struggled with his commitment to following public health guidelines, feeling that his dad deserved a large event. Yoon Tae explained how difficult this experience was: "We had to limit attendance for everyone's health and safety. When I got up to give the eulogy, it was really heartbreaking. I was able to look out at this small gathering of people and know that it would have been a packed room if it weren't for COVID. I felt like my father deserved better."⁴¹

In thinking through why these funerals were unfulfilling, Pastor Craig Taylor emphasized the disconnect between expectation and reality: "You have this expectation for what a service should be and who should be there because you have been going to funerals your whole life. But the rhythm of grieving was disrupted, and so many of the families I worked with felt that. You expect your loved one's funeral to look a certain way; you expect sympathy and comfort to look a certain way, and it just doesn't."⁴² During the early months of the pandemic, several of Craig's congregants died of non-COVID related causes, and he found himself organizing socially distanced funerals. He noted how physical disconnection led to deeper forms of disconnection in the community. Reminiscing on one funeral that he led during the pandemic, he said, "All the chairs were spread out for social distancing, which was the good and right thing to do. But when you were in the room, you didn't really feel together. It's like the chairs being distanced represented more than physical space between everyone—it was emotional distance as well."[43] Julia, who lost her younger brother to COVID-19, had similar emotions about the physical space necessary due to public health precautions:

> The worst part of the funeral—I guess there were so many worst parts of it—but the worst part I am thinking of right now is that we can usually stand close by when they lower the casket into the ground. However, because of COVID restrictions, we had to stand more than ten feet away. I just remember my mom crying out "Bye, John! Bye, John!" As they lowered the casket into the ground from so far away. He was developmentally challenged, so we had been next to him for every moment of his life—except this one; it was a crushing blow."[44]

Despite attempts by funerary and religious professionals to offer alternative modalities for preserving ritual's power, many individuals felt that these innovations only further emphasized the alienation from community.

Maintaining and Negotiating Ritual During the Pandemic

Dan's description of a funeral as a "parody" reveals that for many of those who lost loved ones, there was a gap between the imagined ritual and the reality of what could be accomplished under the conditions of a pandemic. The ideal funeral has the power to comfort because the ritual draws on the weight of both community and tradition. If these connections are not felt, the magic of ritual fails; the actions and utterances lose their power and can seem trite, meaningless, or even silly. Conversely, those who expressed a degree of gratitude for their funeral services had found some way to maintain this sense of connection with community and continuity with tradition, even in the face of a pandemic.

Sabila, a Pakistani American woman living in New Jersey, described how grateful she was that her family could retain a few elements of traditional Muslim funerary rituals, despite what felt like society breaking down around her:

> In the Muslim tradition, we're supposed to bury our dead right away. But the funeral homes were so crowded in April 2020 that we were told it would be at least two weeks until they could bury my father. For us, this was simply another trauma. One of my cousins stepped in and reached out to every contact he had in his central New Jersey mosque. He found someone able to collect my father's body that very day. Traditionally, the body is washed and wrapped by men in the community, but I am not sure how much of that could be completed since he was a COVID patient. I didn't ask, as it would have been too painful to hear the answer. He was buried the next day in a Muslim cemetery forty minutes from us. Watching his burial on a livestream was a horror for our family, but I held on to the fact that we were able to bury him in accordance with the Muslim tradition—that was the one small mercy we were shown in all of this.[45]

Indeed, the need to bury the body quickly became difficult for many Muslim communities during the height of the pandemic. Speaking in April 2021, Imam Sheikh Attia Omara of the Islamic

Center of Lake Travis explained, "Death continues to go on despite COVID-19, and sometimes because of it. In Austin, we have a small Muslim community with only one cemetery where we can perform our own rituals. The body must be washed in a specific way, wrapped in specific cloth, and buried as quickly as possible; this all can't be done in a funeral home, so we specially train individuals to do it."[46] Imam Attia elaborated on how these practices were the subject of great debate among Islamic legal scholars. As a religious tradition, Islam values a commitment to performing the relevant religious rituals appropriately and correctly. Before radical changes are made to any traditional rituals, therefore, Muslim scholars look at a variety of scriptural sources like the Quran, the life of the prophet Muhammad, and prior legal thought known as *shari'a* to determine if changes are needed and how best to make them. Imam Attia noted that, based on this process, the Austin Muslim community reached a consensus on handling a COVID-positive body:

> Within our small community in Austin, we decided that if we are completely certain the individual died from something besides COVID, we continued to wash and prepare the body in the regular way. If we were uncertain or we knew it was a COVID-positive body, then we would not wash it for everyone's health and safety. Generally, other Muslim communities in the U.S. have agreed with our rulings, though I know some Muslims globally have made different decisions. It is not ideal to change the funerary ritual, but prior *shari'a* ruled that preservation of the living was more important than following the necessary rituals for the dead, as much as that hurt our families.[47]

The concrete issues of burial within the Islamic tradition became important topics of religious debate as communities struggled to balance comfort for the bereaved with health and safety concerns.

Islamic jurisprudence during the pandemic extended beyond care for the dead body itself to larger, community-wide debates concerning how best to perform specific funerary prayers. While Americans of many religious traditions suffered from an inability to congregate during the pandemic, Muslim Americans were especially concerned that the need for a small funeral might have potential ramifications for the salvation of the deceased. Imam Attia explained:

> The second major decision our community had to make was about offering funerary prayers in absentia. We make supplicatory prayers for those who have died at every service, but the funerary prayers at the mosque are special. Many Muslims believe the more people in attendance, praying for your soul, the greater your chances are to attain salvation. In specific circumstances in the past, *sharī'a* law has said that one could do the prayers in absentia, without the community or deceased body present—say if someone were lost at sea, or their body was destroyed, or they were kidnapped. But in this case, we know there was someone present to pray the funerary prayers; it just wasn't a big number. Ultimately, we decided that absentia funerary prayers would not qualify, though we hoped Allah will look on the supplicatory prayers with the same intention. Allah is, above all, merciful, so I have faith They will.[48]

In the extraordinary time of the pandemic, Muslim leaders had to use Islamic scholarship to make potentially unpopular decisions in ways that balanced cultural expectations for funeral practices with the unexpected coronavirus.

Jewish religious leaders faced similar problems to Muslim imams when debating appropriate funerary practice in the pandemic. Like Islam, Judaism shares a concern with the appropriate performance of religious rituals. Jewish leaders looked to prior scholarship in the Talmud to determine what ritual practices could be changed and which could not. The Talmud is the central text of Jewish law preserving centuries-old debates and discussions over how best to fulfill the 613 *mitzvoth*, or commandments, found in the Torah. Rabbi Blumofe of the Conservative synagogue Congregation Agudas Achim, explained:

> A lot of necessary modifications are discussed in the Talmud, because this is not the first pandemic the Jewish community has faced. The highest value in Judaism surrounding death is *"Kavod HaMet,"* a Hebrew phrase that means honoring the dead. Until the burial, the priority is respecting the dead—there's a washing process and a dressing process, where the body is wrapped in a white shroud. All of that had to be truncated to keep everyone safe, so we followed the guidelines in the Talmud and other literature as appropriate."[49]

Other important components of Jewish funerals that require community involvement also had to be transformed. Most notably, Jewish tradition states that the deceased is never to be left alone and a watcher, called *shomer* or *shomeret* dependent on gender, is to sit vigil with the body and read psalms until burial. Before the pandemic, this was done in coordination with the funeral home, where the local *Chevra Kadisha*—the community of volunteers who help organize and complete the components of the Jewish funeral—would hand off a key and ensure that for twenty-four hours a day, someone was with the body. Mitzi

Chafetz, director at Austin Natural Funerals, which serves the majority of Austin's Jewish population, explained that she had to make the difficult decision to not allow *shomrim* during the pandemic: "We talked about putting a camera on the body and then having someone sit *shomrim* over Zoom, but that seemed a little creepy. Now, it is just on an honor system. If you sign up for 3–5 a.m., we just trust that you will get up and do it privately at your home."[50] While most local rabbis agreed with Mitzi's decision to protect her employees, she did note that "Some families have pushed for things that we weren't comfortable doing, and we have had to tell them no. I remember once someone told me I was undermining the heritage of the entire Jewish community by not allowing in-person activities with their deceased loved one. As a Jewish woman, that hurt deeply. Yes, I know the families we work with are mourning, but this is a particularly vulnerable event, and I have to protect my people."[51] Rabbi Blumofe echoed how central these experiences are for contemporary Jews and spoke of his community's eager anticipation to return to these practices: "This is probably the thing we miss the most. We can do *shomrim* at home, but there is no substitute for physically taking care of a friend of yours who has passed. The first day it is safe to, that is something we will be doing again."[52]

WHERE DOES RITUAL COME FROM?

These obstacles did not mean that ritual was not happening during the pandemic. Rather, as many lost their sense of connection to both their religious communities and traditions, they began spontaneously creating their own rituals to fill the void. While many of these rituals were initially personal and private, they were often taken up by others experiencing similar trauma and adopted within the ad hoc communities formed during the pandemic period. Invented rituals like these, therefore, allow us to think about what may drive the larger development of religious ritual itself.

Rituals Among Medical Professionals

Due to public safety guidelines, medical professionals found themselves intimately involved with the lives of their COVID-19 patients. They held up iPhones so that families could say a virtual goodbye, they followed the instructions of religious leaders for reciting prayers over unconscious patients on ventilators, and they were often the only ones present at an individual's last breath. In my interviews, medical staff repeated what an emotional toll this work took on their own lives. Mary, a COVID-19 nurse in Austin, Texas, explained how her hospital made it a priority to provide emotional support for the medical team: "Remarkably, at this site, every single member of the COVID team is in counseling at the urging of the hospital. We also do weekly Critical Event debriefings, where we meet with a social worker to talk through our experience."[53] She explained that these debriefings grew out of daily huddle events that the team first instituted back in March 2020. Ostensibly, these events took place to share new information about the virus, but they quickly transformed into daily meetups where medical staff could lean on each other for support: "Policies and scientific information were changing so rapidly, we needed a designated space where we could get updates. But we also needed each other. Just to hold hands in a circle quietly for a moment and feel each other's terror and exhaustion in a single space was critical. It was a time apart for us, time to just be together."[54] This daily event came to function as a ritual in that it was time demarcated from what had become the nurses' new normal.

Kristel, a hospital chaplain in Chicago, described similar stresses that were heightened by her role in the medical system: "People kept looking to me to emotionally guide them through the early months of the pandemic. I was something of a wreck too, so it was sort of the blind leading the blind."[55] In the midst of this confusion, she found that emphasizing the ritualistic elements of her work provided assistance for herself, the medical staff, and the families that she served:

> To get through that time, I thought about all sorts of things in my work as a ritual that could help start the process of grieving. I often was called on to walk with families visiting their dying COVID-positive loved one; that was some of the hardest work. There were two rituals—the ritual of the walk up to the room and the ritual of the walk down. The walk up to the room began at the hospital doors and we would ride the elevator up into the ICU together, during which the family member was generally very nervous. They didn't know what to expect as they hadn't seen their loved one in a while. They had simply gotten a phone call that things were bad, and it was time to come in. On the way up, there were a lot of procedural things to discuss before we began getting dressed in the PPE—that itself could take over fifteen minutes, if the person had never put on PPE before. Then there is the ritual of leaving the room, where the family start to process with me. Often, they will say things like "I didn't know I wouldn't be able to talk to him" or "I didn't know there were so many machines." As we go down in the elevator together, I try to begin talking them through

their experience; that's my part of the ritual, as I think this is where the grief process can start to be put in motion.[56]

Framing this time as a ritual helped Kristel make sense of the repeated experience of leading families into the ICU to say goodbye to their COVID-positive family members. When she discussed her interpretation with other hospital staff, they also found it a helpful hermeneutic to make sense of their own experiences. In this way, the weight of tradition and community—albeit both relatively novel—provided comfort to those confronting death on a daily basis.

Perhaps in reaction to the intimate work with their COVID patients, hospital staff also spontaneously developed rituals to honor those who died under their care. One doctor I spoke with who led a hospice and palliative care team described how one of his nurses would gently touch the feet and head of each COVID patient who died during her shift: "It was this moment of acknowledging their humanity—even if their family were far away, even if no one else was there, she was there, she saw them. They were not alone, and she knew they mattered."[57] Christine, a clinical nurse specialist at Ascension Seton Medical Center in Austin, Texas, described creating similar rituals extemporaneously:

> We made informal rituals to help us when the pandemic was really bad—to feel like those who died while under our care weren't forgotten and that we were doing them justice and honor. We've done a monthly community reading of the names for everyone in our hospital who passed from COVID as a way to honor those we have cared for. We have also created an art space for nursing staff that has a mural of a dandelion releasing its fluff to

the wind, with the fluff then turning into stars. We started writing the names of those who died under the stars.[58]

Invented rituals like these became a way for those working with the COVID dead to commemorate their deaths when no one else was able to enter the hospital setting.

Healthcare workers also utilized these innovative rituals to connect the loved ones who passed with their families unable to see them. In the initial months of the pandemic, Mary traveled to Detroit to assist overwhelmed medical workers. She explained that the colleagues she worked with in Detroit—child life specialists, death doulas, and hospice nurses—shared several rituals with her that they used to commemorate sudden or otherwise traumatic deaths that often happened apart from families, like stillborn infants and dementia patients. These included making handprints of the deceased, framing a photograph of their final heartbeat, and cutting locks of hair. Mary began reframing these rituals for COVID patients on ventilators, who, like patients with dementia, were often unable to speak their goodbyes:

> It's honestly hard to know whether these rituals were more for me or more for our patients' families. Doing them and giving the family something tangible from their loved one let me feel like I was at least giving them something. And it was obvious how meaningful these small items were to people. One patient had his handprint done on his anniversary with his wife. I was able to give it to her and say, "I know he couldn't be with you on your anniversary, but we took this handprint on that date, and you will forever know that." This was some of the most meaningful work I did.[59]

Invented rituals among medical professionals were important strategies of meaning-making during the pandemic that both helped make sense of a chaotic and swiftly changing medical landscape and provided comfort to grieving families.

Spontaneous Personal Ritual

While many families were unable to perform the funerals they had envisioned after their loved ones' passing, several of my conversation partners created their own rituals to express their grief. Carmen, a nursing student studying in Florida, described setting up a personal altar to honor her mother who had died in New York City. She put things on the altar that reminded her of her mother—elephants, a shot glass, statues of Divino Niño (an image of the child Jesus, particularly revered by Columbian Catholics), and so forth. Ritually interacting with these things provided Carmen comfort as she worked to make sense of her mother's death: "I always have a halo of small electric lights around her photograph, and I bring flowers to the altar most mornings. My mother had really good luck, so I also have a small money tree there. Every morning, I greet her presence. Every night, I thank her for watching over me. This is how I remember my mother best. If I can't have the funeral she deserves, at least I can have this."[60] In remembering her mother who died from COVID-19 in January 2021, Amanda also invented small, daily rituals she could do while grieving:

> I have been putting out luminaries every evening for my mother—paper bags in which you place tea candles. For me, it has become a big part of letting go and celebrating my mother's life by

lighting her a pathway to heaven. It's a way to honor her. We'll be doing that on a bigger scale if we're ever able to have a funeral. I also use sage daily around the house we shared to bless her and let her know I am thinking of her. It just helps me connect with her in some way.[61]

While radically personal, these rituals connected Carmen and Amanda to their loved ones and frame their grieving in ways similar to community-wide rituals.

Martha B. Heymann, who is a certified end-of-life doula working with clients and their families through the process of dying, sees these personalized rituals as crucial to healing after the death of a loved one: "Rituals are immensely powerful; they help remove us from our everyday and bring us into a sacred space where we can listen and feel and react in ways not normally available to us."[62] Heymann explained that the more personal the ritual, the more it builds connection between the family and the deceased, the more powerful it can ultimately be:

> I recently had a client who did a ritual with her dying mother. When I first brought the idea to them, their initial reaction was "No thank you. We're not going to need that." That is entirely OK, of course, and I validated that. But after talking with me more, she and her sister ended up creating a few rituals—they just took them and ran with them! As their mother began preparing to die, they would wash her face, feet, and hands daily with a silver cup that had been used by them as babies. It was beautifully meaningful.[63]

Heymann noted that during the pandemic, not everyone was able to have this type of ritual with their family members. In her estimation, this missed opportunity for ritual foreshadowed a coming mental health crisis: "I anticipate there's going to be a lot of trauma coming out of this period—just the trauma of rituals and feelings and goodbyes not able to be fulfilled, not able to be spoken. I worked with one family who was not able to be with their loved one as he died. We would sit in the driveway together and talk through their feelings and try to create honoring rituals there, but in so many ways it wasn't the same."[64] In light of this absence, invented personal rituals among those who lost loved ones to COVID-19 became exceptionally important to provide an individually meaningful framework for the loss of their loved one.

Spontaneous Rituals in Virtual Communities

These individual rituals were not the only rituals invented during the pandemic. Beyond the medical professionals and those grieving a COVID death, virtual communities became an important site of invented ritual. When asked about the impetus behind these new rituals, I was told that they often arose due to the lack of public recognition of their suffering. Sabila, who helped to organize the particularly sizeable Facebook group COVID-19 Loss Support for Family & Friends, explained, "No one saw our pain, so we had to take care of each other. As we came together, it just seemed natural that we would create traditions for ourselves."[65] Such rituals often moved between various social media platforms and virtual communities, starting in one and being taken up quickly by another. Through the performance of these rituals, COVID grief communities came to recognize and participate with each other.

Prominent among these invented traditions were public photo sharing rituals. In the COVID-19 Loss Support group, members would post photos of their loved ones at a happy moment. Theoretically, these posts could happen at any time, but they often served as a commemoration of a specific, painful period—the anniversary of a COVID diagnosis, entering the hospital, or being put on a ventilator. The original poster would then prompt other members to share a happy photo of their loved ones. A cascade of photos would follow in the comments, often with messages proclaiming, "I'll never forget you," "Gone, but not forgotten," or "They won't silence our loss." Individuals would comment on how meaningful it was to see all these photos together, both to think of how much was lost, but also to simply remember their loved ones when they were happy. While it is easy to look at these events as simply sharing photos on social media—an activity most people engage in at some point—the framing of the event through commemorating a significant day, as well as prompting the shared community to participate, sets it apart and removes it from regular time—turning the normal act of photo sharing into a ritual.

Members of the COVID-19 Loss Support group would also virtually acknowledge the annual anniversary of a loved one's death. Annual commemorations of a loved one's passing are central in religious communities across the globe. Some of the oldest recorded Chinese rituals involve honoring the anniversary of ancestors's passing,[66] and Chinese Buddhist scriptures relate a series of offerings to be made during the hundred days after someone passes away.[67] The eldest male in a Hindu family is expected to annually perform a ceremony known as *shradda* to honor deceased parents and grandparents in the paternal line.[68] Jewish families hailing from Eastern Europe will light a special candle known as the *yahrzeit* to burn for twenty-four hours on the anniversary of loved one's death.[69] In the COVID-19 Loss Support group, individuals would often commemorate monthly or annual death anniversaries with public posts, and commemorations have continued past the two- and three-year marks as the pandemic has stretched longer. In marking her mother's death, Carmen framed these virtual commemorations as a form of ritual remembrance: "I post those on the online group because at least someone remembers. I want to be seen, but the world has just moved on already. I am not ready to move on, not yet, not on that day. So, I make it a habit—post there so everyone remembers. And I get responses too, comforting words, little emojis, others who share my grief. For a few moments on what is often a very hard day, I don't feel so alone."[70]

In response to its perceived neglect from larger society, the American COVID-grief community adopted a specific symbol that is central to many of these invented anniversary rituals: a yellow heart ornamented by a black ribbon. The symbol plays on established semiotic conventions involving the color yellow in American wartime commemorations.[71] Its use here, seems designed to specifically equate the COVID pandemic with a form of warfare and call upon American society to remain united in the face of a common enemy. While my conversation partners said the symbol's use first began in Great Britain, the symbol of the yellow heart with a black ribbon quickly took hold across virtual communities and became a component of both personal and public invented rituals. Individuals who joined the community while their loved one was still on a ventilator would frequently post the yellow heart on the public forum to communicate that their loved one had passed on. Hundreds of members chose to tattoo some variation of the yellow heart on themselves in remembrance of their loved one. In a Facebook post, one woman described getting her tattoo as "the most spiritual experience of her life" and stated that she "prayed the entire way through it." Another woman said in a social media post that she continually replaced the yellow and black wreath hanging on her door—what many in this community call a "COVID wreath"—when it became tattered or sun-bleached. When making and hanging a new wreath, she noted that she prayed for her father, who had died from COVID-19, over every twist of ribbon or staple holding the wreath together. She said in a Facebook post, "I will keep a yellow wreath up to the day I die, because I want anyone else who has lost someone to this virus to know that they're not alone."

CONCLUSIONS: WHAT DRIVES RITUAL

The spontaneous, invented rituals discussed in the last section of this chapter are important in thinking about where ritual comes from. We discussed *what* ritual does, *how* ritual does it, and the need to draw on both the continuity of tradition and the support of community to feel as though the ritual was effective. However, these do not get to the heart of *why* people do rituals. Sociologist Robert Bellah hypothesized that humans are hardwired to perform rituals as a consequence of our evolution.[72] While a claim as big as this cannot necessarily be proven, it can still be useful as a tool to think with. At a time when traditional grieving rituals failed for many Americans, there remained the fundamental need to perform some sort of ritual, even one made up on the fly. In these moments, it was the act of doing itself that provided comfort. Perhaps it is that ritual fulfilled a need to acknowledge that we were still there, that we were still present, and that all of us—even those who had just died—still mattered in the midst of the sorrow, horror, and confusion of the pandemic. This type of claim cannot be verified with evidence, but perhaps we can see reflections of its truth in the tenacity of ritual behavior during the pandemic.

Above all, this chapter has shown how drastically rituals changed in the early months of the COVID-19 pandemic. There was incredible innovation and transformation as funerary and religious professionals attempted to comfort the grieving and honor the dead within the confines of local health guidelines. However, for many of those who lost loved ones to COVID-19, these efforts fell far too short. Ritual requires difference from normal time, but when our normal is itself shattered and remains shattered for months, for years even, ritual itself may stop working. Our expectations of a funeral or other grieving ritual could not be fulfilled because our normal had changed.

Our shattered sense of normal goes deeper, however. As the COVID-19 pandemic continued on, Americans' shared experience of normal was further disrupted by the widespread disagreement over what was happening. For some Americans, the pandemic was a reality happening every day, experienced through case counts, news stories, masking laws, and vaccination appointments. For others, the pandemic was a nuisance at best, but oftentimes something more sinister—a shadowy conspiracy bent on personal ruin and global domination involving profit-driven drug companies, engineered illness, and injected microchips. Government advice continually changed, or even contradicted itself, as federal institutions advised Americans to assiduously wipe down packages and sterilize industrial air systems, while some politicians advised taking Ivermectin (a drug used for treating parasites), and even openly mused about the possibility of injecting disinfectants into the body.[73] If the engine of ritual is the difference from a shared experience of normal, and a large, vocal minority disagrees on the normal that most everyone else is experiencing, then ritual faces a fundamental challenge that undermines its efficacy. An important function of ritual is building connections to community, but during the pandemic, when our communities became divided and transformed, these connections became much harder to form. It is to the transformations that death and COVID-19 caused in our understanding of communities that we now turn.

2

COMMUNITY

An interesting phenomenon in American society is that affiliation with a religious community follows something of a U-shape: many Americans belong to religious communities as children, fall away as young adults, and find their way back after marriage and the birth of their own children.¹ While this fact is changing somewhat as more individuals join what scholars call the "Nones"—those who do not report a religious affiliation—it is a compelling indicator that religion might be about more than just belief. People might fall away from their childhood beliefs, and people might grow to have beliefs, but few people believe, then dis-believe, then believe again—all right after they have kids.

Scholars have long thought that religion might provide substantial community engagement and benefit beyond the simple affirmation of belief. In her seminal study of vodou practitioner Mama Lola, Karen McCarthy-Brown noted that Mama Lola functioned as much as an ad hoc social worker as a religious leader.² Joseph Laycock has studied the Satanic Temple as a religious group of like-minded individuals who provide each other with social support while specifically eschewing belief in a supernatural power.³ Erik Braun argues that the prevalence of *vipassanā* meditation among nineteenth and twentieth-century Burmese lay Buddhists was, above all, an effort to preserve the Buddhist religious community in light of English colonialism—not simply a sudden change in belief.[4] None of these studies strictly invalidate belief as the foundation of religious participation. Rather, they point to the fact that individuals might "get something" out of the experience of being part of a religious community.

There are scholars who go even further, however, to argue that a supportive community is not just an important by-product of religious participation but is in actuality religion's true purpose—the community *is* the religion. We will examine that idea and some of its implications in this chapter by tackling the following three questions:

1. **Are all communities religious?**
2. **When do communities break down?**
3. **Can grief foster new communities? What might that mean for the future?**

This chapter will consider how religious communities responded to the COVID-19 pandemic and how encounters with death—both on a personal level and one society-wide—transformed individual understandings of what it meant to be part of a religious community. Some of my conversation partners described their religious community as an invaluable resource of phone chains, food trains, and unofficial funeral planners that leapt into action during the crisis. Others felt themselves irreparably alienated from their community by the experience of encountering death and sought out new forms of connection in virtual spaces. These experiences not only speak to the human need for kinship in a time of extreme isolation, but also represent an important direction for what the future of religious communities might look like.

ARE ALL COMMUNITIES RELIGIOUS?

There is no way to talk about religious communities without talking about Émile Durkheim. A founder of the field of sociology, Émile Durkheim is almost always the first name spoken when trying to make sense of how and why religious communities operate, despite writing his seminal work over a century ago. In the intervening time, scholars have expressed legitimate critiques of his work. As we will see, Durkheim radically privileges society over the individual. His definition of religion is so broad that almost any social institution might fall under it.[5] He was also the essence of the "armchair academic," reading accounts of Indigenous peoples from across the globe and then writing complex theories explaining how their societies worked, without ever leaving his comfortable office in France. Despite these criticisms, his work remains pivotal in the field, and it will necessarily provide the foundation for our discussion.

Society as Religion

Based on his analysis of ethnographies of Australian Aboriginal tribes, Émile Durkheim published *The Elementary Forms of Religious Life* (*Les formes élémentaires de la vie religieuse*) in 1912 as an attempt to identify the origin and function of religion. Revolutionary for his time, Durkheim was not interested in detailing why Aboriginal religions were false, or otherwise evidence that the tribes needed to be "civilized."[6] Rather, he believed that by studying religion in less industrialized—and therefore less socially stratified—settings he could ascertain both religion's origins and its social purposes. His argument has become foundational in thinking about how religion creates and maintains communities.

In Durkheim's estimation, society and religion are inextricably bound together. He states that "religion is a thing eminently social. Religious representations of the world are collective representations that express collective realities."[7] By this, he means that religion is not about gods and the belief in supernatural or transcendent forces, but fundamentally about creating, replicating, and deifying a given social group or a way of life. This process creates a "moral community" that approaches and interprets the world in the same way, with similar values, attitudes, and beliefs. His analysis is based on totemic religions in Australia, where tribal groups historically form identities around specific totem animals. The tribal totems are honored in elaborate rituals involving sacred objects that can only be displayed during the ceremony. Durkheim argues that by honoring the totem and its symbols, the tribe is actually recognizing itself—the community that protects them, ensures their survival, and creates shared feelings of joy. However, the feelings of being a part of something greater than oneself—ecstasy, belonging, patriotism, and so forth—cannot be articulated in language, so that feeling becomes attributed to a symbol that then becomes sacred to the community.

While Durkheim based his theories on Indigenous Aboriginal societies, he argued that his claims were not limited to such communities. Rather, all human societies operate through similar methods: a cross, a flag, or a brand is no less "sacred" than an Aboriginal totem if it shapes its viewers into a moral community. He writes, "The cause we are capturing at work is not exclusive to totemism; there is no society in which it is not at work. Nowhere can a collective feeling become conscious of itself without fixing upon a tangible object."[8] Whether we accept Durkheim's theories in whole or in part, he importantly shifted the analysis of religion away from belief and toward the significance of community. Participating in a religion is not merely about expressing a belief—one could just as easily do that alone in one's bedroom—but about publicly affirming your membership in a shared moral community. This sentiment was evident in Jennifer's explanation of her decision to convert to the Church of Jesus Christ of Latter-day Saints (LDS):

> I became interested in the LDS Church when my marriage began falling apart due to my husband's drinking. There was an LDS couple across the street, and it dawned on me that they're always happy, they're always together—that's how a marriage should be. They invited me and my daughter over for dinner at some point, and I began asking questions. It just was so obvious that these people were happy and fulfilled. They must be doing something right, and I wanted that.[9]

Jennifer did not frame her decision with a discussion of LDS beliefs or her faith in the revelations of the Book of Mormon. Rather, Jennifer reflected greater interest in the shared values and ethics of the LDS community and a lifestyle of which she wanted to be a part.

Feelings of belonging to a moral community often intersect with our sense of belonging to cultural and ethnic communities, as well. In discussing his father's participation in the local Korean Evangelical church, Yoon Tae explained, "I always had a bit of a language barrier with my dad. He immigrated from Korea in the late seventies and settled in Georgia where he ran a gas station. On Sundays, we would drive an hour each way to attend the Korean-speaking church—I don't know if my dad was religious, exactly, but he liked getting to speak Korean on those days and to be with other Korean immigrants."[10] For Yoon Tae's father, attending church was as much about being with other Korean-speaking people as it was about the religious truths of Christianity. Perhaps we do not think that we are worshipping the sacralized community when we go to temple or participate in the Eucharist, but—from a Durkheimian perspective—we are affirming our connection to, and participation in, a group of people that views the world with certain shared assumptions, ethics, and values.

Moral communities become especially important when considering rituals surrounding grief, or what Durkheim titled "piacular rites." These observances represent a critical moment for the community to come together and perform activities that address the grief of one person as, to some extent, the grief of everyone in the community. Durkheim observes, "Mourning is not the spontaneous expression of individual emotions … it is an obligation imposed by the group. One laments not simply because one is sad, but because one is obligated to lament."[11] In this sense, COVID-19 lockdown restrictions did not simply prevent people from expressing their grief; many mourners found themselves unable to perform important moral obligations. This problem was apparent in my conversation with Kay, who lost her father and grandfather to COVID-19:

> In Puerto Rican culture, when someone passes away, you know you have to get ready. Company is coming now! Make

reservations! Clean the house! Make food! That is how it is supposed to work. But we didn't have that—no one could come visit us because we were sick. Even after that, it was strange. With everything being online, it really limited my ability to mourn with my church community. You can't just say to the person next to you, "I lost my dad," or "I lost my grandfather this week." People were dropping off groceries, but they weren't there the way they would have been.[12]

As seen in chapter 1, Kay expressed her frustration over her inability to have a traditional funerary ritual after her family members' deaths. However, in this analysis, she also missed the opportunity to experience the benefits of a moral community that requires certain behaviors from its members and makes grief a shared reality.

We have discussed changes to funerary rituals and other piacular rites in light of the COVID-19 pandemic, and while such rituals necessarily involve community, here we want to focus on Durkheim's theories in action. How do churches, mosques, temples, and so forth act as moral communities? How did such communities take on new meaning in the transition to a virtual space? When might a moral community fail? And how will we make new moral communities in the future? While these questions deal with more than simply our experience of death in the pandemic, the crisis of COVID-19 and the related intimacy with death and dying raised the stakes on these questions, so to speak. Turning to my conversation partners' voices, moral communities can be analyzed, on one hand, for *what they do* (moral integration) and, on the other hand, *how they are constructed* (social integration). Both will be the focus below as we explore how communities themselves may be religious.

Social Integration: Moral Communities in the Virtual Space

The unprecedented and society-wide move to virtual space during the COVID-19 pandemic laid bare the fact that it is collective rituals performed as a social unit—not just shared beliefs—that build moral communities. Therefore, religious leaders adapted by using technology to maintain some sense of social connection in the midst of transformed religious practice. Reverend Chuck Kuhlman, C.S.P.—a Paulist priest leading St. Austin Catholic Parish in Austin, Texas—describes how the Paulist order, and St. Austin specifically, employed a variety of means to build vital social connections with parishioners:

> St. Austin is part of the Paulist order; Paulist.org ran over sixty Masses a week at the height of lockdown. Here at St. Austin, we did our virtual Masses, but we found we had to do more to connect with everyone. We ran a parish-wide newsletter and several smaller discussion groups, though I heard some of those faltered due to Zoom fatigue. We just wanted to make sure everyone knew what was going on and felt like they were a member of a community—here in the parish offices, in the city, and in the Catholic community worldwide.[13]

These connections that religious leaders like Rev. Kuhlman created—some to fellow members of the St. Austin parish, some to fellow Austinites, and some to Catholics around the world when they might never meet—served as the underlying social architecture of a moral community. Bishop Kathryn Ryan of the Episcopal Diocese of Texas had similar experiences deploying virtual tools to build and maintain social relationships among parishioners. Like the St. Austin community, the Episcopal parishes she worked with used Zoom Masses, small groups, and digital newsletters to maintain and develop connections between parishioners who, previously, had seen each other every week. While this required more work, she also noted how the virtual interface, in some ways, allowed the community to develop even closer ties than before by crafting unique opportunities to participate in grieving rituals and other piacular rites: "Zoom became critical for us. Before, when priests were allowed to enter the hospitals to do Last Rites, funerals, and other death-related ministries, it was often only the priest and, maybe, one local family member allowed in the room. But if we were able to do it over Zoom or FaceTime, they could have a much larger community present, the entire church even."[14] When faced with the crisis and isolation of the pandemic, religious leaders used virtual tools to maintain and build social connections between parishioners in the digital space as a means to sustain the moral community.

Indeed, as Bishop Ryan highlighted, some religious professionals found unexpected benefit in virtual religious practice. Pastor Craig Taylor of the Willow Meadows Baptist Church explained that the move to virtual interface deepened many of his parishioners' personal religious understandings:

> We have tried to virtually keep our community as much as we can, and, in many ways, it has worked! Our attendance numbers have actually gone up! Some community members have said that the online format has helped them understand the transcendence of God—everyone there in their own little computer or phone screen, but together as one. Sometimes, people might think "I have to have exactly these things to worship. I have to be in this room, with these people, and have this music." In doing this, they become like little gods themselves, and it disconnects them from

the true meaning of worship. Just holding to our old practices can really limit and restrict our view of God, but by tearing all that up, we are able to think of God in new ways and see that He is bigger than all of us. I have been trying to teach people this for forty years, but they're just getting it now![15]

More practically, the move to virtual practice made space for those who were disabled, ill, or otherwise homebound to fully participate in the religious communities from which they had previously been isolated. Pastor Taylor went on to explain that "In our church, there are people who have not been able to come to a service for years, but now are a part of every service. This is a game changer for them. We used to think the internet was the enemy and that you could never have church online, but we had to and, to be honest, it turned out pretty good."[16] As we have seen, many found virtual religious rituals personally unfulfilling; however, such virtual rituals and virtual communities also created a more inclusive environment that allowed greater participation for all individuals. This speaks to what may be a future avenue in the creation of moral communities that will be explored later.

In the perspective of Durkheim, moral communities have existed for millennia. Yet, the crisis of the pandemic and the move to virtual spaces revealed, at least in part, the forces that contribute to their formation in the modern world. Despite various tensions between in-person and virtual engagement, activities that promote social integration and relationship with others—even those globally that you may never meet—serve as the central ingredient in maintaining the moral community. Beyond their formation, moral communities had important roles during the pandemic as sources of both emotional support and education. Some scholars have called this "moral integration," wherein moral communities possess "a set of shared beliefs about morality and behavior."[17] If the pandemic allowed us to look at *how* moral communities formed via social integration, we might think of moral integration as what moral communities *do*, activities which became critically important in the pandemic.

Moral Integration: Sources of Support

It might seem from the discussion above that any group of humans who are connected for a period of time form a moral community. However, moral communities are not based around mere affiliation. Durkheim argues that there needs to be an element of moral integration as well—people need to care about one another, share resources, and agree on values. People waiting in line for concert tickets are certainly connected, but they are not a moral community. They have agreed to a social contract allocating resources (access to concert tickets) organized around a given system (time of arrival), but they do not feel compelled to look after each other or share resources. In contrast, a moral community takes on an important role in times of crisis to look after and aid its members. As people throughout the United States experienced grief and loss, religious communities were at the front line in providing various forms of financial, emotional, and social support.

Every religious professional I spoke with described setting up formal systems that reached out to those isolated individuals through emails, phone calls, or outdoor visits. These systems often extended to completing errands and other small chores for those who were especially vulnerable. The head priest of the Houston Zoroastrian community, Ērvad Khursheed Dastur, explained that "Some of our youths have taken it upon themselves to pick up groceries for the elderly and call them on the weekends. We have several priests who have been able to maintain our sacred fire that must never go out and have been praying several prayers intended to ward off evil spirits—not only of our community, but for all of Houston."[18] Similarly Ajit Giani of the Austin Bahá'í community explained that creating opportunities for connection not only benefited individuals' emotional health, but also ensured that certain important social skills were not lost by the isolation of the pandemic:[19]

> We have undertaken the responsibility of calling people on the phone to try and bring cheer to people's hearts, especially the elderly and disabled. Bahá'í are a prayerful group and invoke the divine at every opportunity, so we have been praying a lot together. There are many Bahá'í here who have come from other countries, who are very uncomfortable in isolation, and we are doing our best to comfort them during this period.[20]

Ajit went on to specify that some international members of his community were especially worried that their English-language skills would falter in the isolation of the pandemic. As a result, his community saw these phone conversations as important tools to not only raise their spirits, but also maintain their linguistic resources.

Echoing Ajit Giani, Rev. Rich Andre of St. Austin Catholic Church spoke about his efforts to connect with parishioners over the phone:

> Right now, we're doing something called Caring Connection, where we are working our way through the parish database and calling everyone to ask just how they're doing with everything. It is a slow process, but it has been really important. In November

[2020] most people were doing fine, but this second time around in February [2021], it has been a lot sadder. The people really struggling are the isolated ones. I have worked closely with three parishioners in the past month who I have had to help check into psychiatric hospitals or who have elected to do intensive outpatient therapies. There's a lot of people struggling now with all sorts of things.[21]

As Rev. Andre notes, the isolation of the pandemic was not the only difficulty that had to be combatted; many struggled with issues of mental health and addiction that required medical intervention. As a result, this support network—already strained by the pandemic—sometimes had to stretch even further to accommodate additional social crises. Many of my interviews with Texans happened in the weeks after the February 2021 winter storm Uri, when the Texas power grid catastrophically collapsed and close to three hundred people died of hypothermia. The crisis amplified the stress of the pandemic, as many were unable to secure groceries or were without power, heat, or water for days. My own family had power but was not yet fully vaccinated at the time, so we had to choose between strict COVID precautions and housing friends who had been without power for three or four days in subfreezing temperatures. (In Durkheimian fashion, we felt obligated to our community and chose to shelter others). Rev. Andre spoke about the Herculean efforts that his church community undertook to ensure all their parishioners had heat, food, and water. He noted, "During the [2021] freeze, one of our staff members was stuck in her house—an elderly woman. Someone here ran over a space heater, discovered she had no food, then ran to the grocery store to look for food. Of course, there was none, but we raided the school's pantry, our [rectory] pantry, and we have enough to give her to get her by for a few days. We might eat a bit lean, but I think we'll be OK."22

Beyond providing emotional and physical support, religious communities during the pandemic were often able to step in at the moment of a loved one's death to assist with the mundane details of planning funerary rituals. Jennifer, who we discussed earlier for her decision to convert to LDS, lost her mother to COVID-19 in March 2021. She described the incredible support that she received from the LDS community in taking care of various unexpected necessities afterward:

> My mother's memorial service was held in the chapel and the whole community helped me prepare it. I didn't have to plan any part of it; our local LDS Relief Society took care of everything—the reception, the music, the readings, the programs. I just told them her favorite hymns. They got me groceries and drove me to appointments at the funeral home so I wouldn't have to be alone. I always knew the support was there, but I never experienced it before this moment.23

Bishop Bruce Baillio of the San Pedro Ward in San Antonio's North Stake elaborated on the LDS commitment to supporting community members by connecting it to the religion's pioneer heritage:

> There is power in fellowship. The persecution of the early pioneers affected our church culture. It has caused us to become very strong in internally supporting one another. In the last twenty to thirty years, we have started to feel comfortable turning that mechanism outward and supporting the community at large. Although we sometimes face suspicion from other religious communities when we come to help, we really just want to share our

resources—there is not a catch, nothing hidden behind it. Indeed, I sometimes think there is an animosity towards God and religion in our society because faith is not necessarily seen as a tangible benefit, so it appears irrational. The reality is actually the opposite—we love others and sacrifice our own time, money, and resources because we love God and seek to follow His teachings.[24]

Drawing on their history of persecution, the LDS community developed significant internal support and self-reliance that became an asset during the pandemic.

Indeed, the LDS community—often colloquially known as Mormons, although LDS leadership affirmed in 2018 that this term is considered objectionable—stood out for its ability to successfully adapt to the pandemic. Beyond the support structures referenced by Jennifer and Bishop Baillio, the LDS community benefited from recent changes to ritual practice that allowed for greater at-home worship and more flexibility surrounding the timing of certain coming-of-age rituals. The LDS community also relies on a volunteer priesthood attainable by all adult men, making the transition to at-home worship relatively effortless. Reflecting their belief in continued revelation by the sitting LDS president, Bishop Baillio affirmed his understanding that this preparation in the years before the pandemic represented "an act of God" preparing the community for the future.

While scholars of religion generally do not comment on the authenticity of such claims, the experience of the LDS community is an important example of the social benefits provided by religious communities. New religious movements scholar David Feltmate has argued that marginalized religious groups like the Church of Jesus Christ of Latter-day Saints—which has often been viewed with suspicion in wider American culture as somehow fundamentally different than other religions—have primarily been studied through the lens of a "social problems paradigm."[25] In this framework, the group is discussed for its ontology—Is it good? Is it bad? Should we combat it, or should we tolerate it? However, if we look at the examples of the LDS community discussed by Bishop Baillio and Jennifer and ask better questions, we can see what the LDS community was able to do uniquely well in a time of social emergency. A priesthood open to all adult men made the switch to at-home worship easy; the flexibility of continued revelation allowed for immediate changes in the face of crisis; the self-reliance nurtured by centuries of outsider status created a network of autonomous support. All these qualities combined to make the LDS community remarkably adaptable to the pandemic. For those thinking about religion academically, the case study of the LDS community during the pandemic reveals the benefit of moving beyond the social problems paradigm to view marginalized religious communities as laboratories producing novel solutions to universal problems.

Moral Integration: Building Shared Perspectives

In addition to providing material and emotional support, moral communities create a framework through which members come to understand the world and their place within it. As such, religious leaders often held a central role for parishioners as interpreters of current events during the pandemic. Imam Sheikh Attia Omara of the Islamic Center of Lake Travis explained:

> At the beginning of the pandemic, there was a dire need among people to hear something from myself and other Islamic leaders.

I remember early in the pandemic, many Muslims came to me with questions about how to cope with fear, how to find inner peace, how to remain strong. As people became more used to the pandemic, their questions changed, and they became more interested in the socio-political things happening around them. I often find myself educating people on what is happening.[26]

Rabbi Neil Blumofe of Congregation Agudas Achim experienced similar needs from those in his synagogue community: "People above all just wanted to be seen and have someone be present with them. So many times, during lockdown I was asked, 'Rabbi, can you just come over and sit with us outside? Just talk to us about what is happening.' I often found myself trying to give perspective or contextualize what was happening."[27] In the chaos of the pandemic, many people looked to religious leaders for perspectives on how they and other members of their moral community should understand political and social realities.

Sometimes, the role of religious communities in creating this shared perspective involved framing complex medical and historical information. While all religious communities played some role in educating the public about the pandemic, African American churches had an especially important place in combatting disinformation. Pastor Lou McElroy of the Antioch Missionary Baptist Church in Houston, Texas spoke about his efforts to provide trustworthy information for his predominantly Black congregation:

> At the onset of this pandemic, there was a stigma that the church—especially the Black church—was a petri dish for COVID-19 because of the close contact of fellowship and worship. But we had a big role in limiting the pandemic that needs to be appreciated! The Antioch community organized two COVID testing

sites at the church around the holiday season to be sure everyone was safe. We partnered with the Texas Children's Hospital and the Houston City Health Department to do a virtual town hall on the vaccine that targeted Black and Brown communities who were a little hesitant. We bought airtime on the Texas Southern University radio station to promote vaccination and ran a three-day vaccination site. While we were certainly a site of spiritual comfort, the church became the main source of information for many in the Black community.[28]

Pastor McElroy's experience speaks to larger historical trends in American religion. Broadly speaking, church communities have a more central role in the Black community than in the non-Black community. Sociologists C. Eric Lincoln and Lawrence Mamiya explain, "As the only stable and coherent institutional area to emerge from slavery, black churches were not only dominant in their communities but they also became the womb of black culture and a number of major social institutions."[29] Therefore, African Americans often look to their moral communities not only for spiritual development, but also for practical medical and social information. This role has been amplified by the painful history of the Tuskegee Syphilis Study and similar cases of medical experimentation and mistreatment of African American patients that have caused significant suspicion of the government and medical establishments. Pastor McElroy later related to me the success of his efforts—ninety-eight percent of the Antioch community was vaccinated, in comparison to just under sixty percent nationwide.[30]

The moral integration of various religious communities was not only related to medical or political information, but also to a shared perspective framing the death of a loved one. After her mother's death in January 2021, Amanda, a member of the

Apache tribe who identifies as Christian, described feeling lost and desperately seeking reassurance that her mother was in a better place. While leaders at her local Christian church did little to reach out and met her requests for guidance with unfulfilling platitudes, she explained how her Apache elders more successfully framed her mother's postmortem reality:

> Unlike the church leaders, the elders from my tribe have given me so much support. They have reached out and done meditations or blessings with me on the phone. There has been so much communication and conversation about my mother, which is honestly what I wanted—to not let her be forgotten and to just have some sort of certainty of her place in the afterlife. There are two elders I speak with—Esther and Lavita. Lavita is a medium who is very concerned about my mother being released to the ancestors. She told me that my mom was OK, but that I have to let her go so that she can come back and guide me. She says that I have to trust our Creator has her and only then can I feel her presence again when she returns as an ancestor. Esther is Christian like me. She explained that you are placed on this earth for a limited time to attain ultimate peace in heaven. Esther told me my mother was with my father and the ancestors in heaven, watching over me.[31]

By deploying a shared perspective on what happens after you die, the Apache elders were able to console Amanda. This example serves as an evocative case study as to the effects of social integration on making the moral community believable. Amanda identifies as both Christian and Apache Indian—two distinct but overlapping moral communities. She sought comfort from both communities in grieving her mother's death, but the Apache community provided a more powerful and comforting perspective due to Amanda's greater experience of social integration. While Durkheim's initial theories about Aboriginal tribes focused only on single moral communities, here we see his ideas still have merit in situations where people might belong to multiple, intersecting moral communities with various levels of social integration.

As will be discussed later, the formation of shared perspectives within moral communities had a negative effect as well, with many churches spreading misinformation about the seriousness of COVID-19 and the pandemic to parishioners. While I strived to get a diverse set of political viewpoints in my interviews, no Evangelical Christian leaders who publicly expressed suspicion of the pandemic or vaccines responded to my requests for conversation—possibly because as an academic, I too was regarded with suspicion. But the fact that some churches became places where disinformation spread reinforces the central role of moral communities in shaping worldviews. Moral communities do not have to form an understanding of the world that is accurate—it only has to be coherent. This reality leads to our next topic: that sometimes moral communities do not provide the necessary social and moral integration, especially when confronted with grief in a convoluted and confusing time.

WHEN DO COMMUNITIES BREAK DOWN?

Durkheim believed that an encounter with death is an important time when members of the moral community have the opportunity to come together and share the burden of sorrow. In his own words, "When an individual dies, the family group to which he belongs feels diminished, and it comes together to react to this diminishment. A shared misfortune has the same effect as the approach of a happy event. It enlivens collective feelings, which lead individuals to seek one another out and come together."[32] However, Durkheim acknowledged that things did not always happen in this way. If the death remains unacknowledged, serious harm would befall the moral community's social integration, because "for a family to tolerate that one of its members should die without being mourned would give witness thereby that it lacks moral unity and cohesiveness: it abdicates, it renounces its existence."[33]

Not every moral community—religious, national, cultural—*worked* during the pandemic. Some religious communities could not switch to virtual practice due to doctrine or practice, while others found their ideas of what it meant to be a religious community challenged. Thinking through this particular concern, Bishop Ryan of the Episcopal Diocese of Texas eloquently explained:

> Every aspect of the normal functioning of a religious community has been challenged in the pandemic. You want to care for the poor and unhoused? How do you do that while keeping your volunteers safe? You want to keep your lights on? What if your community has mixed feelings about accepting federal aid? Do you ask your parishioners for funds when they are already financially hurting?[34]

Still others that I interviewed found their participation in the larger community of Americans suddenly under suspicion on account of their ethnic background in a politically charged climate, where social media and fringe news outlets warned of the "Chinese virus," the "Wuhan bug," or the "kung flu." And many of those I interviewed did not see their personal experience with death, loss, and grief reflected in their moral community's discourse, causing feelings of isolation and abandonment. All these examples show us the limits of community, and places where moral communities might fail to adapt in a swiftly transforming environment.

Difficulties with Virtually Replicating In-Person Communities

Despite the success of many religious communities' shift to virtual practice, grief and grieving rituals complicated that transition. Chapter 1 highlighted how many mourners found virtual funerals unfulfilling; this dissatisfaction extended to the experience of grieving more generally in isolation from religious communities. Among those I spoke with who lost loved ones to COVID-19, a frequent refrain was how isolated they felt because they could not physically be with other people in the aftermath of their loved one's death. While virtual communities sufficed for some, others felt that the virtual space was inadequate. One of the most painful interviews that I conducted was with Paul, an elderly Roman Catholic widower living in New York City who lost his Jewish wife, Joannie. He spoke about the extreme isolation he felt as COVID-19 robbed him of the only community he had remaining in the aftermath of her death:

> I would have loved to go to Mass, but I am afraid to be around people. I am alone. I have no siblings and my wife lost her only sister. All of our parents are gone. My aunts and uncles are gone. I have a few friends, but they have all started to move away. Once I can go back to the [Catholic fraternal order] Knights of Columbus and establish face-to-face friendships again, that will be a

big help, but I just don't feel safe yet. I always joked with my Joannie that I would be in Christian Heaven, and she would be in Jewish Paradise, and they're just a short bus ride away. But I feel so alone now. I need her. I need people, but this illness doesn't let you see them.[35]

Perhaps because of my own aging parents, or my fears about what will happen to my childless partner and I as we get older, I sometimes still find myself thinking about Paul, and my heart breaks all over again. What Paul, and others who expressed similar feelings are describing is a lack of the tools necessary to build a moral community—despite all the virtual options for participation, they were unable to socially integrate. Indeed, while reflecting on mourning his father, Yoon Tae poetically expressed the central problem of grieving in the time of COVID-19. He stated, "That's the worst of it—the vehicle of COVID is other people, so there's this sense that the virus is the monster, but the actual foot-soldier of the virus is other people just doing normal things. It isolates you."[36]

Durkheim highlighted issues of grief and death as particularly vulnerable times in the architecture of moral communities, and many religious communities attempted to overcome that obstacle with virtual participation. However, it is important to acknowledge that, for some religious communities, the move to a virtual space was fundamentally impossible due to doctrines or belief systems. While many Christian communities perform a reenactment of Jesus's Last Supper, Roman Catholic theology is unique for positing that the bread and wine become the literal body and blood of Jesus Christ—a doctrine known as transubstantiation. As such, Rev. Rich Andre explained that virtual religious practice could not be a substitute for attending Mass in person:

There's a lot of Catholic theology that says you have to be in person for the Mass, because Catholicism is extremely sacramental, and sacraments are tangible. The most important part of a Mass is receiving the sacrament of the Eucharist, which Catholics believe is Jesus Christ present in body and blood, soul and divinity. So, the theology has always been that you must go to Mass—you can't do that online!

Traditionally, Catholic theology states that Christ is present in four ways during the Mass: imminent in the gathering of people, in the proclamation of the scripture, in the figure of the priest presiding the Mass, and in the Eucharist itself. Christ was powerfully present during our virtual Masses in all ways except the Eucharist. Some days we would have two hundred to two hundred fifty computers logging on to our weekday 8 a.m. Masses, which was unheard of before the pandemic. But we can only take the sacrament in person.[37]

Due to belief in transubstantiation and the sacramental nature of the Eucharist, virtual practice, if continued long-term, cannot serve as the entirety of social integration and religious practice for Roman Catholic communities.

Similarly, the religious beliefs of the Zoroastrian community inhibited the move to virtual practice—even in short-term situations. One of the oldest continuously practiced religions, Zoroastrianism originated in ancient Persia. Due to persecution, the community eventually moved to India in the ninth century CE, where they became known as the Parsis or "those from Persia." To this day, the Zoroastrian religious community is largely coterminous with the specific Parsi cultural community. Zoroastrian religious practice centers around offerings to a sacred fire that must be constantly maintained by priests, known as *ērvad*. When discussing the response to the pandemic with Ērvad Khursheed Dastur, head priest at the Houston Zoroastrian Center, he explained:

> We have not had many changes due to the pandemic. We were unable to go virtual, as we believe electric energy interferes with our rituals and reduces the efficacy of the prayers. However, priests remained in the temple to maintain the sacred fire. We also had always been wearing masks, because in the Zoroastrian faith, you cover your face during important rituals so that your spit does not touch the sacred fire and make it impure.[38]

The physician and historian of science Jeremy Brown notes that Orthodox Jewish communities faced similar concerns, as "computers and smartphones are forbidden to be used on those holy days, and in any event a quorum of 10 men is needed for much of the prayer services. Unless that quorum, called a *minyan*, can meet in person, the thrice-daily prayers may not be recited, at least not in full."[39] For religious communities like these, even short-term virtual practice was not an option. While this significantly limited the community's social and cultural activities—important parts of a moral community's social integration—Ērvad Khursheed Dastur reflected that it did not fundamentally change their religious practice, as this had always been limited to the priests.

Even when communities were able to make a switch to virtual practice, this transition often brought up complicated ethical and social questions when considering its long-term role. My conversation with Rabbi Neil Blumofe of the Congregation Agudas Achim occurred in February 2021—a transitional time when some were vaccinated, and others were not.

Passover is one of the most important Jewish holidays, commemorating the Jews' escape from slavery in Egypt. As Passover 2021 approached, Rabbi Blumofe explained the difficulties he faced as a religious leader blending virtual and non-virtual participation:

> The virtual format has raised some difficult ethical questions. Passover is coming up; it is the most observed Jewish holiday of the year. This holiday is based on sitting at a table together and sharing a meal, which is the one thing we're being told not to do. Last year [2020] we skipped it, but this year, some of our community are vaccinated and some are not. What do we do? Do we open up an in-person event only for those vaccinated? What about breakthrough infections? We have been looking at other Jewish communities to see what they are doing and the Halacha [Jewish law] is clear—you join together in the face of warfare, discrimination, disease, this COVID pandemic is just another difficulty like any other.
>
> But this whole pandemic raises bigger questions: What is the job of a synagogue? Is it just community? People can get community in all sorts of places, but synagogues are about Jewish traditions—how do those remain vibrant when you can't do them? We're not financed by some world-wide organization like many Christian denominations; we're a membership model and our numbers have gone down.[40]

After a brief pause, Rabbi Blumofe expressed his concerns over the future of synagogues if religious communities remained entirely or predominantly virtual, saying, "I think many people just aren't sure this community means as much to them in the virtual space as it did before."[41]

Rabbi Blumofe's thoughts, as well as the experience of other religious leaders highlighted in this section, speak to some of the limits in constructing moral communities virtually. As a tradition, Judaism generally values the collective performance of specific religious laws and festivals over private belief, making a move to virtual practice comparatively difficult. We saw earlier that Roman Catholic, Zoroastrian, and Orthodox Jewish communities faced similar struggles in fully transitioning to virtual practice due to their theologies. This reality suggests that the move to creating virtual moral communities was most effective for Protestant Christian communities and others that emphasize personal belief over specific ritual practices. While this claim is necessarily limited by my relatively small sample of interviewees, it speaks to an arena for future research and discussion as virtual religious communities become more common in the future. More importantly, though, is the question of who is lost by the move to a virtual community. Paul's extreme isolation in the wake of Joannie's death demonstrates how many people still rely on face-to-face interactions that cannot be easily replicated in virtual spaces. Such a challenge demonstrates that the move to socially integrated moral communities in virtual spaces is neither an easy nor a sure one.

Undermining Social Integration in the American Moral Community

To this point, we have discussed moral communities rather synonymously with individual religious communities. But it is important to remind ourselves that Durkheim said that many types of groups and organizations can function as moral communities if they have shared values and cultural practices. While one may be understandably hesitant to say America is a "religion," when we say things like, "That's un-American" or when we salute the flag, we are acknowledging a set of values and totemic sacred objects that we share. During the pandemic, however, many individuals, especially those of Asian descent, felt their participation in the moral community of "America" questioned because of racist accusations about the pandemic's purported origins. Others confronted ableist assumptions about whose deaths were acceptable expenditures in the uncomfortable math of the pandemic. By causing people to question where they belonged, the pandemic threatened the social and moral cohesion of the American community as a whole.

The COVID-19 pandemic led to an unprecedented uptick in racist discourse and racially motivated attacks against Asian Americans. A recent review of twelve nationally representative public opinion polls found that thirty-nine percent of Asian Americans reported personally experiencing racism, significantly more than before the pandemic.[42] Among the four Asian Americans that I interviewed, two personally experienced, or had a family member personally experience, offensive comments that were racially motivated. With Scandinavian, Chinese, and Peruvian Quechuan Indian heritage, Arla identified herself as multicultural in our conversation about her father's death from COVID-19. However, her daughter was adopted from the same Chinese province where her grandfather had been born and experienced racial remarks in school: "The spring of 2020 was not easy for my daughter because she was born in China. Classmates and even some teachers would joke about the coronavirus being from China and tell her not to touch them."[43] Arla later elaborated that although her family had attended the same church in Southern California for most of her life, she and her mother witnessed there disparaging remarks about the Chinese origin of the virus:

> In the church I grew up in, people would say the virus was made in China, that it was manufactured to hurt us. I was aghast! Could they not see my face? I am one-quarter Chinese. My mother is half Chinese. Do you not see how embarrassed she is? How hurt she is? We worry for our daughters after the [March 2021] shooting in Atlanta—what can happen to Asian women in this country is appalling. People are more scared of the coronavirus because it came from China, rather than somewhere in Europe. They are taking those fears out on Asian women.[44]

Arla's concerns were echoed by Taiwanese Buddhist nun Venerable Jue Ji. Working at a Fo Guang Shan temple in Austin, Texas, she explained that many of her Chinese parishioners living in central Texas expressed concerns about the potential for racist attacks: "In the beginning, COVID-19 was called the Wuhan epidemic. As a result, many of my Chinese parishioners worried about their safety and chose to stay out of the public. It has been hard for our Chinese community."[45]

Beyond the explicit racism faced by Asian Americans during the pandemic, data repeatedly showed mortality rates higher among minority communities and people of color.[46] While the reasons for this are likely complex and multifaceted, many of those who lost loved ones to COVID-19 believed the greater infection and mortality rates to be symptomatic of culture-wide neglect of people of color. Sikh American Manpreet noted that when her Punjabi father was admitted to the emergency room in the spring of 2020 for COVID-19, the hospital failed to provide appropriate translators and, as a result, his medical information was incorrect: "When my father was finally admitted, they immediately put him on a ventilator. I couldn't go in with him, and I feel like he was so neglected. On his medical records, they had all this incorrect information! They said he was an alcoholic, they had the wrong age, they put the wrong language translator—Hindi instead of Punjabi!"[47] While she was quick to explain that as a medical professional herself, she understood mistakes could happen, she said she could not shake the feeling that her father was provided inferior medical care because of his ethnicity: "I know doctors are human and make mistakes, but I worry they looked at him and just saw a dying immigrant, so they stopped trying."[48] Amanda shared similar sentiments while reflecting on her mother's death from COVID-19, expressing that wider American society disregarded how the pandemic disproportionately affected Native American communities. She elaborated, "There has been so little discussion of how this is affecting the Native American population. We are already a forgotten people; we know we're not accepted or acknowledged, but with COVID, we got to see that neglect firsthand."[49]

The pandemic also forced questions about the allocation of medical resources and systemic ableism. Medical data consistently showed higher rates of death among COVID-19 patients with comorbidities like diabetes, asthma, or other immunocompromising diseases.[50] For many of those who lost loved ones to COVID-19, these medical facts became strategies to dismiss the death of their loved one as somehow less tragic or more explainable. Later in our conversation, Amanda returned to the question of neglect, explaining, "When I tell people my mother died, the first question they ask is, 'How old was she? Did she have any pre-existing conditions?' Our loved ones deserved better than this; they didn't deserve to die like this. Who cares if they had asthma or heart disease? Who cares if they struggled with their weight? What matters is they're gone, and we could have done better by them. Whatever was going on, they didn't deserve to die."[51] Carmen related similar experiences when describing her mother's death: "I have had friends who know my mom and ask, 'Did she REALLY die of COVID?' It is a slap in the face. She had a lot of medical problems, but to deny her death like that—it hurts."[52] As part of this sentiment, the hashtag #Mydisabledlifeisworthy began trending on social media in early 2021 as individuals expressed their frustration with public discourse about pandemic deaths that reflected ableist sentiments. A comment made in January 2022 by the CDC's director that the majority of those who died of COVID-19 while vaccinated were "unwell to begin with," drew ire from disability rights activists for implying their deaths were somehow negligible or acceptable.[53] As COVID-19 has become endemic, such debates balancing public safety and public life have only intensified and are ripe for further discussion.[54]

Social Isolation Mourning a COVID Death

While minority and disabled communities found their experience of the pandemic especially isolating, those who lost loved ones to COVID-19 also felt isolated from their religious and social communities due to lacking the shared experience of a COVID death. This experience ultimately led them to question their participation in communities that had formerly been important to them. In my conversations with those encountering death during the pandemic, almost everyone expressed feelings of abandonment by larger American society. Over a million Americans died from COVID-19; however, many lived lives personally unaffected by a COVID-19 death and individuals felt anxious to return to "normal." Manpreet explained that "When I see my friends—my grief is actually worse! My dad used to drive these friends home and they knew him, so they're a trigger rather than a comfort. My friends have kind of put me down over this too. They tell me I am obsessing too much over it, but I think they just don't understand. They don't have to deal with this every day." After her father died early in the pandemic, Sabila similarly felt frustration and resentment at watching others on social media return to their daily lives with little concern for the pandemic:

> I think I speak on behalf of many people in the community when I say it feels like the country has abandoned us. Everyone is just out there, moving on and living life, and we feel left behind. I have gotten into arguments with two different sets of cousins about going out and eating while the pandemic is still raging. On social media, I see all these smart, educated people in my extended family and friends who are taking risks I just can't believe. It feels like a slap in the face for us, for my father, and for our experience. If it doesn't affect you first-hand, it's not real. People are willing to take risks because of FOMO [fear of missing out], but it is just spreading death and illness to more people. I would get so angry in the summer and fall of 2020, just seething with rage, but now I have become numb to it.[55]

Julia echoed Sabila, explaining how the lack of a shared experience with death during the pandemic made her feel isolated from larger society following the death of her brother: "I know everyone feels this way after they lose someone—why does the world keep going?! I understand the world is going to move on eventually, but I am not ready for it now; I don't want to forget him. I can't stop talking about him; I can't stop talking about the pandemic. It is not some person off in the far edge of the world who died, but someone right here, in their community."[56] Durkheim's moral communities require both social and moral integration—shared experiences and shared values. During the pandemic, however, Americans had fundamentally different experiences of death, social activity, and public health needs. Without such a shared foundation, many felt their moral communities breaking down.

Those who lost a loved one to COVID-19 often found themselves isolated even within their own families. After Olivia's father died of COVID-19, her family was eager to return to the politically conservative church where she believed he contracted COVID-19—a decision she vehemently opposed:

> Family has not been a source of strength for me right now. Their views are just so different—even though my father died of COVID-19 they still claim that the pandemic is not a big deal, that he is the outlier, that you won't be harmed if you are washed in the blood of Jesus. My dad was washed in the blood—he was a devout and holy man! Why did he die then? The whole thing makes my grief so much harder. If my mom goes back to church, the church that killed my father and gave him COVID, I don't know if I can have any relationship with her.[57]

Bianca found herself in a similarly antagonistic relationship with her family in the aftermath of her grandmother's passing:

> My uncle wanted to have a huge party after my grandmother's death. I actually threatened to call 311 and tell the authorities that

he was having this huge party at a time when it was against California regulations. I didn't do it, but I wanted to. It's hard as the oldest granddaughter in a Mexican American family. While I was out there, it was just expected that I would make the meals, clean the house, plan this party, but I didn't do that. Someone had to stand up to my uncles.[58]

Olivia and Bianca's experiences demonstrate that even if the intimacy of losing a loved one to COVID-19 is shared, relationships within one's communities and families may still be threatened by conflicting values and moral perspectives.

This experience of different, competing perspectives on whether the COVID-19 pandemic was a "big deal" or not will be discussed further in chapter 4. While those who directly lost loved ones to COVID-19 were, perhaps, most affected by this discourse, many individuals found themselves confronted by the breakdown of our shared moral community. Working as a COVID-19 nurse at a major hospital in central Texas, Mary told me:

> Frankly, we nurses, we're not OK. We're able to put our work mask on and get through the day, but ever more frequently, the mask isn't covering it. So many nurses are leaving the profession. I have been told by patients with COVID, by their families, and by people online, that I am lying. The pandemic isn't real; these people aren't really dying of COVID. Another nurse was told by her neighbor that she was a government crisis actor hired to make us all scared. It is a real punch in the gut.[59]

As discussed in chapter 1, if America lacks a clear idea of what is happening during the pandemic—a shared belief in its causes and experiences—our ability to mourn and to grieve together is fundamentally undermined. Such need for a shared experience extends to our moral communities as well, causing many to feel their religious, professional, and national communities failing.

CAN GRIEF FOSTER NEW COMMUNITIES? WHAT MIGHT THAT MEAN FOR THE FUTURE?

While this chapter began by examining how existing religious communities made the move to virtual spaces in the pandemic, some individuals found that they no longer felt like they belonged. As demonstrated in the last section, a lack of shared experience in the pandemic—and as a result, shared ethical commitments—alienated many from the various moral communities that had previously formed their identity. However, social media allowed for those who shared the experience of losing someone to COVID-19 to create new communities that transcended local boundaries across America and around the globe. These virtual communities may be a harbinger of the future religious landscape, where it is not geography or location that determines one's affiliation with a religious community, but social or political identity.

Moral Communities on Social Media

As Americans became ill and died from COVID-19 during an unprecedented lockdown that limited access to social services, many scoured the internet for information on how to care for their loved one, ensure that they received adequate medical treatment, and, in some cases, handle the various legal obligations after their passing. In the isolating period of lockdown, the virtual space also became the place where many worked through their grief by joining communities on social media. Among these, the COVID-19 Loss Support for Family & Friends group on Facebook became one of the most prominent, with over twenty-five thousand members at its largest. While many groups and tags developed on social media to connect those who lost loved ones to COVID-19—including the Instagram hashtag #covidgrief, the Reddit group r/COVIDgrief, and various TikTok users making public memorials—the blend of photo and text posting, link-sharing, non-anonymous posting, and possibility for immediate person-to-person interaction through comment chains made the Facebook group exceptionally popular.

Like in-person moral communities, the COVID Loss Support Facebook community has a set of shared values. Anyone espousing vaccine denial, scientific misinformation, or fraudulent claims about COVID-19 is immediately banned. They also have rules for appropriate behavior and etiquette. While anyone can join, the COVID-19 Loss Support group strictly enforces its posting policies, allowing only those who are grieving to post or comment. Researchers or media inquiries must first send their request to a moderator who posts the call on their behalf. Members identify the page as a safe space to share stories. Arla explained that she joined the group because, "I have found it difficult to share with other people. I feel like Peter in the Bible after Jesus died, because I just want to run around with a sword and cut people's ears off. I have that same raw emotion right now. Some people publicly pretend they know you and support you—like Judas did when he kissed Jesus—but he was the betrayer. At this point, I have come to realize that I can't trust the people I thought I could."[60] The community has also spawned smaller, offshoot groups focused on specific types of grief such as parents who lost children to COVID-19 or spouses mourning spouses. These groups generally disallow members who do not share that grief, and they do not respond to media or research requests.

Sabila, who sat with me for an interview, started the COVID-19 Loss Support group after her father died in March 2020 and has remained its lead moderator in the years that followed. For her, running the community has represented an important piece of healing:

> I started the Facebook support group three days after my dad died. That has been a huge source of comfort. If I didn't do it, I don't know where I would be emotionally, psychologically; it gave me a sense of purpose after losing my dad. It's a lot of emotional labor to run the group, but I feel I could very easily drown in my own sorrow if I was not doing the work. I have seen my mother struggling with her grief even more than me because I have the large Facebook group to turn to when I need support. She has only me and our relatives.[61]

Yoon Tae agreed with Sabila's assessment on the group's capacity for healing. He explained that "The Facebook group lets me be creative and talk through ideas. It's an outlet where I could write five paragraphs about my feelings and people will actually read it. We're all just trying to figure this grief thing out together."[62] The group features members from around the globe, although the majority of its members are based in America and membership seems to fluctuate based on need. Having observed the group for over two years, I realized its membership served as a type of macabre monitor for the pandemic's spread: when India featured an especially terrible pandemic surge in April and May 2021, more South Asian names suddenly began appearing with posts and comments. As the community almost exclusively uses English, the imprecise measurement afforded by this group can only document the coronavirus's spread among English-speaking communities, but other virtual linguistic communities featured similar groups.

Chapter 1 discussed the COVID Loss Support community's development of specific rituals and emblems used to commemorate their deceased loved ones at death or on specific anniversaries. Further forms of moral integration are evident in the community's other activities. They host weekly meditation sessions, coffee hours, or phone check-ins. There are dozens of individual contemplations, musings, and responses posted each day by members. Beyond these personal observations, individuals share diverse articles on recovering from grief and how to mourn the dead, as well as memes or images meant to comfort the viewer or express frustration with the situation. The comment section underneath these posts becomes the arena for lively disagreement and theological debate. In a post on January 30, 2021, that became particularly controversial, one individual shared a meme about how—just like a glow stick that must be "broken" to activate—God sends us difficult experiences like the death of a loved one to help us "glow." One woman responded, "Yeah, no. I don't want to be broken to fulfill whatever purpose," while another supported the original post with the comment, "This is beautiful. God is good in all things. Exactly what I need to hear." The debate continued in the comment section for several days before eventually dying out. In this way, these posts represent an especially dynamic form of theological discussion.

In many ways, the COVID-19 Loss Support group community functions as a moral community, with shared rituals, values, and social integration. The mutual experience of grief fostered connections and recognition of shared values between members who, though they had never met each other, became incredibly close. Reflecting on the death of her father, Arla told me that "The COVID-19 Facebook group online has been the most helpful community for me because they get it. I strangely feel I can be my most authentic self with strangers rather than people I have known for twenty years."[63] Manpreet echoed this sentiment. She described the community on the COVID-19 Loss Support group as the only people who truly understood her experience:

> I joined the COVID-19 group because there just weren't people to talk to at that point. I've watched it grow, which is both a good and a bad thing. It is terrible so many people are still dying from this disease, but there are now more people who can relate. While there is important information on there—how to have a funeral, how to cremate the body, how to get the death certificate—I go mostly for the emotional support. They seem to be the only people who get it.[64]

Despite being a devout Catholic, Paul explained his involvement in the community as a greater source of comfort than relationships with those in his church: "I have spoken to a priest, but I find most comfort in the online grief group. Every day, I read stories of people who have lost sometimes their whole families—both parents, or both parents and a sister and a brother, or a husband and a sister—I don't know how they go on, but if they can, maybe I can too."[65] For those like Paul, the virtual moral community of the COVID-19 Loss Support group did not replace his participation in other religious communities, but rather augmented his identity by providing a service that he felt he was not adequately receiving at his local church. This multifaceted participation in diverse communities reflects what scholar

Heidi Campbell calls a "networked community" and "networked religion." Rather than participating in a single moral community, virtual moral communities allow individuals to seamlessly move between online and offline religious identities "that are emergent, varying in depth, fluid, and highly personalized."[66] In this way, social media groups like COVID-19 Loss Support for Family & Friends can become the foundation of new moral communities that intersect with their other identities to address specialized grief, trauma, or other experiences.

The Future of Religious Communities?

An oft repeated, but not entirely true, claim is that the Chinese word for "crisis" is made up of the characters for "danger" and "opportunity." The implication is that widespread crises like the pandemic may serve as an unexpected catalyst to develop radically new ideas and new ways of being. From that perspective, the rise of virtual communities like the COVID-19 Loss Support group may be a herald for what religious communities will look like in the future. Among the religious leaders that I spoke with, nearly everyone expressed the conviction that virtual practice was here to stay in at least some component of their community. As noted above, virtual religious practice allowed the community to broaden its outreach to include the disabled or otherwise homebound. In the words of Rev. Chuck Treadwell, rector of St. David's Episcopal Church in Austin, Texas: "The pandemic helped us leap the digital divide. We got people back, even—people who could no longer drive or moved away or didn't feel safe coming downtown at night. We will definitely keep a virtual element going forward."[67] Speaking in April 2021, Bishop

Suffragan Kathryn Ryan of the Episcopal Diocese of Texas echoed Rev. Treadwell: "I am absolutely not saying that God sent us the pandemic that killed half a million Americans so that we can learn to connect through Zoom. But we can say that in the midst of this crisis and this great loss, there have been surprising treasures that have been uncovered for us."[68]

Beyond providing greater connectivity, the move to virtual practice allowed for doctrinal innovation as well. Jason, who worked with local missionaries in the San Antonio LDS community, noted:

> The pandemic turned everything on its head, but it has been a great thing in many ways. Our missionaries were isolated to their apartments during the lockdown, so they moved online. They built social media platforms and websites with all sorts of virtual materials. It has ultimately increased the connectivity of the people we speak to throughout the congregation. When the missionaries teach people online, they can connect with individuals much more easily.[69]

Rev. Chuck Kuhlman of St. Austin Catholic Church explained how, despite the issues surrounding transubstantiation and performing the Eucharistic sacrament in a virtual space, there would likely continue to be some virtual element: "There's been a long tradition in the Catholic Church of 'spiritual communion,' where you ask Jesus to be with you spiritually, even though you can't receive him sacramentally. It is an old idea and was not intended for the virtual domain, but it has been used for quite some time to justify televised Mass. I think that virtual communion will remain for many parishioners after the pandemic is over."[70] Indeed, many of the religious leaders that I spoke with explained that the continued push for virtual service was coming, in large part, from parishioners. Pastor Lou McElroy of the Antioch Missionary Baptist Church in Houston joked with me during our conversation, "The truth is that some churches won't recoup a certain percentage of the congregation for in-person worship because they have gotten acclimated to home worship in their pajamas, so I think we have to keep that element."[71]

Perhaps the most significant transformation afforded by the move to virtual environments, however, is the opportunity to participate in moral communities outside of your geographic locale. Rev. Rich Andre explained that he and the other religious leaders of St. Austin were unprepared for the influx of parishioners from outside of Austin regularly joining their virtual Masses:

> Many of the people attending Mass used to live in Austin, but never found a good community when they left, so they wanted to come back digitally. And then, there are people who we've never met, who find us online and want to be part of our community. There's a couple in New York who sent us a letter and a check, saying that as long as we're doing Mass online, they are our parishioners. Sometimes people log on and say, "Greetings from California!" Or "Greetings from South Africa!"[72]

When I pressed him on what he thought this meant for the future of his parish, he explained that he saw a larger move toward more intentional communities that aligned with individuals' personal values:

> I think the pandemic is going to speed up a lot of changes that were already happening for quite a while. Our understanding of parish is going to change. At the Council of Trent in the 1500s,

the whole world was divided into geographic regions—the smallest of which was a parish. All over the world, no matter where you lived, you were in some parish. There has been some fracturing of this, especially in the United Sates, as more families purchased cars and people could choose which parish to attend. The move to virtual is only making that change greater. Parishes that weren't really dynamic before the pandemic, that weren't really drawing people in are going to struggle. In some ways, churches are like businesses and many other social organizations. A lot of priests I know worry, "Are people going to come back?"[73]

While virtual practice offered a greater opportunity for social engagement and experimenting with new doctrines, it also opened the door to a greater era of self-choice between religious communities.

As highlighted by the religious professionals that I spoke with, this entrepreneurial initiative may presage a move to joining virtual communities that affirm one's political beliefs or convictions. Pastor Craig Taylor of the Willow Meadows Baptist Church explained:

> I think the idea of how community is expressed is going to change. What we long for in community will still be the same, but we will have different ways of validating our community. In the future, I think we will see churches that are entirely online—centered around a specific socio-political bent or a specific cultural community. That was probably going to happen anyway, but I think COVID-19 just accelerated the changes.[74]

Many national religious groups exhibit deep divides between liberal and conservative factions. Such communities—especially in small towns—used to have to exist under one roof with one pastor, priest, or spiritual leader, but the introduction of virtual religious services means that, in the future, people may be able to select a church that aligns with their views. Yoon Tae explained, "Being in the South, the selection of churches that match our values was limited, so my wife and I have been Zooming into my friend's church in Chicago. We don't do it every week, but it is nice to know the option is there."[75] Arla echoed Yoon Tae's experience. After the death of her father, the social chaos of the summer of 2020, and the continued GOP support for Donald Trump, she began examining her own spiritual and faith commitments—a practiced she called "pruning the tree." The result was her decision to leave the church she grew up in and had attended for decades to join a church community over an hour's drive from her home that she had never set foot in:

> When George Floyd was murdered, the church I had attended said nothing—they didn't do anything at all. Roughly eighty percent of them voted for the most vile man on the planet. It was an utter betrayal. It made me not trust that church, and I haven't been back. My husband actually says that he will never again step foot in a church with an all-white leadership team. I found a church that was led by an African American pastor in Monrovia, and we have been attending that church virtually. Racism has been discipled into us by the church and it needs to be discipled out. Pruning the tree is painful, but I know my spirituality and my relationship with Jesus will be better for it.[76]

As demonstrated in Arla's experience, the proliferation of virtual religious communities caused by the pandemic has given individuals more options than were previously available and may speak to a future where politics and personal values determine participation in a given community, rather than geographic location.

CONCLUSIONS: THE DANGERS OF POLARIZATION

So, is this where we are heading? As we have seen, many religious communities are not able to make the jump to virtual practice due to doctrinal beliefs. It is unlikely that all, or even most, religious communities will become entirely virtual. However, a virtual component to religious communities seems an inescapable truth. Indeed, as seen in the example of the Facebook COVID-19 Loss Support group, virtual communities can step in and serve all the functions one might normally see in an in-person moral community. Our lives are increasingly virtual and for those, especially, who are disabled, sick, or unable to leave their homes, this can be a very good thing. But it might also give us pause. If we have the option to select our religious communities based entirely on political commitments, or to interact only with others entirely like ourselves, we may never have to socially integrate with those with whom we disagree. In the 1980s, sociologist Robert Wuthnow argued that this process has been underway in America since the end of World War II, but technological innovations, and now COVID-19, seem to have drastically accelerated it.[77] There is evidence that Americans are socially isolating themselves from those with whom they disagree politically and this trend may be a bad thing for a civil society.[78] In civil society's social media extensions, Cass Sunstein has identified "cybercascades," where group polarization on a social media site is brought about by a virtual echo chamber.[79] Such a possibility is certainly both a cause for concern as well as an arena for future research. Regardless, while our ideas about which moral communities we belong to might be changing, our necessity for them as human beings—at least according to Durkheim—is not.

Beyond his work on the relationship between social communities and religion, Durkheim is well-known for his work on suicide. In Durkheim's typology of suicide, "anomic suicide" refers to suicide in response to a social state in which a group's social norms or ethical standards are rendered irrelevant (what sociologists call *anomie*). After Hurricane Katrina devasted New Orleans in 2005, two police officers took their own lives. Not only had they lost their homes and property, but the police as an institution were in disarray. Many abandoned their posts, and those who stayed had to scrounge for supplies along with other survivors.[80] This experience represents a powerful example of anomic suicide. For Durkheim, human beings can bear almost anything except a world that is no longer coherent. Our survival requires a world in which to meaningfully dwell, as much as it requires food and shelter. A major factor in making such meaningful worlds are the stories we tell ourselves about it. Now, we turn to consider narrative and identity: How do stories provide the keys to telling us who we are? And what happens when, during an unprecedented crisis or when confronting death, those narratives are destroyed or fundamentally challenged?

3

NARRATIVE

To be human is to tell stories. Some stories are small, like how you went to buy a roll of toilet paper at the pharmacy but were distracted by a billboard for the new ramen place and subsequently rear-ended the car in front of you. Some stories are big, like how you decided to talk to the cute girl at the bar because she had on a T-shirt of your favorite band, then you went on a date later that month, and now she is your wife. Some stories become the foundation for a whole country's self-understanding, like the narrative of a group of rebellious gentlemen farmers dreaming of a country built on freedom and standing up to a king an ocean away. Regardless of size, stories have a way of communicating more than the simple details related in their telling. They give us a window into another person's world—what they value, what they fear, and how they arrange the plotline of their lives. Our lives are literally ordered by the stories told about them and those stories, therefore, have a central role in the function of religion. Indeed, Stephen Prothero has argued that religions might best be understood as "story systems."[1]

There is, however, little agreed upon theory about "narrative." Mircea Eliade discussed mythic stories as a means by which human beings transcend the mundane world and connect with an eternal reality,[2] but the grand, de-historicized work epitomized by Eliade has been left behind in recent years in favor of focused analyses of discrete texts in specific cultural and historical arenas. Accompanying that shift has been a disregard for theory that makes similarly universal claims. Indeed, maybe stories do *too* much to rely on a single intellectual tool kit. Scholars have studied narrative influencing arenas as diverse as ethical debates on the permissibility of torture;[3] the success of the Taliban in Afghanistan;[4] the portrayal of human nature in premodern India;[5] and the relationship of American law with morality.[6] Narrative is essentially a tool of interpretation and, as almost the entirety of human culture is an act of interpretation, making a theory to encompass all that narrative does is, perhaps, a hopeless task.

So, a single, overarching theory of narrative eludes us—awash as we are in a sea of stories. But we can focus on one of the most important interpretative functions of stories as represented in the examples that open this chapter: its role in making meaning and building identities. Paul Ricoeur, Charles Taylor, and others have argued that identity is essentially a story we tell ourselves about ourselves. That is not to say that it is a lie or a falsehood, but rather, "Knowledge of the self is an interpretation."[7] More poetically, we might say that deep in our hearts lies a story about who we are, who we have been, and who we hope to be.

By paying attention to how individuals make and use stories we can understand the significant role that narrative has as a lens to interpret experiences of death during the pandemic. As such, this chapter is organized around three questions:

1. **How can a story tell you who you are?**
2. **What ingredients make meaningful stories?**
3. **What happens when stories no longer work?**

Those who encountered death during the era of COVID-19 had to make sense of themselves and the world around them through stories. Many of those I spoke with used established stories from their home religious tradition or their personal family history to make new stories after the death of a loved one. In this, they recommitted to their religious identity by fitting their experience into a larger spiritual or cultural narrative. But others found their former stories lacking. COVID-19 was an unprecedented situation, and it caused a crisis for many as the narratives that had been central to their identity in the "before times" suddenly did not work. Some even questioned the wider, socially accepted narratives of the pandemic's origins and vaccine safety. In this environment, a variety of materials became the building blocks of new stories, including interpretative signs of postmortem contact and histories of spiritual communities' resilience in the face of prior struggles. Therefore, analyzing the way in which stories function as an interpretative lens becomes a place to think about methods of meaning-making employed during the pandemic.

HOW CAN A STORY TELL YOU WHO YOU ARE?

Narrative, Time, and Plotting Our Lives

As described in this chapter's introduction, we understand ourselves largely through stories. Stories serve as a way of arranging information to put emphasis on one particular moment in time. Physicists and philosophers have explored the idea that time is not as simple a thing as we might think. Paul Ricoeur, who is one of most prominent philosophers of narrative and identity, explains that there is chronological time (at 3 a.m. last

Tuesday my daughter was born; on the following Friday afternoon, I purchased a minivan) and phenomenological time (my daughter was born, so I bought a new minivan for traveling with her to see my parents). These two types of time put information in a sequence, but they communicate that information in different ways: the first is a list of what happened, while the second relates the events to each other in a causal pattern and, through that, gives them meaning and significance.

Reconstructing a sequence of events with an eye to phenomenological meaning is called "emplotment." First discussed by Hayden White in his dissection of how historians narrate their work in conjunction with established plot lines, emplotment is at play in a variety of environments—including how we think about our own lives.[8] In Ricoeur's framing of emplotment, putting diverse events into an established order, with meaning and significance, mediates between the chaos of our everyday experience and our idea of the way things should be. By imagining events as a story, where one thing leads to another, rather than just a chronology, it becomes possible to answer "why" questions: "I never learned to play guitar *because* my parents urged me to study piano" or "I got that raise *because* I work so hard." Connecting facts together into stories allows places, things, events, and even people to become meaningful and understandable. Furthermore, it is this narrative that tells a person what to value, what the right thing to do might be, and who they are as a character in this story.

This strategy of emplotment was especially evident in my conversations with medical professionals about their experiences during the pandemic. Repeatedly, I heard the refrain that, rather than bow out of their professions, it was their duty as doctors and nurses to stay—some even delaying retirement to continue working when they felt that they were most needed. One doctor that I spoke with, Dr. Black (a pseudonym), was a primary care physician. He explained that his work during the pandemic was not only his duty as a doctor, but also a spiritual calling:

> I am glad to be working in the pandemic—I wouldn't miss it! My God, this is what I prepared for my whole life! Of course, I am not thrilled to be walking into a medical facility filled with the sick and dying, but if not me, then who? I don't dwell on theism vs. atheism or whatever—I gave up on that in Genesis. I don't think humans have the hardware to contemplate infinity: if there is a God, I can't understand it, just like I can't understand how Moses could have a conversation with God and come down the hill with commandments. But I know this is what I am supposed to be doing. This is my calling.[9]

In reflecting on his time during the pandemic, Dr. Black used the guiding narrative of what it means to be a doctor—what a doctor is "supposed to do"—as the framework that gave his decision to continue working spiritual meaning. While not an especially religious person by measurements like synagogue attendance or holy day observance, Dr. Black understood his work as, at least in part, a practical expression of his spiritual convictions.

Dr. Black's experience was echoed by Jack and Larry Kravitz, two brothers who had entered the medical profession as a hospice doctor and family care doctor, respectively. Working closely with the dying, Jack explained, "The idea that I would walk away from my profession at the beginning of a pandemic was just inconceivable. This is what I was trained to do; I had to be there."[10] Like Jack, Larry had also elected to continue working during the pandemic, even taking on extra volunteer work at a local shelter for those experiencing homelessness. When I spoke with him, he was in the middle of recovery from COVID-19, which he believed had been contracted while working at the shelter. Larry used his Jewish heritage to explain the decision to practice medicine with the unhoused during the pandemic: "There's a Jewish concept called Tikkum Olam—essentially it means to repair the world. That's our job and every day you should wake up and ask, 'What can I repair today?' That's why I am a doctor and continued working in the pandemic. That's why I began volunteering at the homeless shelter. The world is scary out there, but this is the little area where I can repair the world."[11] While many other things surely influenced the decisions of Dr. Black, Larry, and Jack—401ks, mortgages, a fear of boredom—they plotted the time, the duties, and the meaning of their actions through narratives on the role and duties of a doctor seeking to fix the world. In this, we can see that framing identity through narrative is not merely a passive process; we are both readers and writers of the stories around which we shape our lives.

As both a thing received and a thing composed, narrative has an important role in mediating between contradictory ideas—I am a Christian, but feel myself losing faith in God; I am an atheist, but crave a community to share a sense of spirituality and belonging; I am a Sikh, but going to the gurdwara is painful. Philosopher Arto Laitinen has called this the distinction between "'what is' and 'what ought to be.'"[12] Narrative is the intellectual bridge that helps the individual make sense of such coexistent, but contradictory, frameworks. A Christian losing faith in God might rely on stories about Mother Teresa or C. S. Lewis to understand those doubts as part of a spiritual struggle that will ultimately deepen their faith. However, narrative can also be the tool that moves an individual from an older identity to a newer one. Perhaps our unnamed Christian will adopt an enlightenment narrative that celebrates their personal transition from the ignorance of Christianity to the intellectual light of atheism. Or perhaps they will decide that religion is socially valuable, regardless of its truth, and grow comfortable with attending church for their children's sake, while personally believing that there is no God.

It is on this mediating role of narrative—both when it succeeds and when it fails—that we will spend the rest of our time in this chapter. Many of those confronting death found themselves approaching their religious tradition in new and different ways, and the religious identities that they had before their encounter with death became critical flashpoints in how they interpreted the COVID-19 pandemic. Many used scriptural stories from their home religious traditions to make new stories about the death of their loved one and, in that, strengthened or reinvigorated their religious identities.

Building Identity with Familiar Narratives

Almost everyone who confronted the death of a loved one due to COVID-19 acknowledged initially feeling existential anger and spiritual doubt. However, many eventually came to resolve these negative feelings through narratives from their home religious communities that helped put the death into a larger spiritual context. Chicago resident Kay exemplified this trend. After a period in the hospital, Kay's father was released. Unfortunately, like many COVID-19 patients, he quite suddenly took a turn for the worse and collapsed in his bed while Kay was talking to her mother on the phone. Although the experience first caused her to doubt her faith, she described finding comfort in the story of Lazarus from the New Testament:

> After my dad passed away, I would read scripture and Lazarus's story just seemed to be so much more important than it was before. When Jesus talks about Lazarus dying, he says he did it with a purpose—to show that "I loved you." I realized for my dad's passing away that was true. My father's death was really traumatic, but I realized it happened in the best way possible. My father came home. My mother was with him. I was with him on the phone. That couldn't have happened in the hospital! I can't believe now that I was so mad at God, that I would have rather him been at the hospital—alone and scared.[13]

Olivia also used Christian narrative to make sense of her complicated feelings after her father's death. While the experience ultimately inspired her break with the nondenominational church that she and her family had attended for years, the Christian narrative of John the Baptist served as a lens in making sense of her feelings of sorrow, grief, and isolation:

> I felt the Lord calling me to a specific scripture, the one when John the Baptist was beheaded. And I realized, Jesus went through this too. He had to watch someone chop his cousin's head off and put it on a platter; he had to watch someone die in a horrifying way. I had felt so distant from God because I thought Jesus never knew my sorrow, but I see He does. God says that He is close to the broken-hearted, and He is.[14]

For Kay and Olivia, the narratives of death, grief, and resurrection found in the New Testament served to frame their fathers' traumatic deaths and their resulting, complicated emotions. In this way, these narratives emplotted the death of their loved ones into a larger pattern that mediated between their initial feelings and the ultimate meaning that they found in the experience.

Sabila, a Pakistani American woman who also lost her father, found in the experience an opportunity to reconnect with her Muslim heritage. She explained:

> I had never really felt connected to my Muslim identity before this, but I have been reading the Quran since my father passed away. I read the Quran in Arabic a million years ago as a child, but I didn't really understand a word of it. After my father's death, I began reading an English translation of the Quran, and I actually really love it. It makes me feel closer to my father, my family, and my heritage in a way I just never did before.[15]

The Islamic tradition prizes not only the words of Allah, believed to be preserved in the Quran, but also the sayings and teachings of Muhammad, which followers gathered after the prophet's death. In one particular collection, *Sahih al-Bukhari*, Muhammad seems to be struggling with a plague sweeping through the Arabian Peninsula. Muhammad gives important advice to the people he leads—including what appears to be a precursor to social isolation policies in which he commands his followers, "If you hear of an outbreak of plague in a land, do not enter it; but if the plague breaks out in a place while you are in it, do not leave that place."[16] In other moments, Muhammad is comforting the bereaved; he tells grieving families that those who pass away in a plague are deserving of heavenly glories.[17] This story became influential in Sabila's interpretation of her own father's death from COVID-19: "Muhammad said that if someone loses their life in a pandemic, they are considered martyrs and given the highest ranks in heaven. My aunt told me this after my father died. That has given me so much comfort. It tells me that he is in a better, much better place."[18]

Following her grandmother's death Bianca similarly found, through narratives, an opportunity to deepen connections with a religious heritage from which she had felt distant. Coming from a large Mexican American family, she eventually became alienated from her Catholic upbringing, developing something of a "love/hate relationship," she joked during our conversation. But with the death of her grandmother, the creation story found in the Book of Genesis became a framework for memories of her grandmother's life:

> For whatever reason, the creation myth in Genesis is providing a lot of comfort—birth, creating a life with as much care as God's creation of life. It reminds me of my grandmother taking care of the life around her. Her plants were everything to her—bushels of herbs, peppers, things she used to cook and make moles, salsas, and tamales. When she moved into the retirement community and lost her backyard, she had to bring the plants to the front of the house. The old white ladies complained, but she kept right on caring for them despite that. I want to care for things now like she did, I guess like God did.[19]

While the death of a loved one due to COVID-19 allowed many to deepen a connection to a religious tradition with which they already strongly identified, for others like Sabila and Bianca, it meant reconnecting with the stories and narratives of their religious heritage. Sabila elaborated that the year her father died was the first year she had successfully completed the fast during the month of Ramadan—one of the central practices of Islam. While

Bianca still maintained a somewhat measured distance from her Catholic heritage, she said that she continued to feel drawn to the elements of Catholicism that her grandmother had found comfort in: saint figurines, rosary prayers, and metal charms known as *milagros* that are used as votive offerings in many Latin American cultures. In her own words, "I don't really know if I believe in God, I guess. But I believe in my grandmother."[20]

These examples demonstrate how, for many encountering death during the pandemic, the narratives of their home religious traditions became tools that mediated between the "before times" and the "after times" of the death. These stories helped, at least in part, to turn the reality of a loved one's death from a chronological to a phenomenological reality—something that was not simply a fact, but rather was enmeshed within a larger framework of significance and meaning. In this way, the death of a loved one became the opportunity to deepen the connection to their home religious identity.

Scripture Interpreting the Pandemic

The existential chaos of a "before and after" time was reflected not only in those who personally lost loved ones, but in the experience of entire religious communities as well. Religious leaders often found themselves in a position of having to render the suffering, confusion, and death interpretable and understandable. As such, religious narratives found in sacred scriptures became important for developing meaningful responses to COVID-19. As leader of the Antioch Missionary Baptist Church in Houston, Pastor Lou McElroy, like many pastors, initially faced skepticism from some of his congregation concerning the lockdown in March 2020. However, he drew on the Old Testament

Exodus story of Passover to help his parishioners frame the need for a lockdown:

> Scripture has been our guide. As noted in Exodus 12:21–31, in the last plague against Egypt and prior to the coming of the Angel of Death, the Israelites had to put blood on the doorpost. God then says to them essentially something like, "Go in your homes while this plague passes. Pray in your homes until it is OK to come out." This is a type of quarantine! That's the lockdown! That's the message I preached to tell my community why the citywide lockdown was necessary, in order to protect the citizens of Houston from COVID-19. I was able to encourage the community that we could still pray together—the church was within us, within the people of the Christian faith.[21]

Here, we see how the narrative of the ancient Israelites escaping Egypt became a way for Pastor McElroy's community to make sense of the sudden lockdown and adapt to at-home worship. By framing their experience as analogous to the Jews awaiting the Angel of Death to pass over, the unprecedented experience of the early pandemic becomes a part of phenomenological time.

Similar examples of using narratives as guidance during the pandemic were seen among the leadership of the San Antonio Latter-day Saints community. As discussed earlier, the Church of Jesus Christ of Latter-day Saints (LDS) does not have a full-time priesthood and, instead, relies on adult men in the community to volunteer for spiritual and administrative roles. In San Antonio, their missionary efforts were coordinated by Jason, who discussed his work mentoring the men and women serving in the area. He described how many of the young people were confused and upset in the early months of the pandemic:

In the scriptures where it discusses "the latter days," which we believe we're in, they talk about famines and pestilence and so forth. So, from our perspective, this pandemic certainly isn't anything that caught God by surprise—it is all part of the plan. For our missionaries, we talked about how this is life, not just a bump in the road of life, but life itself! And life has challenges! You can address those challenges with either faith or with fear.[22]

Through using the narrative of the "latter days" found in LDS scripture to interpret the experience of the early pandemic, Jason mediated between the way the world had worked before March 2020 and after, ultimately turning the pandemic into a meaningful phenomenon.

Indeed, the mediating function of narrative often becomes a cyclical process. While religious narratives can make sense of our pandemic experience, the pandemic experience can also make better sense of the religion. Venerable Jue Ji, leader of the Fo Guang Shan Xiang Yun Buddhist temple in Austin, Texas, related how the stories that her congregants shared about the pandemic allowed her to teach the Buddhist doctrine of interdependence more effectively. Sometimes called dependent origination, interdependence reflects the foundational Buddhist belief that identity and the self are not discrete, self-existing categories, but instead come into being through relationship with other things around them:

> My Master always says that when a person is living in a paradise, it is difficult to teach them the *Buddhadharma* [Buddhist Teachings]. As a person coming from Taiwan, the United States really is a paradise for me—the quality of living is better than in Taiwan. What I miss in my home country is the people there: When

you teach them that there is suffering, they accept that very easily and understand it. In the States, it is so difficult to get people to understand this kind of teaching. But COVID-19 has made Americans understand the *Buddhadharma* better; they start to understand intimately the interdependence and inter-relationship between all beings. A person contracts COVID-19 in a faraway place, and the next day it can immediately be among your community. That proves the truth of the Buddha's teaching. It is making us understand the world actually is one and that we are not all isolated in our own community. The COVID-19 deaths in New York and in California, they aren't just strangers out there, but rather part of us ourselves![23]

The pandemic provided the opportunity for Venerable Jue Ji to engage in novel interpretation of doctrine in other ways, as well. A major part of Fo Guang Shan Buddhist practice is the promotion of vegetarianism. Venerable Jue Ji used the framework of Buddhist conceptions of karma—the idea that actions you take in this life will affect future rebirths—to think through the unintended consequences of using hand sanitizer. She maintained that adopting a vegetarian lifestyle might help individuals counteract the potentially negative karma arising from killing single-celled beings:

> We regard the COVID-19 virus as a living being and every time, we use hand sanitizer to protect ourselves, we are killing hundreds of living beings like the coronavirus. We have no choice. The COVID-19 virus is threatening our life, and it is because we have bad karma with the virus that we are in this situation. I encourage my community to take a vegetarian diet so that they can make more good karma and counteract the bad karma they

make by killing the virus with hand sanitizer. Less killing now not only saves more lives but may help our future selves.[24]

In essence, this is a story created by Venerable Jue Ji about what happens when you use hand sanitizer. It is not the official teachings of the Fo Guang Shan organization, but rather the work of one nun using the resources at hand to make sense of the lifestyle changes brought about by the COVID-19 pandemic. Indeed, most Buddhists will say that viruses are not considered "sentient beings" and therefore cannot be killed in such a way as to create karmic retributions. However, Venerable Jue Ji's attempts to make the pandemic meaningful through reference to Buddhist doctrine, and commitments to more ethical lifestyles, demonstrate the cyclical nature of narrative as a meaning-making machine. Religious narratives give meaning to unexpected experiences, those experiences then become an opportunity to make new spiritual narratives about the right way to be a Buddhist (or Hindu, or Christian, or Muslim, or anything else). In revealing the powerful, evolving tool of narrative in its role both to emplot events and to mediate between old and new experiences, these experiences lead us to our next question: What raw materials besides religious scripture are used to make meaningful stories.

WHAT INGREDIENTS MAKE MEANINGFUL STORIES?

We have considered the technology of narrative—how stories turn chronological time into phenomenological time, to use the categories of Ricoeur. In this way, narrative was able to mediate between our reality before and reality after the COVID-19 pandemic so that events like the early lockdown or the death of a loved one become meaningful. Here, let us consider what elements make a story meaningful, make a story "stick," so to speak. This list is not meant to be exhaustive, nor is it meant to represent especially extraordinary materials. Rather, we are all like Angus MacGyver, the famously resourceful character of 1980s television, who could make a tool to get out of any situation using only the basic materials at hand. We have already seen how scripture was used to make meaningful stories as individuals framed the death of their loved ones and the experience of the pandemic. Here, we look at three further ingredients for constructing meaningful stories that repeatedly appeared in my conversations: (1) signs of contact from deceased loved ones; (2) struggles undergone by religious communities in the past; and (3) stories advising on how we can produce a more satisfying ending. Each serving a different group, these worked to emplot a sense of phenomenological meaning through the creation of a new narrative.

Postmortem Contact

For those who lost loved ones to COVID-19, seeing signs from their dying or deceased loved ones became an important interpretative framework. Carmen, a nursing student living in Florida, knew that she had to immediately return home to New York City when her mother contracted COVID-19 the week before Easter, in April 2020:

> I saw a bald eagle—an honest-to-God, American bald eagle! It was pretty soon after I learned my mother was in the hospital,

that she had refused intubation and was going to fight as hard as she could. But the bald eagle was flying strangely, almost wobbly, because in its claw it had a bunch of dirt and sticks for building a nest. I had never seen one before and here it was building a nest—that told me I had to fly home as soon as possible. To be with my mother because some part of me knew then she wasn't going to make it.[25]

Carmen's mother passed away soon after and she has since taken comfort in seeing signs that her mother is still with her: "I have had all sorts of signs from my mother. Right before one of my upcoming exams, I was walking in the park trying to clear my mind, and I heard my mother's voice clear as day yelling her nickname for me! I also see butterflies all the time now—so many butterflies! She loved butterflies and every time one brushes against my cheek, I know it is her coming to say hello."[26] Speaking to the cyclical nature of narrative, such signs and images are themselves stories built around seemingly random events—a stray insect or a misheard sound. But through narrative emplotment, they also become evidence of metaphysical realities of postmortem contact that provide comfort.

In COVID-19 loss support groups on social media, there was an abundance of stories similar to Carmen's, as well as widespread community affirmation as to their validity. These posts were often accompanied by popular media to justify these claims. In the spring of 2021, the docuseries *Surviving Death* (based on journalist Leslie Kean's book of the same name)[27] debuted on Netflix and garnered significant interest from those mourning the loss of a loved one. In the months after its debut, nearly every day saw a different post from someone who found consolation in watching the series and feeling that there might be life after death. One woman stated, "I only started the first episode [of *Surviving Death*] but I found it very comforting to know what my dad may have experienced as he crossed."[28] Almost one hundred people commented on her post, echoing her reassurance and thanking her for bringing the show to their attention. Intense discussion in other posts dissected the show episode by episode, often with links to the studies it cited or to the social media presence of the people interviewed. Popular and widespread media like *Surviving Death* became important touchstones for those grieving as it described their own hopes that their loved ones were still present and reaching out in some way.

Despite expressing her suspicion of such postmortem contact, Manpreet shared her own experiences in the aftermath of her father's passing from COVID-19 that made her feel like her father was still spiritually present:

> One night, when my father's urn was in the house and we were preparing to spread his ashes the next day, I was falling asleep and suddenly heard the door open and close. See, my dad had a habit; he worked late nights as a cab driver, so every night when he came home, he opened the door of every child's room before he went to sleep to check in on us, make sure we were OK. That is what I heard that night and all of my siblings heard it too. Dad, come home one last time to make sure we were all OK.[29]

Manpreet went on to describe dreams that she and her partner experienced in which her father appeared to be giving them messages about where he wanted his ashes scattered, or relatives they needed to contact. In another incident, she found a small, meaningful token in the cup holder of her car—one that she swore had been lost—at a critical moment when she desperately needed comfort. Like Manpreet, Julia was apprehensive about claims of communication from beyond the grave. However, in recounting her experience of losing her brother to COVID-19, she noted:

> My sister gets these moments where she feels like my brother has contacted her. One night, my niece was crying, so my sister began telling her all these funny stories of what her uncle, my brother, would do when they were kids. She's laughing and when they turned to look out the window, the moon was the most strange rose-gold color. My brother was very artistic and loved to make interesting, different colors; the color of the moon was so strange that both my niece and my sister perceived it as my brother reaching out to them. I take great comfort in that.[30]

Postmortem contact became an important ingredient in the stories of many people who lost a loved one to COVID-19. While some expressed hesitation in giving these incidents their full faith, the veracity of the stories ultimately became secondary to the goal of providing reassurance.

The importance of these narratives of postmortem contact is especially apparent in the words of those who did not experience such signs and, as a result, felt reinjured by their loved one's death. After losing her father to COVID-19, Sabila had only a few dreams of him, which added to her significant grief:

> My older brother and mother have way more dreams than I do—my mom dreams of him every single night! But to me he feels far away. Sometimes I look up at the stars and realize that my father is more distant from me than those little stars are. I have young children, so laundry is a big part of my life; I had this idea one night that even if I were to take all the endless

loads of laundry, all the folding, everything, and pile it up to make a big stairway to the stars, my father would still be remote and out of reach.[31]

Amanda echoed Sabila's frustration in narratives of postmortem contact after her mother's passing. During our conversation, she linked her mother's lack of contact from the other side with the indecorous way in which her mother's body was handled in the hours after she passed:

> It was so inhumane how the coroner handled my mother. She died at our home, and they had to put her body inside a plastic bag when they arrived to prevent infection. They tried to cover it up with a velvet bag afterwards, but the whole thing felt disgusting. I have PTSD [post-traumatic stress disorder] from that, from finding my mother dead, from thinking of her little body lying there, wrapped in plastic. I try to pray in the hopes that she will reach out to me, and I can have a final memory of her that is not lying in that tiny plastic bag, but she never does. I get annoyed when people say they saw a bird and that was their loved one who had died . . . it's just a fucking bird.[32]

Various signs, perceived as loved ones reaching out from beyond the grave, gave comfort to many during the COVID-19 pandemic. But they also isolated those who did not share such experiences and furthered the disconnection that they felt from their loved one. For them, postmortem signs were unable to act as a building block in a new narrative of connection. Rather, the lack of any postmortem connection reinforced their profound experience of absence and loss. This comparison makes the central role of narrative in forging connection apparent, as those who did not experience postmortem contact felt reisolated from their loved ones.

Historical Struggles

A second ingredient used to make meaningful narratives that was especially employed by religious leaders during the pandemic was the resiliency of their religious communities in the face of prior struggles. Danièle Hervieu-Léger describes religion not just as a set of institutions and communities today, but also as a "chain of memory" that situates individuals as members of a transhistoric lineage.[33] While the transformations brought about to contemporary religious communities were discussed at length in chapter 2, the struggles confronted by these communities in the past came to serve as inspiration for the narratives of hope offered by religious leaders in the face of the pandemic. Many religious leaders drew upon narratives of the tribulations faced by their historical compatriots to render the experiences today as understandable and, most importantly, survivable.

Throughout my interviews, religious leaders used narratives of a spiritual community's perseverance to make the pandemic meaningful. As stake president of a San Antonio LDS community, Greg Neuberger found himself referencing the early history of Latter-day pioneers to his concerned parishioners repeatedly in the first months of lockdown:

> For anyone familiar with the history of the Latter-day Church, they know we had a rough time while we were driven westward. Some individuals have compared the difficulties we're in now to that time of persecution. It helps us remember that we are a

resilient people, and the [LDS] Church has come about in an inspired way. We can be flexible because we're being led by God. We talk a lot in our church about our pioneer heritage because we're very proud of it, even though the vast majority of the [LDS] Church today does not have pioneer heritage themselves. However, it is still something that you can look back to and learn from—people driven westward and facing enormous hardships who survived because they trusted in God.[34]

President Neuberger noted that some in his community felt particularly persecuted early in the COVID-19 pandemic for the state government's refusal to allow in-person worship and subsequently took inspiration from early LDS pioneers who were violently forced from town to town as a result of their religious practices. Others, however, felt a more general connection to the early pioneers for maintaining their faith in God while living through isolation and hardship. These stories of perseverance offered by religious leadership served as models for new stories, created by contemporary believers in response to the pandemic.

As the leader of one of the most prominent African American churches in Houston, Pastor Lou McElroy echoed President Neuberger as to the importance of looking to historical narratives to guide his community during the pandemic. He explained that his church's history went back centuries, to both enslaved peoples brought to Texas and freed men and women who came after the U.S. Civil War. He was proud of the church's heritage and saw in its narrative a promise of the community's ability to persevere with strength and fortitude:

> The pews that we sit in today were made by our former enslaved ancestors, freed men and women who came to Houston to have a better life. That same legacy of determination and resilience still

guides our congregation today. Our church was there during the Spanish flu; we were there during both World Wars, during the Korean War, during swine flu, during the fight for civil rights. Just last week, we celebrated the Women's Suffrage Movement where Antioch served as a place of education and organization for the African American suffragettes. That same history and determination guides us today.[35]

In the words of Pastor McElroy and President Neuberger, the message is clear—if our religious forebears made it through this, we can too.

Rabbi Neil Blumofe of the Congregation Agudas Achim in Austin, Texas similarly found the resilience of the Jewish community an inspiring example. The synagogue branded masks and various paraphernalia for congregants with passages from the Hebrew Bible, heralding the overcoming of adversity. The Hebrew Bible, however, is not the only source of authority in the Jewish tradition. Rabbinical literature relies on a wealth of stories including exegesis of Biblical narratives, parables, and more than a few jokes. Rabbi Blumofe shared a story that he personally felt was significant to understanding the pandemic today:

> There was a rabbi in 1930s Warsaw. He had a yeshiva school and some folks in New York wanted to fund it. So, all these wealthy New Yorkers make the long and arduous journey to Warsaw to see the school. It is a big, beautiful building, but inside it is just cinder blocks, crappy chairs, and a folding card table. They laugh at this famous rabbi sitting in such a dump. They walk up to him and ask, "Rabbi, what's going on? You need to step it up! Present yourself a little better! Do an Instagram or something."
>
> The Rabbi looks at them and asks, "What about you? You have nothing but a suitcase and a fancy hat!"

The funders laugh and say, "Well, we're just passing through; we're only here for a little while."

The Rabbi laughs and says, "Exactly, now you understand me. We're just passing through." I [Rabbi Blumofe] love the idea of temporality, of realizing what is really important. We're just passing through. And no matter what, it's all going to pass. The pandemic, the election, the protests; it's all going to pass. This point gets hit over and over in Talmudic literature—we've been in some difficult situations before like this, but it is going to be OK. It may be horrible for a while, but it is going to be OK. Honestly, this is the foundational story of Judaism.[36]

Judaism is sometimes described as a tradition of laws and stories.[37] In addition to formal legal opinions about properly following the *mitzvoth*, the Talmud also contains stories called *midrash* that themselves can provide legal opinions and offer creative perspectives on Biblical narratives. Such narratives make the Hebrew Bible applicable to a much wider range of circumstances, while also creating continuity between the concerns of the present Jewish community and that of the past. Although this particular narrative is not explicitly a *midrash*, Rabbi Blumofe's reference to the "Talmudic logic" it represents demonstrates how rabbis' strategic deployment of stories can serve to frame congregants' individual experiences.

While stories of religious communities overcoming adversity together became an especially important ingredient in creating new stories of resilience during the pandemic, a common subtheme relied on by religious leaders was the specific hardship endured by prophets and religious founders. Imam Sheikh Attia Omara, an Egyptian American cleric serving the Islamic Center of Lake Travis, connected the difficulties experienced by the prophet Muhammad to the strength that contemporary

Muslims could find through relying on God. As an Abrahamic religion, Islam shares in the narrative tradition of Christianity and Judaism—although it understands Muhammad to be the final messenger in a long line of prophets that includes Jesus, Elijah, and Abraham:

> All the prophets have experienced hardship or hostility in the places they were sent by Allah—not just Muhammad, but Jesus, Isaiah, Job, all of them. Because of that, you will find so much in the Quran about struggling through hardship. In the hadith, we see the struggle of Muhammad losing his three sons as infants, as well as the deaths of three married daughters with children, his beloved wife, and his uncle. Muhammad relied on God through all that, and we can too.[38]

Pulling from two sets of religious scripture—the words of God found in the Quran and the stories of Muhammad's life, known in Arabic as *hadith*—Imam Attia uses the suffering endured by Muhammad as inspiration for the contemporary community that he leads to persist through the pandemic. Similar strategies were employed by Ajit Giani in his role as a spokesperson for the Austin Bahá'í community. Arising in nineteenth-century Persia and growing rapidly across the Middle East, the Bahá'í tradition follows the prophet Bahá'u'lláh, who is understood to be the latest prophet in a globally diverse series that spans from Abraham to Lao Tzu to Jesus. For his ministry, Bahá'u'lláh was imprisoned by the Ottoman leaders in an isolated penal colony. Ajit Giani repeatedly referenced the difficulties faced by the prophet Bahá'u'lláh as a source of strength during the COVID-19 pandemic: "Bahá'u'lláh was imprisoned in 'Akká during the height of winter. In those days, the prison was made of solid rock and was quite cold, especially in the winter! These stories of

Bahá'u'lláh's suffering for the Bahá'í faith provide the basis of our prayers for protection and healing. They have been a great comfort to many in our community. They tell us that we too can prevail."[39] As demonstrated in these conversations with Ajit Giani and Imam Attia, religious leaders used the narratives of suffering endured by historic prophets and founders as the foundation of new narratives, providing solace and encouraging resilience in the face of contemporary suffering. In this way, the struggles of one's historical community became an important ingredient in the construction of meaningful stories.

Changing the Ending

Every story has an ending. For many religious or medical leaders confronting death during the COVID-19 pandemic, spiritual narratives that spoke to the critical need to take action in the face of suffering became compelling inspirations to reshape their own endings. These then became further elements in new narratives that sought to control even a small piece of the world. Like the other religious leaders discussed in this chapter, Rev. Chuck Treadwell of St. David's Episcopal Church in Austin, Texas, found solace in stories of his religious community's perseverance through earlier times of crisis. He also saw in them a call to work for the betterment of those around him:

> I take inspiration from every minute of Christian history. If you read the psalms, half of them are basically reacting to crisis: "Where are you, God? What is going on? Why is this happening?" There has always been some sort of conflict, some sort of pain, some sort of loss—religion exists to help us swim through the pain, suffering, and conflict of the world. A pandemic is a

pretty big bit of suffering, but we have been here before. We'll get through this now, and I am called to help make that happen.[40]

Rev. Treadwell's inspiration to serve was reiterated by Bishop Kathryn Ryan of the Episcopal Diocese of Texas. She similarly found herself drawn to the narratives of Christian mutual aid: "The Bible and Christian tradition is full of stories of people who have endured challenges and suffering but helped each other along the way. In those difficult moments, they had the surprising discovery of God's presence in unlooked for ways—these are the stories I find really sustaining right now."[41] Reflecting this theme, Bishop Ryan pulled upon the specific narrative of Episcopal leaders responding to pandemics in the past as inspiration for her own role: "I have been meditating often on the Martyrs of Memphis during this pandemic—six men and women ordained in the Episcopal Church who died while caring for people during the 1878 Yellow Fever epidemic. They gave comfort, sustenance, and relief to the poor and sick, though it took their lives."[42] As both Rev. Treadwell and Bishop Ryan reflected on the narratives of Christian obligation to public service in the face of painful circumstances, these inspirations became woven into their own narratives of serving those in need.

This phenomenon—in which stories from the past became a call to service—was especially prevalent among medical professionals. Dr. Black, who spoke earlier about his calling to continue his work as a doctor during a medical crisis like COVID-19, found guidance from the Jewish tradition:

> Since the start of the pandemic, I have gotten more knowledgeable about the Torah and Jewish history. It's really just the story of one disaster after the next, yet the Jews have survived, and we

will too. It helps me frame the pandemic by thinking about how these people worked together just one step at a time and survived... well most of them did. There are similar themes in medicine—maybe that's why so many Jewish folk become doctors. Whatever the disease is—allergies, heart attack, pneumonia, sepsis, you name it—it will not go on forever. One way or the other, you will get to the other side, be it death, recovery, or some new normal. My job is to help make that transition as easy and painless as possible.[43]

Indeed, the early 2020 lockdown became a time of significant uncertainty for many Jews about how best to practice their religion. Many of the commandments given to the Jewish people by God require Jews to gather together. This forced the question: Was there greater responsibility to public health guidelines or the commandments (*mitzvoth*) given by God? The Jewish tradition uses a variety of narratives outside of those found in the Hebrew Bible to decide best practices. During this period, the story of Rabbi Israel Salanter's Yom Kippur 1848 feast went viral on social media. Yom Kippur is considered the holiest day in Judaism, during which Jews atone for the past years' sins and traditionally fast for twenty-four hours. However, during the 1848 cholera epidemic, Lithuanian rabbi Israel Salanter defied local rabbinic rules and encouraged his congregation to eat. A blog post by Rabbi Elisha Friedman describes the legend:

> [Rabbi Israel] Salanter felt that fasting on Yom Kippur would put lives in danger and that it would desecrate Judaism if Jews died trying to observe the fast... On the morning of Yom Kippur, Salanter walked to the front of the synagogue with wine and cake,

made *kiddush* [Jewish prayers over food] and ate in front of everyone. The people were in shock... but Salanter was not cowed. According to [Rabbi Dov] Katz, he remained in place until everyone in the synagogue had eaten. According to some accounts, he then proceeded to other synagogues in town to encourage worshippers to eat.[44]

Salanter's actions reflect what, in Hebrew, is called *pikuach nefesh*—the principle that the preservation of human life can override every *mitzvah*. While there is significant debate among scholars as to whether the story of Rabbi Salanter happened exactly as described, this did not stop it from becoming a touchstone for many Jews during the pandemic. As one Facebook user put it in her post sharing a version of the story, "Fasting is not pikuah nefesh when you need to keep up your immune system! Gathering is not pikuah nefesh when we might make others ill!"[45] Rabbi Blumofe also told a version of this story in our conversation, describing it as an inspiration for his own efforts to think through the competing needs for public safety and observing the *mitzvoth*. The story of Rabbi Salanter, therefore, is an important example of building contemporary stories around actions that work toward a desired end.

As is apparent, new narratives are built largely out of old ones. Seemingly random events narrativized into signs of contact from beyond, histories describing a religious community's resilience, and examples of how we should respond to social crises all became important ingredients in making new narratives. Perhaps this is not surprising, as humans are fundamentally narrative creatures. However, such a reliance on other stories also leaves many in a precarious position—what if all your prior stories fail? Indeed, not everyone was able to find comfort in the narratives and histories of their home religious traditions during the pandemic. Some experienced a catastrophic failure of these stories, leading to confusion, innovation, and a widespread questioning of authority.

WHAT HAPPENS WHEN STORIES NO LONGER WORK?

While narrative became an important way to frame the pandemic, for some, the stories around which they had previously oriented their lives no longer held true. This section explores what happens next, and there is not a single answer to this. Some people abandoned former religious identities entirely; others creatively integrated new stories into their old ones; and still others questioned the stories told to them by government officials, doctors, and public authorities. This does not mean that these people lived without stories—Ricoeur would say that identity is largely impossible without a story—but rather that they began to arrange phenomenological time in different ways that created new narratives.

Rejecting Religious Identities of the Past

In contrast to those who deepened their religious convictions after losing a loved one to COVID-19, there were those who rejected prior religious identities entirely. The stories that they had previously used to structure their identities no longer made sense, and, as a result, the deaths of their loved ones became a pivotal moment in their restructuring of phenomenological time. Manpreet, a Sikh woman living in New Jersey who had been trained as a nurse, explained how her father's death transformed her relationship with Sikhism:

> We got a call from the hospital that my father had gone into cardiac arrest, and they asked if we would like to do CPR. I said yes. We all sat down in the living room—me, my mom, my brothers, my grandmother, and one of my nephews—and we started praying. I was looking at the clock the whole time, because, from my work, I know they only do CPR for ten minutes before declaring the patient dead. We got a call at 1:01 for the arrest, and I kept staring at my watch, watching the minutes go by and thinking, "If they did CPR, it should have worked by now." At 1:14, I got the call and put it on speaker, but I already knew. Everyone else in my family was hardcore praying, but I was just looking at the clock. I think a part of me just gave up right then because the prayer didn't work. That's why I am so confused because I just hate my religion right now. It makes me really upset, but I don't know how to get out of this confusion. I am just angry at God.[46]

Manpreet elaborated that the stories she knew—that God listens to prayers, that virtuous people are protected by the shield of God—were contradicted entirely by the experience of her father's death. While she took some comfort in what she thought might be signs that her father was contacting her and the possibility of a postmortem existence, she described her faith in the Sikh religious tradition itself as fundamentally undermined.

Amanda had similar struggles with her religious identity in the aftermath of losing her mother to COVID-19. Despite having what she described as a "rock-hard Christian faith" before, the death of her mother instigated a dramatic reversal in her belief because the stories she had believed about a caring God no longer seemed true:

> I can't imagine God letting this happen; the only explanation I have right now is that God is not there. So, as far as my faith, this is the most Godless time of my life. I am constantly questioning my beliefs. I am so very, very angry at God. The last thing my mother and I did together before she died was to pray for her healing and her restoration. Then, the next thing, she is gone. It made no sense, and it broke my faith.[47]

Amanda explained that she felt guilt about her loss of faith not only within a Christian context, but also because she was not properly living out the values and goals of her Apache culture: "In Apache culture, you live to honor your elders—your life is a testament to them. Our people are dying, and our culture is already limited; our customs and language have been wiped away by years of colonization. But this was a tradition I could do, and I'm just failing. I wish I could maintain my faith in God as a testament to my mother and her own incredible faith, but it just isn't happening."[48]

Dan's grandmother died early in the pandemic while living in an assisted living community in California. For him, the experience was the culmination of his crisis of faith. Formerly a devout Catholic with plans to become a priest, the experience of losing his grandmother to COVID-19, and what he identified as the hypocrisies of many Christians during the pandemic, became the final impetus to reject his former beliefs:

> My grandmother was terrified of COVID. But she was also very devout. My mom and I suspect—given what we know about her personality—she may have made, in her mind, some sort of bargain with God. If you give me COVID, you will spare my family from the disease. On one hand, I find that very endearing and it only makes me love her more. But on the other hand, it also makes

me angry that some people have this idea of such an abusive God that would even take such a bargain. That is sadistic; that is fucked up. I am basically an atheist at this point. I have been headed that way for a while, but the pandemic just really clinched it for me.[49]

Dan is not alone in his feelings of anger. As will be discussed further in chapter 4, some Christians' flaunting of public health guidelines and denials of the pandemic's reality caused many of those impacted by the death of a loved one to COVID to reconsider their religious commitments. Pastor Craig Taylor of Willow Meadows Baptist Church in Houston connected the politicization of pandemic protection measures with a wider ignorance of Christian scripture, even among Christian leaders. He noted, "The pandemic became politicized and as a pastor, I often saw people expressing a really simplistic understanding of Christianity as a result. I consider myself Evangelical, which tends to be more conservative, and I have heard other Evangelical leaders say things like 'God's not going to let anything happen to us,' and I just want to say, 'Have you read *anything* in your Bible?'"[50] While Pastor Taylor defended his own efforts to work with parishioners toward a more nuanced faith, for others like Dan, the hypocrisies of the Christian Right during the pandemic ultimately invalidated all Christian narratives that had previously scaffolded their identity.

Innovating New Stories

While many found their pre-pandemic religious identities challenged by the experience of losing a loved one, a group emerged that I call "spiritual innovators." Such spiritual innovators creatively renegotiated their former religious identity by incorporating new practices not permitted or associated with their existing religious tradition, including contrasting spiritual beliefs, contacting spirit mediums, and using psychedelic drugs. Identifying spiritual innovation as a category is not, in itself, especially novel. Many scholars have noticed that lived religious identities most often reflect a *bricolage* of practices. In the 1980s, Robert Bellah and other sociologists produced their famous book *Habits of the Heart*, which describes a nurse named Sheila Larson and her ad hoc religion of "Sheila-ism."[51] Religion scholar Thomas Tweed notes that religious history does not involve "self-contained traditions chugging along in their tracks." Instead, it more closely resembles a system of "hydrodynamic flows" in which creative borrowing and hybridity are the norm, rather than the exception.[52] Leonard Primiano coined the term "vernacular religion" to talk about the messy reality of religion in practice.[53] The spiritual innovators in this study, however, were those who actively recognized that they were incorporating new practices to create a more fulfilling spiritual identity in the aftermath of a COVID-19 loss. In this way, they were able to creatively negotiate a new narrative that included elements of their former identity combined with novel practices of belief.

Julia lost her brother to COVID-19 in the fall of 2020. Coming from a Filipino American family, Catholicism formed a large part of her religious identity before the pandemic. The death of her brother, however, undermined her faith and confidence in God: "After my brother's death, I still pray, but part of me feels like my prayers weren't heard. And then I get angry, but then another part of me is asking, 'Did I not pray hard enough for my brother when he was in the hospital?' and I start to feel guilty."[54] Julia began reaching out to spirit mediums in an attempt to contact her brother after his death, despite what she knew would be her family's disapproval: "After all this doubt and self-blame, I have been searching for presence of my brother somewhere. I have reached out to different spirit mediums, even though I know my family would disapprove and think it was of the Devil. But there are times when I get the feeling that he is trying to communicate with me, and I just desperately want that."[55] While Julia ultimately found her first experience with a medium unfulfilling, she continued to make appointments and, at the time of our interview in February 2021, seemed confident that she would continue to work with them in the future.

Indeed, contacting spirit mediums for the first time was a common experience among those who lost loved ones to COVID-19. A significant number of the posts on the COVID-19 Loss Support Facebook group were seeking recommendations for mediums, as well as discussing what constituted an appropriate "going-rate," how to tell if a medium was a fraud, and best practices for visiting or contacting a medium.[56] These sites also became the venue for theological debate concerning the use of spirit mediums more generally. At least once a week throughout 2021, a new post asking about mediums would appear and inevitably erupt into hundreds of comments debating the validity of spirit mediums and whether their use violated Christian, Muslim, or other religious beliefs. While those in favor often discussed how they had integrated their personal religious practice with seeking out or even developing mediumistic abilities themselves, those against mediums frequently cited Leviticus 19:31, which prohibited the ancient Israelites from seeking out the services of mediums. Beyond these religious arguments, a common concern was fraud, especially when intimate details of lives could be uncovered with relative ease online.

To gain a greater understanding of how spirit mediumship affected the way that Americans were approaching death during the pandemic, I reached out to several spirit mediums who were recommended by individuals on the COVID-19 Loss

Support group. While they acknowledged fraud in the field, the individuals that I spoke with were passionate about their work in the grieving process. Carla, a medium working in the New York metro area for more than a decade, explained, "Clients have said that working with me has healed them more than any therapy ever has, I consider what I do as a service. I'm not a saint, but I am helping people heal every day."[57] Carla herself did not identify with a specific religious institution or community, but she acknowledged her role in leading people to a better understanding of their own spirituality: "Death is the great leveler; it is the one experience we all have in common. But death can easily cause a crisis of faith. Oftentimes, spirit mediums have to be the ones to guide someone through that; I have to serve them, to let them know that there is something on the other side. It's not all harps and angels; but my sitters take heart that they will see their loved one again."[58] Carla's work reflects what may be a strength, sociologically speaking, of spirit mediums. Because they serve clients, not congregations, spirit mediums have greater flexibility in responding to spiritual crises and may be able to develop a more nuanced response more quickly. Indeed, this fact was reflected in the work of Susan, who currently works as a spirit medium in California. She explicitly identified her role for clients as helping to answer major theological questions of theodicy and the existence of evil: "I try to help them understand that nothing they did caused their loved one's death. Free will is a factor they struggle with a lot: 'If God's really there, why are these things happening?' I help them frame this as a chance to grow; pain is our biggest motivator, and, in this grief, their spirituality can grow—God, spirit, whatever you call it, is too big to fit in one religion!"[59]

The three mediums that I interviewed all agreed that COVID grief was of a particular type. Susan explained that "The grief my sitters experience from a COVID loss is very similar to people losing their loved ones to car accidents or suicide—a feeling of complete powerlessness they have never experienced before, where final words and goodbyes could not be said."[60] Her experience was echoed by Maria, a spirit medium based in New England:

> My sitters constantly ask, "Do they understand? Are they OK that they were alone, and I couldn't be with them?" It is actually harder for the person suffering than the one who passed into Spirit, because those who pass on and wake up in Spirit have an immediate understanding of why. What has come through in my work is people saying, "Don't worry. Your grandfather was with me, or your father, or your mother, or so forth. I wasn't really alone." That has been the most comforting thing for people to hear."[61]

While many were desperate to connect with loved ones who died from COVID-19, all the mediums that I spoke with noted an increase in sitters seeking to contact loved ones who died of drug or alcohol addiction during the pandemic. This reflects overall trends nationwide; a recent research note in the *Journal of the American Medical Association, Psychiatry* found a nearly fifty percent jump in overdose-related deaths in May 2020, as compared to May 2019.[62]

Beyond consulting with spirit mediums, other spiritual innovators describe incorporating the beliefs of religious traditions outside their own to make sense of their loved one's death. A Korean American man from Georgia, Yoon Tae was raised Christian and has a graduate degree in theology. Despite this, he found Christian theologies unable to comfort him after the death of his father, the owner of a local convenience store. Instead, he was drawn to religious concepts outside of Christianity:

We have this vendor who could come into my father's convenience store. I am not even sure of his ethnicity or religion—I think he was South Asian—but he knows my wife and I have a child on the way. He said to me "In my religion, we believe the spirits continue on into another form. A part of your dad will be in that child." I found that way more comforting than any sort of Christian resource. The way he approached it was so different. It wasn't that he was not sorry for us, but he expressed his belief so clearly and confidently. It felt like it was true for him, and so it made it true for me somehow. I've come back to that a few times because that is a narrative of the afterlife I like more. I do have a lot of resources based on the Christian theology I have studied to understand the world, but it was weirdly this random guy at my father's store that gave me the most comfort.[63]

At the time of our interview in May 2021, Yoon Tae said that he had not explored these ideas further than some late-night Google searches. However, he reaffirmed that the idea of reincarnation found in South Asian religions like Hinduism, Buddhism, and Sikhism ultimately provided greater comfort than traditional Christian ideas of the afterlife.

Like Yoon Tae, Gurpreet felt drawn to different religious narratives to reconstruct his identity after the death of his father. Raised as a second-generation Sikh American, the death of Gurpreet's father undermined his faith in Sikhism: "Whenever I feel religious or feel like praying, I do it in a Sikh way. But my dad was the main reason I had so much faith. When he was in the hospital, I put my whole-hearted faith into praying, but it didn't do anything for the one man who made me want to be Sikh, so now I feel like why should I do it at all?"[64] After his father's death, Gurpreet cut his beard—an action at odds with the Sikh tradition, which encourages believers to not cut or remove body hair out of respect for the body God has given them. In the months after his father's death, Gurpreet's conversations with friends became an important resource, first for religious exploration and later religious renegotiation: "I have been talking to my friends who are all sorts of different religions, not all Sikh. I have been reading their scriptures and trying to understand what they believe. I have a much broader look at religion now and think, if God is real, you should strive to know him in every way. I am more spiritual than religious now—no longer just following the Sikh path, though that will always be my religious home."[65] The experiences of Yoon Tae and Gurpreet demonstrate how some spiritual innovators were able to build meaning around their loved one's death by creatively combining new narratives from foreign religious traditions into their religious identities.

While many forms of spiritual innovation might exist, a final one that my conversation partners spoke about was psychedelic drug use. Sofia, a Hispanic college student from south Texas, became interested in psychedelic drug use after the death of her grandfather from COVID-19. While she was clear that she would likely have taken drugs anyway, the experience became a part of processing her grandfather's death and rethinking her own religious upbringing:

> One night, I took too many drugs and lost touch with reality. That was really scary, but it also made me think about my place in the world. When I usually see people having spiritual awakenings from drug use, it is after a really positive experience, but mine didn't happen that way. After my grandfather died, I didn't know what I believed. I don't really identify with being Catholic anymore, but this drug trip—which was scary, like really, really bad—helped me figure out my place in the world and the cosmos and the afterlife.[66]

Sofia later described other members of her family exploring alternative spiritual or religious ideas previously unthinkable to them:

> I know I am not the only one in my family looking at other ideas about the afterlife. My grandmother is the most religious person I know—she would make us pray the rosary every night at her house. But after my grandfather died, she began looking up about Near Death Experiences online. I think she didn't want us to know, but I found out after she borrowed my computer. When I asked her, she said she found comfort in that. It wasn't the Catholic Church's official line or teaching, but she was comforted by it still.[67]

Sofia's experience reveals how many individuals relied on alternative strategies of meaning making outside their home religious traditions after the death of loved one from COVID-19.

Between deepening connections to home religions, rejecting them, or creatively transforming and renegotiating them, we have seen a variety of ways in which individuals used narrative to mediate between identities before and after a loved one's death from COVID-19. It is important to note that these are ideal types, reflecting differing styles of engagement with a tradition, not ontological realities set in stone. A person may employ these narrative strategies in various ways throughout their grieving process or in their life. Such stories, however, share a concern with bridging the gap in phenomenological time between the before and after of the death of a loved one. They accomplish this by telling a story of who they see themselves as, who they were, and who they might hope to be. However, these narratives of personal religious identity are not the only stories that "didn't work" during the pandemic. Some experienced a narrative failure on a society-wide scale that caused them to doubt our accepted public realities and seek out new sources of authority.

New Sources of Authority

The pandemic shattered not only our individual stories of religious identity, but also our socially shared stories about the way life works—children leave the house for school during the day, you go to work in an office, the wedding planned next month will certainly happen. As a result, some individuals began questioning other stories we were being told about the origins of the virus, best treatment options, and the safety of vaccines. As information about the virus rapidly changed, and government officials publicly argued with medical professionals, conspiratorial thinking became prevalent in many online and public forums.

This questioning of government narratives was especially evident among alternative spiritual practitioners who operate outside of religious institutions. Of the three spirit mediums I spoke with, two espoused conspiratorial views. In expressing her belief that COVID-19 was made by the government, Susan relied on her unique relationship with Spirit as evidence: "The spirits tell me that the narrative our governments are telling us is a lie. I think powerful people created COVID in a lab, but Spirit tried to warn us. When the news reported on the laboratory in Wuhan, I asked Spirit if it was connected to all this, and the spirits told me it was. Where evil can exist is only in the minds of man, I tell you, but Spirit can help us grow."[68] Carla echoed Susan's claims that the COVID-19 virus was manmade, while also expressing mistrust of the vaccine based on spirits of the deceased that she was contacting:

I recently brought through a twenty-five-year-old who died from the vaccine—of course, that wasn't on the news! I read his sister and brought him through. She offered that he was given the vaccine and within several minutes he dropped to the ground. My logical mind went immediately to an anaphylactic reaction, but as a medium I must move past my logical mind. I asked the young man in Spirit, "Was it anaphylactic shock?" The young man said, "No it was not shock." I offered this information to my sitter. She confirmed it wasn't shock and, at that time, believed it was a bile duct reaction—bile went into his lungs, and he passed less than twenty-four hours later. In other readings, I am also bringing back people who worked in pharmaceutical companies, and they're telling living relatives to be cautious with the vaccines. I mean, it does seem rather strange how it all happened, doesn't it?[69]

While it is unclear if the sitters working with the mediums agreed with such claims, these conversations reflect what Charlotte Ward has called "conspirituality," a movement representing the intersection of female-dominated, alternative spirituality and male-dominated, conspiratorial thinking.[70] Humans deploy narratives to take an unprecedented situation and render it interpretable. The conspiratorial thought of these spirit mediums demonstrates how, when the accepted narratives do not make sense or are otherwise considered suspect, creating new narratives based on novel information can become an important interpretative tool.

Oftentimes, what makes a public or socially accepted narrative *not* work can be located in a community's prior experience. As explained by Pastor McElroy, the painful history of exploitation of and experimentation on African Americans resulted in significant hesitancy to accept government narratives about COVID-19 and the coronavirus vaccine:

Black and Brown people have been more hesitant to accept the government's story about COVID and the vaccine because of our history. We as a community have endured some horrible experiences at the hands of the government. I found that many were scared to take the vaccine due to misinformation that was out there. As an example, there were conversations among some that there was a microchip of some kind in the vaccine. Several felt that "Big Brother" was watching them or that the vaccine was going to destroy natural antibodies.[71]

In Pastor McElroy's opinion, the church that he led—the Antioch Missionary Baptist Church in Houston, Texas—had an important role in helping to alleviate his community's fears: "The only way to combat that mistrust is education, so our congregation went canvassing door-to-door and had large events aimed at educating the community on the virus and the vaccine. We took a three-pronged approach, where we worked closely with the healthcare system and the local government to develop a consistent message."[72] As discussed in chapter 2, these efforts were so successful that only two percent of the Antioch Missionary Baptist Church community remained unvaccinated. While Pastor McElroy acknowledged the legitimate origins of his congregants' suspicions, he also saw his church as an important partner in fighting against such misinformation.

Beyond specific histories that engendered suspicion for public narratives of the pandemic, other communities expressed suspicion of the government as the sole source of truth. In leading the San Pedro Ward of the San Antonio LDS community, Bishop Bruce Baillio explained his belief that forces of secularism were actively working against the Christian community. While he eschewed conspiracy theories as a whole, he also explained that he did not blindly trust the government in all things:

> There is a real militancy out there in society that I think came to the forefront in the pandemic. People, some of them in the government, have been militant against the nuclear family, against religious institutions, and against our values, because we serve a higher authority than the government. I don't necessarily think people are sitting around tables and conniving to get rid of religion, but I do think there is a cynical view that a belief in God is antithetical to obedience to the State. The [LDS] Church tries to be good citizens in whatever country we live in and the current president of the LDS Church [Russell M. Nelson] is a doctor who was very public about when he got his vaccine, but that doesn't mean we trust the government without question. We trust God.[73]

Bishop Baillio reflects a view, common in many communities, that forces at play in the government did not always have the public's best interests at heart. While this narrative may not have originated in the pandemic, COVID-19 created new opportunities for individuals to interpret public events and construct an alternative narrative of what was happening.

Such conspiratorial narratives that led to COVID denial and vaccine refusal were often traumatic for medical professionals and those who lost loved ones to COVID-19. Working in the medical system, Manpreet explained, "I am out there every day traveling to nursing homes and to medical facilities to vaccinate people, and I encounter people who don't want to take it—some of them are even nurses! It makes me so angry. Do you know how quickly I would have leapt at the chance for my father to have this vaccine? But he can't. Because he is dead."[74] While such trauma is certainly understandable and warranted, from an academic perspective it is important to try and imagine why these conspiratorial narratives might make sense to intelligent and thoughtful people. The popularity of such subversion narratives may reflect the general confusion of the pandemic reality into which we were all unexpectedly thrust. Information on the virus changed almost daily in the early months of the pandemic, and many of the narratives we had previously lived by had to be reevaluated entirely. As a result, the usual sources of information appeared suspect and many looked to alternative sources of information—social media, the internet, or alternative religious practitioners—to interpret the chaotic events around them. This does not make them correct, of course, but it gives some context as to why such narratives became so prevalent during the pandemic. As stated earlier, to be human is to tell stories. When our stories no longer work, we do not live without stories, but rather create new ones with the materials at hand.

CONCLUSIONS: *THE THING*

This chapter has shown narrative as a fundamental tool of meaning-making for those who encountered death during the COVID-19 pandemic. For some, it mediated between the "before and after" times of a loved one's death in ways that strengthened religious identities or offered the opportunity to reconnect with their religious heritage. Others rejected prior narratives entirely, or creatively renegotiated them through incorporating novel practices and beliefs. Religious leaders drew on narratives of their communities' historic struggles to frame responses to the contemporary suffering around them. Medical professionals contemplated what it meant to be a doctor or nurse. And some, rejecting our public stories of viruses and vaccines entirely, searched for new narratives.

A few days before lockdown came to Austin, Texas, my husband and I went to see John Carpenter's 1982 horror classic *The*

Thing. It was eerie—we sat in a mostly empty theater for what had previously been a sold-out show, watching a movie about a virus-like entity that leaves a community isolated and paranoid, constantly guessing who is infected. In this case, art and reality reflected each other in an odd coincidence that I still find myself thinking about. COVID-19 was just beginning to dominate the airwaves, events had been canceled, and lockdowns were beginning in major cities on the East and West Coasts. The air of the theater was pregnant with anxiety, and we all knew something was coming as we stifled any stray cough and surreptitiously moved seats to put distance between ourselves and other moviegoers. I wondered if the movie on the screen in front of me was a portent for the coming weeks. I had no idea how long it would be our reality.

I relate this story because there is no Archimedean point with narrative—no space outside the stories. I watch a movie about a community slowly devolving into isolation and fear over an unknown virus, and that influences my actions when a novel virus finally arrives. Did watching *The Thing* provide a prophetic map of the coming lockdown and social chaos of 2020? Or did I just select that moment in my own arranging of phenomenological time? We are always enmeshed within the stories that we construct; as such, we must choose our stories carefully.

4

TRAUMA

In so many ways, every chapter of *Shattered Grief* has led to this one. My conversation partners repeatedly described feeling traumatized by the deaths of their loved ones, traumatized by their complex experiences of grief, and traumatized by the neglect of larger society in attending to it. Like a gold thread in a tapestry or an intricate musical refrain, trauma was threaded throughout each and every one of my interviews.

Perhaps, this is the way it has to be when talking about death. There is some debate among anthropologists and philosophers as to whether death is, by its nature, inherently traumatic. Terror management theory argues that belief in an immortal soul, a loving God, and other such religious ideas grows out of our deeply-held fear of death and dying.[1] Some archaeologists have even traced this fear to our earliest Paleolithic ancestors, claiming that ancient burial practices reveal an anxiety of annihilation in death.[2] Anthropologists, however, have noted a diverse approach to death in certain cultures that complicates the claim of death as necessarily traumatic.[3] Jewish philosopher Baruch Spinoza hypothesized that, when a state of complete rationality is reached, we need not fear death because the rational ideas held and cherished by our mind are eternal.[4]

In previous chapters, we started by introducing a theoretical framework and then using that to analyze the voices of those encountering death during the pandemic. Here, we will save our theoretical framework, such as it is, for the end. It feels, in some ways, almost disrespectful to subject the raw emotions that my conversation partners shared with me to aggressive analysis. It threatens to rob such feelings of their power if understood only as the evidence of a particular theorist's ideas or a given phenomenon. But this switch also acknowledges that we are walking in largely uncharted territory. Ritual, narrative identity, community—these conceptual tools have been the foundational building blocks of religious studies almost since the discipline's founding. Our vocabulary for acknowledging and thinking about trauma in religious settings, however, is relatively new.

In social work today, trauma is generally defined as an "event that overwhelms a person's ability to cope and that is threatening or damaging in some way."[5] The fifth edition of the *Diagnostic and Statistical Manual of Mental Disorders* (DSM-V) goes further, specifying that an individual must be exposed to an event involving "actual or threatened death or serious injury, or sexual violence" to be diagnosed with trauma.[6] And indeed, many of those I spoke with witnessed the death of their loved one or feared significantly for their personal health and safety. Regardless of whether their experience rose to a clinical diagnosis of trauma, these individuals found the rhetoric and framework of trauma useful for conceptualizing their experience of the pandemic. These feelings of trauma were also inextricably bound with feelings of rage and anger toward the various forces that created the pandemic and allowed it to continue. To begin exploring this topic, this chapter is organized around three questions:

1. What does trauma look like during a pandemic?
2. What happens when you are angry at your church? At your country? At God?
3. Does religion always comfort those in pain?

While these questions will not be the final word on the topic of religion and trauma during the COVID-19 pandemic, they can help focus our attention on the confusion, rage, and upheaval endemic to my interviews. As End-of-Life doula Martha B. Heymann explained, "There is going to be a lot of trauma for those who lost loved ones during COVID—even if it wasn't from COVID—because it radically changed how we say goodbye to people. There is so much grief going on that hasn't had a chance to be expressed. We celebrate life, but death should also be celebrated. It is one of the most important experiences we go through, and we don't get a practice run at it."[7] More research will be done on these topics, but this chapter serves as a small snapshot into the pain and suffering of those who encountered, experienced, and worked with death during the pandemic.

WHAT DOES TRAUMA LOOK LIKE DURING A PANDEMIC?

Between the upheaval of established norms, the omnipresent fear of infection, various political and social unrest, and widespread confusion over appropriate medical protocols, the COVID-19 pandemic was an overwhelming and terrifying time for many Americans. Such experiences were exponentially more so for those Americans who became intimate with death through their work or the loss of a loved one. This section aims to highlight their voices as more than just a catalogue of trauma. Rather, their stories represent a significant and immediate interpretation of the experience with death during the pandemic.

Distance from Dying Loved Ones

By and large, the factor that inspired the most pain for those who lost a loved one to COVID-19 is that they could not be together through their loved one's illness and death. Describing her father's death early in March 2020, Sabila explained, "He died such a traumatic death—I can't stop thinking about what he went through in his final days, and I think that is one thing that will haunt me for the rest of my life. The idea that he spent three days in the ER during the peak of the pandemic. He was never put on a ventilator, so he was awake for all of it, but his throat was so sore he could not speak. That part just brings me to my knees—how do you get over that?"[8] Olivia echoed Sabila's experience. A veteran mourning the loss of her father, she described driving the forty-five minutes every day to the hospital where her father was intubated. Although she was not allowed inside, she would sit in the parking lot just to be as near to him as she could. Several religious leaders who worked with parishioners struggling with a COVID-19 death affirmed the difficulty of being separated from loved ones. Pastor Lou McElroy of the Antioch Missionary Baptist Church in Houston, Texas explained that "It is important to understand that the grief of many didn't start at the point of death from COVID-19: the grief started when the people were admitted to the hospital and their family members couldn't go in. Many people have not been able to properly grieve; there is an absence of grief when we are not physically there, with our dying loved ones."⁹

In this way, the hospital became, for many of my conversation partners, a prison—the enemy itself, even more so than the disease. Bianca described her Mexican American father's hatred and anger at the hospital during her grandmother's illness, saying:

> He called it Auschwitz and said once they send you there, you don't come out. He didn't believe she died from COVID; he said it was the hospital. His brothers said similar things. They just didn't want to accept that their mother could die. They didn't want to seem weak. In Mexican culture, men aren't supposed to show any sort of fear or sadness. The one emotion they can have is anger. Anything else is a vulnerability. This has completely fractured my family, and I am not sure we will ever be the same again.¹⁰

Working as a nurse in several COVID-19 wards across the country during the pandemic, Mary explained that this anger directed at hospitals was omnipresent in her conversations with families:

> It's highly charged in the hospital, lots of difficult decisions that family members don't understand and then get angry. It's one thing if they can be there at the bedside and can see the care everyone is giving their loved one. But during the time of COVID, they couldn't. I understand in my gut that anger is just fear expressing itself in a new and different way, but it can still be hard as a nurse to experience that. At some point, our society is going to have to understand how much we have lost to COVID—that

we couldn't even hold the hand of our loved ones as they died. The trauma of that is going to be felt for a long time.[11]

Dr. Jack Kravitz echoed Mary when describing his work leading a hospice ward filled with COVID-19 patients. He stated, "Hospice work is ten percent medicine and ninety percent emotion. It is understanding that all of us, but particularly those whose loved ones are particularly ill, are working off of our emotions. Families of COVID patients are very angry; they need to blame something or someone. It is not our place to validate their accusation, but we can validate their feeling."[12] While loved ones were dying, anger at hospitals and medical staff became an ever-present reality for many families of COVID-19 patients, isolated from their loved one.

As the pandemic progressed, some hospitals began allowing a designated family member to visit a COVID patient, although they often could not enter the room. Julia's brother contracted COVID-19 in late December 2020 and was intubated in January 2021. Because the rest of her family was either recovering from COVID-19 or had small children, she served as the designated family member to visit the hospital, which was especially emotionally challenging:

> It was really hard, looking at him through the glass, seeing him there by himself. The doctors and nurses stayed with him because he was the youngest person in the ICU at the time, so they couldn't bear to leave him alone. In Filipino culture, we're firm believers in being with our loved ones until the end—we move in rotations to be sure someone is always with the person who is sick or dying. So just staring at him through the glass and not having that—the prayers, the hugs, the handholding—it was traumatic.[13]

Similarly, Catholic widower Paul was unable to participate in any sort of grieving rituals when his wife Joannie died in their New York apartment. Her local synagogue organized a funeral, but he was unable to attend since he was, himself, still recovering from COVID-19. He explained the pain that this caused, saying, "I thought I had killed her, that I had given her the disease. I ask God all the time, 'Why did you take her from me? Why did you make me alone?' They sent me a few digital photos from the funeral of the rabbi standing over the coffin, but I am not sure anyone was in attendance—it was just Joannie and me here in the city. I feel abandoned by the city of New York, the government, by everyone."[14] Scott, a counselor based in Austin, Texas specializing in issues of complicated grief, explained how feelings of isolation like Paul's and Julia's were the seeds of more serious concerns that might manifest down the road for those suffering a COVID loss: "Being geographically or medically isolated from our loved ones changes the dynamic. It creates guilt and shame, which can lead to what we clinicians call 'complicated grief.'"[15] While "complicated grief" is a clinical diagnosis that may or may not fit everyone's experience, the inability to be with loved ones in their final moments was a recurrent source of trauma throughout my conversations.

Arbitrary Death

As a disease, COVID-19 seems to be recklessly arbitrary in terms of both who survives and who dies. While certain factors might increase the likelihood of death, stories abound on social media and the news outlets of unexpected individuals who beat the disease and made full recoveries. COVID's capricious and inconsistent nature caused some to obsess over their loved one's death.

As Carmen declared when ruminating on her mother's death, "I can't stop asking myself, 'Why my mom? What did she lack? Why can other people beat this disease and not her?'"[16]

COVID-19's arbitrary nature caused traumatic feelings in two ways. The first was simply, as we saw with Carmen, the erratic nature of who lived and who died. Dr. Jack Kravitz noted that "Unlike terminal cancer or terminal heart failure, many people with COVID survive. So, when I sit down and have to say to a family, 'YOUR loved one is not going to make it,' it can be very hard to accept. They will see these things about new medicines, new treatments, someone being in the hospital months, then getting discharged with everyone clapping. It's hard to explain that this is not going to happen for their loved one."[17] Yoon Tae agreed with Dr. Kravitz's assessment of the emotional toll caused by COVID-19's seemingly random selectivity: "My dad's passing really made me realize the human capacity for hope in what are utterly hopeless situations. Even though the doctors and nurses were telling us that it didn't look good and that the chances of recovery were less than one percent if my dad was able to string together four or eight good hours, then you could believe he was still fighting and still had a chance."[18]

After a loved one's death, many described significant fear that any small illness might represent their own bout with COVID-19. Julia explained that "This experience has increased my fear of death. If anyone gets even a little sick or makes a small cough, it sends me into a frenzy, and I am sure they are going to die. I am always on this edge of fear; it wakes me up in the middle of the night."[19] Even medical staff found themselves constantly wondering if every sneeze or cough was "their turn with COVID." In the words of Texas primary care physician Dr. Larry Kravitz, "This is a Russian roulette disease—most people are OK, most don't have long COVID, most survive, but then some people die catastrophically. Other people's stories haunt you and hang over you—every time you have a symptom. You start to wonder if it is going to become more serious, like the stories you hear."[20] The seemingly random nature of COVID-19 deaths undermined any sense of security that individuals felt around small or minor illnesses.

A second factor in the apparent arbitrariness of death during the pandemic was the fact that family members could not see their loved one's decline until death was near. This fact made the death feel like an unpredicted shock. Reflecting on her work as a hospital chaplain in Chicago, Kristel explained that "For a normal ICU stay, a family can adapt over time. They get updates; they see the concern on the medical staff members' faces; they see their loved one get worse and worse—that does a lot for the pace of grief. During COVID, however, that was not an option."[21] In this environment, nurses and doctors deliberated as to their role in preparing families for a COVID-19 death. Dr. Paul Tatum led a hospice and palliative care team at Ascension Seton Medical Center in central Texas. In our conversation, he emphasized, "A lot of hospice work during the pandemic was being the family's eyes and ears—translating and passing on information for them. If you hear that their oxygen is 91, that doesn't sound too bad, but you might have no idea the number of interventions being done to keep it there and that there are no more interventions to add. We provide information to help manage emotions."[22] Nurses also began considering techniques to signal to families the gravity of illness earlier in the process. Working as a clinical nurse specialist in Austin, Christine explained:

> In the ICU, once visitors were allowed to visit while wearing PPE [personal protective equipment], we tried to make the room look

nice, make the sheets straight, the tables cleaned. But underneath all of that, the patient was falling apart. We began to wonder if maybe we shouldn't make them look so perfect, so the family would understand how sick the patient really is. We've isolated ourselves from the ugliness of death in this country, but it can be important for the healing process to see it up close earlier on.[23]

Because individuals were often kept separated from their dying loved ones and unaware of their decline, their deaths seemed all the more sudden. Jennifer lost both her mother and best friend to COVID-19 in a period of a few weeks. While she had medical training and understood that, often, someone's decline is relatively quick, the sudden loss still stung: "You don't have time to prepare. It is like a sudden accident—boom! They're gone! My best friend had things on her calendar for the week after she died; my mother had just put her winter clothes back in storage and had brought out her spring clothes."[24]

In wider American culture, it is common for people to say that they prefer a sudden death with little time for suffering or fear; "I want to die in my sleep" or "At least he didn't suffer" are common refrains. However, from the perspective of many religious traditions, knowing your death is approaching, and being prepared for it, is understood as the preferred way to die. The Roman Catholic Church defines a "good death" as one that "will include the knowledge that death is approaching and one's treatment choices will be respected, the confidence that one will not suffer useless pain or be abandoned by friends and family, and the opportunity to be reconciled with one's life project."[25] According to Dr. Mohammad Zafir Al-Shahri and Dr. Abdullah al-Khenaizan, a good death in the Islamic tradition allows for the opportunity to reflect on past sins and seek forgiveness as one is surrounded by family.[26] Buddhist traditions state that the mental state at the moment you take your last breath is crucial for determining your next rebirth—if you are asleep or mentally incapacitated, you may not approach death with the appropriate awareness.[27] These statements, of course, are not meant to make claims about the postmortem fates of those who died from COVID-19 while intubated or otherwise unconscious. Rather, they demonstrate how the unexpected and sudden nature of death during the pandemic lacked proper closure and produced complicated grief for those who survived their loved ones.

Lack of Acknowledgment

Perhaps the greatest cause of trauma for those who lost loved ones was the widespread lack of social acknowledgment surrounding their loved one's death. Those who died in other national disasters like 9/11 or Hurricane Katrina were widely mourned with public memorials, ceremonies, and events. In contrast, the drawn-out nature of the United States's COVID-19 death toll and the politicized environment surrounding the virus meant that many could not agree that a tragedy had occurred at all, let alone how to commemorate it. In her work with the COVID-19 Loss Support for Family & Friends Facebook group, Sabila discussed the apparent apathy experienced by many who lost loved ones to COVID-19: "This whole community is just dealing with trauma. We want our voices heard; we want to talk about the trauma our loved ones went through and the trauma we go through every day without them. Our country is facing a tsunami of the most unprecedented grief in history, and no one seems to care."[28] Julia echoed Sabila, "The people who experience this loss, we're on a rampage. We try to tell people around us to please just stay safe. I have told people online, 'I lost someone. You could die from this.' But some call us liars, sanctimonious, or say we're filled with bullshit. A woman I know was told that she was a crisis actor. We really need our neighbors to support us in this time. And we're just being completely abandoned by them."[29]

In our conversation, Rev. Rich Andre of St. Austin Catholic Church emphasized his perspective on how the lack of society-wide commemoration affected those in mourning. He stated, "We have not grieved as a nation; we have not acknowledged these deaths. This was made so much worse by the political situation, where there was a real effort to downplay how many people were suffering. It stopped us from having any type of public grieving. There is a really strong denial of what is happening and wanting to deal with it."[30] These feelings led many of those who lost loved ones to create their own makeshift memorials. Beyond commemorating the deceased, these memorials also forced the topic of COVID-19 deaths into public view. Such ad hoc public memorials included stones on a New Jersey farm painted with the names of those who died,[31] ribbons tied to a central Texas bridge,[32] and local businesses who placed hundreds of memorial plaques in their storefronts.[33] Such practices were not unique to the United States. Across the globe, communities built spontaneous memorials to mourn the dead, including lighting a temporary wooden sanctuary ablaze (England), lining a road with thousands of pinwheels (Brazil), and painting white crosses in public squares (Czech Republic).[34] In 2021, as the American government changed leadership, more avenues opened up for public acknowledgment. Prominent among these was *In America: Remember*, in which artist Suzanne Brennan Firstenberg (Washington, D.C.) placed 600,000 white flags along the National Mall to represent the (at the time) 600,000 Americans dead from COVID-19.³⁵ In contemplating the more public acknowledgment of their loss, Carmen explained, "I wept at the moment of silence during the Super Bowl 2021. It was such an unexpected kindness after the lies, backstabbing, betrayals we endured for four years."³⁶ This society-wide neglect and politicization of the pandemic bred intense feelings of resentment and anger in many mourners that remain central to their experience of the pandemic.

Warriors in a Battlefield

While those who lost loved ones to COVID-19 were traumatized by the experience of isolation, those employed in medical and funerary settings found their own work emotionally and psychologically exhausting. As such, they consistently described their experiences as akin to soldiers on the front lines of battle.Ced Dr. Jack Kravitz described his work in hospice with COVID patients as such:

> I wake up every day and feel like I am on a Civil War battlefield, with people just dying to the left and right of me. The immensity of it is striking. I have taken two doctors off of ventilators—both gentlemen I knew for over thirty years. It was personal there. I was a medical professional then, I had to be. But I also really felt it. In the beginning, it was scary because there was not enough PPE [personal protective equipment] and we didn't even know if it would actually protect us. We were taking plastic Walmart bags and wrapping them around our feet with scotch tape. We thought we might die doing this, but we just had to swallow the fear and go. There's a camaraderie between those of us who have been serving in COVID-19 wards. Just like when military

people come home from war and don't want to talk about it; I don't want to talk about it with my family. But I know we'll all be having flashbacks for a while.[37]

Dr. Kravitz later elaborated further, explaining that he was particularly haunted by worry for his wife and family: "If I brought this thing home from the hospital and gave it to my wife, I don't know what I would do. I come home every day and strip off all my clothes in the garage, then immediately go shower. It would destroy me if I gave her that illness."[38] While describing her work preparing bodies for burial, funeral director Mitzi Chafetz echoed Dr. Kravitz's feelings, "Funeral directors are inherently sensitive and empathetic people, so this has been an especially painful time for myself and my employees. We have elderly in our lives like everyone else and it is scary knowing that every time we go to pick up a body, we might be putting ourselves and our loved ones at risk."[39]

This period also witnessed morbid creativity and innovation in hospital settings. Working as a hospital chaplain, Kristel explained:

> In early COVID, it made sense for doctors to pull out all the stops—there were so many unknowns that it made sense to try absolutely everything and see what might work. But eventually, as norms developed around COVID care, we could see what treatments worked with what patients. We developed a palliative pathway in our hospital that included who might not be able to get a ventilator if we ever ran short. It was a set of difficult conversations for all of us, and ones I wish we did not have to have.[40]

A nurse in Houston described the elaborate procedures devised by nurses in COVID wards to limit exposure as much as possible. COVID patients were isolated in a specific room with all medical machines and IV drips located outside and tubes taped to the floor that went underneath the door and into the room. A nurse would then enter the room to examine the patient and write notes on the glass in backwards script to their colleagues on the other side about what medicines or procedures were needed.[41] Indeed, like the funerary directors discussed in Chapter 1, Dr. Black saw analogies to the HIV/AIDS crisis of the 1980s and early 1990s in the pandemic's macabre innovation:

> As a doctor who has lived through both, this pandemic is very similar to the early years of the AIDS crisis, only happening faster. We innovated to try and make it work, and to heal who we could. But there was also just the omnipresent fear and complete lack of information. There was hysteria and conspiracy theories about why this was happening—people blaming doctors, researchers, politicians, pharmaceutical companies. Above all, the fear is similar.[42]

While this may seem a minor comparison, several of my interviews with medical and funerary professionals referenced the similarities between the COVID-19 pandemic and the HIV/AIDS crisis in terms of widespread uncertainty, fear, and public indifference. This speaks to the inevitability of a future pandemic's recurrence and the, perhaps depressingly, predictable human reaction to unknown threats. It also demonstrates, however, the psychological toolbox that such professionals developed during the HIV/AIDS crisis and had at their disposal to address the COVID-19 pandemic. Going forward, the COVID pandemic will likewise become the inspiration for a new toolbox to react to future, novel viruses.

Despite this creativity and innovative spirit, by the spring of 2021, many medical professionals had become despondent at the unrelenting nature of the pandemic. In our interview in February 2021, Dr. Paul Tatum discussed the despair that had begun to set in among some members of his staff in the Hospice and Palliative Care Unit of the Ascension Seton Medical Center: "The last three months have been a lot harder than the first. The first surge was more along the lines of, 'Roll up your sleeves everyone, let's get through this.' This second surge is more emotionally and mentally draining; we're all left asking, 'When is it going to end? How much longer can we do this?'"[43] Mary served as a travel nurse early in the pandemic and spent several weeks in Detroit at the height of a particularly brutal COVID surge in the spring of 2020. She described her experiences as spiritually relentless:

> The nurses, the staff, the doctors, we were all traumatized. We were drowning in trauma; layers upon layers of it all around us all the time. It was an eight hundred-bed hospital, and every square inch was filled with COVID patients. It happened like the flick of a switch, overnight. Many of the patients we were seeing—it was the third or fourth family member to die. In one day, we lost twenty percent of the ICU in a four-hour span. It was breaking the medical staff. The second they came up for air, they would immediately get dragged back down.[44]

Describing themselves as warriors on a battlefield, medical professionals became the vanguard in our national confrontation with death during the pandemic. While many were proud of their tireless work and innovation, every medical professional I spoke with described the experience as, ultimately, one marked by feelings of isolation and trauma.

Trauma was a constant theme in my interviews, as COVID mourners, doctors, and medical professionals struggled to make sense of the pandemic. While the necessity of being distant from loved ones was the start of many individuals' trauma, the lack of widespread remembrance and the seemingly arbitrary nature of a COVID-19 deaths exacerbated the experience. Medical professionals found themselves as frontline warriors in a seemingly endless battle against the disease, often with little recognition by the larger society of their constant fear and exhaustion. This experience of trauma led to overwhelming anger and resentment among those who worked with or experienced death during the pandemic. America was a country divided by its experience of COVID-19, and few avenues existed to alleviate the hurt and betrayal that many felt. These emotions often existed in the context of religious communities that had previously provided important sources of support, leading many to question the validity of their religious beliefs.

WHAT HAPPENS WHEN YOU ARE ANGRY AT YOUR CHURCH? AT YOUR COUNTRY? AT GOD?

Arising from these traumatic feelings of neglect and isolation, the anger of those confronting death during the pandemic coalesced around four major, interrelated themes—first and foremost, anger at President Donald Trump for what they understood as his role in pandemic denial; anger at their predominantly Evangelical church communities for supporting President Trump; anger at other Americans for their negligence and complacency; and, finally, anger at God himself. Individuals that I spoke with understood these four entities as responsible for the continued strength and transmission of the pandemic.

Anger at Donald Trump

Donald Trump was president in 2020 when the pandemic first began, and he repeatedly denied its severity. As a result, anger and frustration with him was ubiquitous. Among my interview subjects who lost loved ones to COVID-19, Paul epitomized this response, saying:

> I am angry at that son-of-a-bitch Trump. His father built the damn co-op building I live in. As a child, Trump used to go around with his father to collect our rent in person. That little shit was probably in this apartment I am in right now, collecting rent from the former tenant. I used to tell people about that, I was so proud—the president of the United States was in my apartment when he was a child. But now, I am embarrassed to say that. How the American public could ever have elected this schmuck, I'll never know.[45]

Although my interviews were taking place in early 2021, after President Trump's electoral defeat in November 2020 and the inauguration of President Biden in January 2021, anger at President Trump continued to be vehemently expressed by many of my research interlocutors.

The medical professionals that I interviewed especially expressed anger at President Trump for his role in hindering the pandemic response. Dr. Larry Kravitz opined, "How many people did Trump murder with his COVID policies? I sometimes wonder to myself if the so-called 'Dark Ages' were so dark as the time we are in now?"[46] Dr. Black echoed Dr. Kravitz, explaining, "I have been disgusted with how Trump fucked it up—I am so angry at that guy. From making masking a political statement, to leaving the World Health Organization, to criticizing the Centers for Disease Control, to undermining medical experts, to playing down the seriousness of his own COVID experience. It makes me angry."[47] The anger at President Trump sometimes extended to other Republican leaders perceived as allies in his COVID denial. In March 2021, Republican Governor Greg Abbot overturned the Texas mask mandate. A few months later, he made it illegal in Texas for any public entity to enforce a mask mandate.[48] Mary, a nurse in central Texas, said, "When Governor Abbott undid the mask order, I wanted to cry. I remember that day seeing nurses with tears in their eyes. I would have said some unkind words to that man if I could, we could have protested or organized, but we had to keep going—we were all just trying to survive."[49]

Beyond the role that his policies and legislative activities played during the pandemic, many individuals saw Donald Trump as a catalyst that transformed formerly supportive people, places, and communities into harmful and hurtful ones. Arla blamed Donald Trump for the pernicious transformation of her Evangelical church—even in defiance of pastoral leadership:

> When Donald Trump came into office, you really saw this crazy transformation at the church. Individuals' rights were more important than the collective community, and they demanded to meet in the church building. It was the pastor's first pastorate and I think he felt pressured by the community. He tried to make everyone wear masks in the church, but there was only so much

he could do. It was really common in the church to hear that the pandemic was a sign of the end of the world. They would say that Trump was chosen by God, that the election was stolen, that the virus was manufactured in China. People would say, "Trump didn't wear a mask, so neither should I." I blame Trump for my father's death—Trump and the people who worship him like a golden calf at the GOP summit. Trump made people feel OK to be vile and evil because he himself is like that. He just lies and gives everyone permission to reveal their own ugliness.[50]

She was echoed in these feelings by Olivia, who described her own Christian community transforming after the election of President Trump:

> I love God and I will always love God. That hasn't changed. But here's the thing: I was part of a congregation that propped up a political candidate as equal to God himself, greater than God himself. God is a loving God, he cares about "the least of these." My dad was "the least of these," but nobody cared about him when he got COVID. These churches say patriotism is godliness—that is the platform that led to my father's death. We have a president who politicized masks, and pastors raging about how the churches need to be open. I am not sure if I will ever go back to church. It would have to be some kind of special leader for that to happen.[51]

The presidency of Donald Trump transformed not only Evangelical religious communities; many religious communities were critically divided by parishioners' conflicting responses to the pandemic. As an Episcopal leader, Bishop Kathryn Ryan spoke about her surprise at the pushback that she received concerning her decisions regarding pandemic safety:

I didn't expect my role as a religious leader to become politicized. Our call is to love God and love our neighbor as ourselves. In the Episcopal Diocese of Texas, we understand that as requiring our congregations to adopt safe practices like masking and social distancing. But myself and the leadership teams who were making these decisions, we were called leftist shills for the Democratic Party by some parishioners and even seen as part of some conspiracy.[52]

During the pandemic, church communities frequently became politicized and divided. For those holding more moderate or liberal views, anger directed against Donald Trump was, at least in part, a response to his role in transforming religious communities that had previously provided a comforting space. These feelings sometimes extended even further into anger at the various church communities themselves.

Anger at Church Communities

The anger that many individuals experienced toward Donald Trump and his COVID-19 policies also manifested as anger toward the religious communities that seemed to be supporting (or at least in line with) his perspective. Arla, who spoke earlier about her decision to leave her church and join one with a more diverse leadership, explained how this betrayal added a layer of grief:

> I am not only grieving the death of my father, but also the loss of my childhood church. My father died on December 18th, and he was part of a small church—only fifty or sixty people total—so

I thought it would be a big deal. But they went on with Christmas Eve services like nothing happened; some people weren't even wearing masks! My father had played piano there for over forty-five years, but it was like no one cared. After that, I couldn't go back. This was the church I grew up in, but it was traumatic to even think about setting foot in there again. My mother tried to tell me the church loved me and wanted me to return, but they obviously didn't.[53]

Later in our conversation, Arla elaborated further on the social failings of her church, framing her criticism as a widespread failure to live up to Christian ideals:

I don't understand how the American Evangelical community allowed this to happen. They are to blame, and the blood of half a million Americans is on their hands. This is not Christianity. If you look at Jesus, he was a radical; he was someone not liked by the spiritual leaders. He hung out with poor people—with widows, orphans, and other marginalized communities. Our country was built by slaves and the Christian Church supported their enslavement, even promoted it as the civilized thing to do! We planted false wheat in the American church from the beginning, but sometimes you just need to burn the field and start over. They talk about reconciliation, but you need repentance first.[54]

Indeed, like Arla, many of my conversation partners used the values of Christianity to criticize Evangelical churches as falling short of their own purported ethical principles. Alongside questioning his Catholic faith, Dan saw a ubiquitous hypocrisy among Evangelical Christians, saying, "A group of people who call themselves 'pro-life Christians' and always talk about 'family values' seem to be just fine with a lot of people dying. People who say they follow Jesus—you know, the man who warned people about being too rich—just worry about the economy and stock market more than hundreds of thousands of lives. They claim to be the moral arbiters of society, but a special sort of cruelty seems to be on display."[55]

While *Shattered Grief* focuses specifically on how COVID-19 changed American religion and spirituality, such claims of hypocrisy and a call to reimagine Christianity are not entirely unique to the pandemic. Within the contemporary Evangelical Christian community, many discuss the process of "deconstruction"—a tip of the hat to the twentieth-century intellectual movement that challenged foundational social categories like the self, language, and culture as historically constructed phenomena. Rather than accepting such phenomena as given, natural features of the intellectual environment, deconstructionist philosophers encouraged investigating them as mutable developments manufactured to serve larger political purposes. Deconstruction in the contemporary Evangelical Christian context aims to similarly investigate, challenge, and reshape what participants interpret as a simplistic and, ultimately, harmful understandings of faith.[56] Like the conversations highlighted throughout this chapter, such a process may be exceptionally painful. The first person to coin the term, Pastor David Hayword, even compares the process of deconstructing one's faith as going through Elisabeth Kübler-Ross's model of the five stages of grief.[57] The impulse to reexamine and reevaluate religious beliefs is not limited to those mourning a loss or those in the middle of a social crisis; rather, it may represent a larger trend in American Evangelical Christianity itself.

Other individuals expressing anger at religious communities during the pandemic found the effort to both retain and make sense of their personal faith more complicated after the death of a loved one. Olivia believed that her father contracted COVID-19 at his church during a choir event. She described the church leaders' use of Christian rhetoric to silence her experience:

> When my dad was in the hospital, the church [leaders] reached out to me to tell me that I was holding on to a lot of anger and resentment, and I needed to let that go. They told me they were praying for my dad, but that for my dad to truly be healed, I had to release my judgments against them. I wanted to yell, "It was your stupidity that got him sick!" And then when my father died, the hospital let the pastor and pastor's wife go in to pray over his body, not my mom. How is it OK that a man is dying because of the decisions church leaders made and the church leaders have more rights to see him than his family? My family is a Christian family, so for them it is a matter of forgiveness. I believe in the Bible; I believe in God; I believe in forgiveness. But there also needs to be some sort of accountability or justice.[58]

While she had been a devout Christian her whole life, her experiences with her father's church after his death gave Olivia new insight into critiques made against Christianity as a whole:

> This experience opened my eyes to many things that unbelievers say about Christians or churches—I never believed them before, but I see why they say them now. While my dad, a Christian Black man, was hospitalized with COVID-19 that he got while singing in a praise band at that very church, the pastors at our church told the congregation that a Christian wouldn't say Black Lives Matter—a Christian would only say that All Lives Matter, because God believes in protecting everyone. They also said things like "Christians don't run scared" or "Christians shouldn't

wear masks because they need to trust in Jesus." The pastor was physically taking people's masks off from the pulpit. Seeing this gave me a compassion and empathy for people who have turned away from the church in a way that I didn't have before. I am broken right now. There is not a pill that could fix me, there is not a pastor who could lay hands on me, or prophesize for me, or take away this kind of pain. These are things that I have to process and work through.[59]

These examples of Olivia, Arla, and others do not fully answer the question that guides this section—what happens when the source of your trauma is your church or religious community? Perhaps, there is no single answer that can be given to such a complex and, ultimately, personal question. But in an effort to make meaning out of the tragedy of the COVID-19 pandemic, many expressed deep anger at the religious communities that they perceived as complicit in the pandemic's spread.

Anger at Complacent Citizens

The engine of the pandemic was people: people gathering, people being together, people celebrating and doing all the things that humans have done for centuries. These were the activities that allowed the virus to thrive. Despite government guidance to isolate or wear masks, many did not follow these directives due to misinformation, complacency, or exhaustion. As medical professionals worked amidst the crisis and mourners grieved the loss of loved ones, this divide in social conduct became a source of anger and acrimony. Dr. Black explained, "Going to work at a clinic and knowing that you're going to have a COVID day, but on the way there you see people milling around at a bar with no masks—it just makes me furious. Here I am walking into a shitstorm, and these people couldn't even be bothered."[60]

While there were certainly many reasons for this difference in behavior, many of those who lost loved ones to COVID-19 were resentful of others unaffected by the virus. Reflecting on the death of her mother, Jennifer told me, "People who haven't had someone pass from it or haven't been very sick—they just don't get it. If you have a mild case and just have one symptom, you just get a two-week vacation where you get to binge shows and watch movies. I think a lot of people think it is just a big joke!"[61] Amanda echoed Jennifer, but expressed her feelings with greater frustration:

> When I read posts on social media, where whole families are decimated by one illness, I want to scream—just because it didn't happen to you, doesn't mean you can look away! People always say, "I can't imagine what you're going through," but that's a lie. They could imagine—they could change their behavior, but they just don't want to. No one wants to talk about my grief. No one wants to talk about my dead mom. They'll just say some platitudes about how she lived a good life and is not in pain anymore, but they refuse to sit in the reality of it.[62]

Those enduring the effects of COVID-19 firsthand felt isolated from other Americans whose experience of the pandemic was fundamentally different, leading to widespread feelings of resentment and rage.

Indeed, feelings of anger toward those unaffected by and seemingly apathetic to the pandemic ran throughout my interviews with those who lost loved ones to COVID-19. While Yoon Tae maintained a fairly calm demeanor throughout our interview, at one point he broke down:

For me, it's just like, God! Humans suck so much! In a moment, when you're trying to find hope, it gets taken away every time you go the grocery store. You're constantly stripped of your hope over and over. I'm mad at anti-maskers, at people who don't care. As we have reached the point of half a million dead, I just want to scream, "Yes! My father is part of that half million! But he's not just a number! He was a whole person! He was going to become a grandfather soon!" But this whole COVID situation feels like I am screaming, but no one hears you; no one recognizes you're screaming.[63]

As seen in Yoon Tae's words, many felt ignored by the larger population, as if their loved ones' deaths meant nothing. Carmen explained, "It has been a year and people are still going to the hospital, still dying, still not listening. Fighting about their rights more than the health of their neighbors. That hurts me more than anything else—it is extreme disrespect, a slap in the face. We're at over half a million Americans dead, more than in all the wars we have ever fought, more than 9/11—did their lives not mean anything at all?"[64] The seeming indifference to the needs of neighbors—what Carmen identified as disrespect—generated anger, resentment, and often seemingly irreconcilable differences between those who were affected by COVID-19 and those who were not.

Anger at God

The arbitrary nature of COVID-19 meant that it was not always clear why someone died and someone else lived. This inconsistency led many to question why their prayers had not been answered and their loved ones not spared. While not everyone that I interviewed participated in a religion that believed in a providential God—one that is concerned with the prayers of individual practitioners—among my research informants who did, many described feelings of confusion or abandonment by a God that did not answer their prayers. As a Sikh man mourning the death of his father, Gurpreet explained, "For me, I just wanted God to be there this one time and it just, you know, didn't happen. We had no control and it felt like God abandoned us. There was nothing we could do; we couldn't hold his hand, sit in the room with him. We could only call the hospital and wait."[65] Sikhs believe in a singular God who is immanent in the world and pervades creation. Prayer in the Sikh tradition, therefore, is sometimes said to represent an act of intimacy between the believer and God.[66] Gurpreet's feelings of abandonment by a God who did not answer his prayers may be especially poignant due to the intimacy that Sikhs are expected to feel with God during prayer. Amanda expressed similar confusion when working through her complex feelings on God's providence after the death of her mother: "People like my mom did everything she could, she was careful, she made sure to take care of her community. She was better than all of us, better than anyone else I know. When I look at everyone still alive in the world—people who are going to bars and restaurants, or not wearing masks—I just don't know if God made the right choice."[67]

For some that I interviewed, the anger they expressed at God became a means to reevaluate and transform their spiritual relationships. While Olivia spoke earlier of her anger at the leaders of the church attended by her father before his death, she also related feeling resentment at God in the immediate aftermath of his death. She described herself as raging, saying, "If someone played Christian music or if I saw a minister on TV, I just wanted to throw something at the TV, turn off the radio. I was yelling at God, 'How could you let this happen to my dad? How could you take him from me? How could you let the pastors do this to your church?'"[68] However, she elaborated later that her anger became a foundation for a greater spiritual understanding: "Maybe now, I am more real with God than I was before; I am not pulling punches anymore, and neither is He."[69]

As evidenced in Olivia's words and the others highlighted here, feelings about religion, God, or the various figures that operate in what William James called the "unseen order,"[70] are seldom simple. We have seen individuals struggling with the question of "theodicy"—how evil in the world can be reconciled with the idea of an all-powerful, benevolent God. As a topic of philosophical and theological debate, theodicy has a lengthy history.[71] Many theodicies argue (like the theodicy that Olivia herself arrives at) that suffering ultimately has some greater, unseen purpose. The question of evil in a divinely ordered world, however, remains a powerful instigator of religious questioning in the face of a crisis. Elie Wiesel famously explored these themes in *The Trial of God*—a farcical play intended to be performed during the Jewish festival of Purim—where three traveling actors put God on trial and Satan serves as the defense counsel.[72] Wiesel states that the play itself is based on an event that he witnessed as a young man in WWII concentration camps, where three rabbis put God on trial over the course of several nights. In his introduction to an updated edition of the play, Robert McAfee Brown notes that Wiesel related to him how, after God was found guilty of crimes against creation in the concentration camp's trial, the rabbis in the concentration camp continued with their evening prayers as they had always done.[73] Such an anecdote is telling, although it leaves us with no easy conclusion. Perhaps, religious practice can exist without a positive faith in God, and actions do not arise from belief but instead have some other purpose (as we explored in Chapter 1). Or perhaps struggles with theodicy and anger at God are not the death notes to religious faith that some believe them to be, and these feelings can coexist with the continued practice of a religious tradition.

We have sought to answer what happens when we experience anger at larger forces over which we have little control—our president, our churches, our communities, and our divine beings. The truth, however, is that we simply do not fully know the answer to this question. On one hand, it may still be too early to tell how the anger resulting from the COVID-19 pandemic will transform our society. On the other hand, tracing the causative effects of emotions like anger through human history can be a difficult, maybe even impossible, task. Beyond the fact that emotions are, at least in part, individually and socially *sui generis* to those experiencing them, few people formally cite their own emotions as the underlying drive behind their actions—no matter how likely it seems to be. One thing we can see is that religion is not always the source of comfort during trying times that it is often perceived to be.

DOES RELIGION ALWAYS COMFORT THOSE IN PAIN?

Many Americans give little thought to religion until there is a funeral or they have the need to confront why a loved one died. Indeed, church attendance has been on a steady decline for decades and in 2020, only forty-seven percent of Americans belonged to an organized religious community.[74] In this sense, the COVID-19 pandemic functioned rather like a giant, national funeral, calling attention to the influence of religious beliefs and ideals on American society. As seen throughout *Shattered Grief*, Americans often did not like what they saw.

Spiritual Wounds and Religious Trauma

While ideas of deconstructing conservative Christianity have come to the forefront of many American vocabularies, so have the terms "spiritual wounding" and "religious trauma." Arising largely in clinical settings with the goal of framing individual experience, these concepts have been rather inadequately discussed in academic literature. Psychologist Marlene Winnell—who argues that we can recognize a specific "religious trauma syndrome"—identifies religious trauma as the "condition experienced by people who are struggling with leaving authoritarian, dogmatic religion and coping with the damage of indoctrination."[75] Others, like Alyson Stone, explain that this trauma is happening predominantly to children when religious communities put prohibitions on certain emotions or behaviors and utilize "spiritual practices and beliefs to 'transcend' or deny problems rather than understand them."[76] Looking at specifically Christian contexts, Alison Downie emphasizes the role of chronic shame in producing religious trauma.[77] Philosopher Michelle Panchuk identifies religious trauma as perceived injury by a closely-associated religious person, practice, or being such that one's ability to participate in a religious setting is diminished.[78] Looking at these authors' thoughts on trauma, we see that there is little agreement on what constitutes religious trauma. The concept, however, remains especially vital. While these authors often take as their model, either implicitly or explicitly, fundamentalist or conservative Christian communities, the concept has had a renaissance in a variety of religious and ex-religious communities, most notably Islam,[79] Judaism,[80] and the Church of Jesus Christ of Latter-day Saints.[81]

What is at stake in these discussions is not illuminating the exact contours or ontological realities of the phenomenon of religious trauma. Scholars of religion eschew terms like "indoctrination" or "dogmatic" and generally understand labels like "religious trauma" as a way of thinking about and framing one's experiences, rather than an objectively real phenomenon. What scholars can say, however, is that emotional or psychological injury in a religious context is particularly harmful *because* of the religious environment in which it is taking place. Religions often involve powerful, divine forces that are said to be all-knowing and all-powerful. They involve mechanisms that may control your postmortem fate and communities that regularly come to define one's social life. The power concentrated in religious institutions and religious communities is significant. Painful and traumatizing experiences happening in religious settings may very well be experienced as worse due to the teleological or salvific framework that surrounds them.

Religious Trauma in the Age of COVID

Returning to our guiding question for this section—is religion always a source of comfort for those in pain?—the answer for many is an emphatic "no." While those I spoke with did not explicitly use the framework of religious trauma to make sense of their spirituality during the pandemic, many explained that the usual guidance given by religious leaders did little to help.

Part of a large Catholic family, Julia described the inadequacy of her priests' statements in light of her unanswered prayers:

> The platitudes of the priests are not appealing to me right now and they provide no comfort. I have a hard time reaching out to them because they all say the same thing: "He's in a better place; he's at peace; he's no longer experiencing the pain on this earth; he's with God." At the end of the day, those just don't help anymore. I was fortunate—but also not fortunate—in the sense that I was the one who got to see my brother. It was always behind a glass door, and I would pray and pray and pray and pray, but it wasn't enough. Sometimes I wonder, "Maybe if I were a better Catholic, prayed harder, said more rosaries, I could have saved my brother." There are moments when I ask, "Did God not hear me? Was God ever listening to me? Have I been praying to air?"[82]

In describing her efforts to make sense of her Sikh faith after the death of her father, Manpreet echoed Julia's uncertainty in the existence of a divine figure, saying:

> If there is a loving God looking out for us, then why did all these people die? I don't want to be clichéd about it, but my dad was the best dad; he had this bright positive energy to him. He didn't deserve to die. I went to the gurdwara [Sikh temple] for Dad's services right after he died, but I haven't gone beyond that. My family shared my frustration and anger right after my dad died, but now they have gone back to their old religious habits. I just cannot.[83]

Similar to what we saw when individuals became angry at the perceived carelessness of a providential God in not answering prayers, such ruminations were a constant source of spiritual wounding throughout my interviews. Yoon Tae described this personal conflict:

> For the past ten years, I have been asking myself if I am still a Christian. While I very much don't believe in a providential God, I was on my knees praying every day when my dad was in the hospital. It was a ritual of needing some sort of help, just hoping it would work—you grasp for whatever you can when you are desperate. And yet, my dad did not get better. I have enough friends in Christian spaces that I knew there were literally hundreds of people praying for him, but he still didn't get better. My analytical mind knew this is not how God is supposed to work, and yet, I kept asking myself if this was happening because my faith was not a true faith.[84]

Indeed, while discussing the death of his grandmother, Dan elaborated on how, from his perspective, struggling with death was an issue where the popular beliefs expressed by many Christians caused more emotional harm than comfort:

> Belief in an afterlife robs us of our grief. I'm coming to terms with the fact that I will never be able to talk to my grandmother again. A lot of people think that is a very sad way to look at life. But for myself, every moment I have with her is more sacred to me because I don't believe that someday we'll both be dead and be together. I saw a Facebook post today that said, "My parents are together in heaven," but I am not going to be in heaven with my wife. If she dies today, she's gone. So, every moment has to be sacred—life is more sacred! Believing in an afterlife actually cheapens life.[85]

Various theologians might counter Dan's argument or explain a vision of the afterlife differently than a Facebook meme. However, popular or "folk" theologies like those expressed by Dan remain important to framing widespread Christian thought at a lived level. From Dan's perspective, trauma is inherent to popular Christian beliefs concerning the afterlife.

In contrast, for others that I spoke with, a sense of religious trauma was oriented less around a God who did not answer prayers and instead around church leaders who led the community in destructive directions. Olivia explained:

> I am a veteran. I know how to keep a mission, and the mission during the pandemic was to stay inside. But for my parents, church was an exception. God is sacred, you don't mess with that. They said we were washed in the blood of Jesus; that this was the enemy's plan to distract us; that we were violating only Biden's laws by gathering, not God's laws. I grew up in the [Christian] Church; I was taught submission to authority, submission to pastoral leadership. These are the people I respected, but they betrayed me with their false words and prophecies.[86]

Olivia's words demonstrate that it is not always the religion's doctrine that causes trauma, but rather the use of that doctrine to promote the destructive decisions of church leaders. Rev. Dr. Kibbie Ruth, a consultant with Kyros Ministry and a significant public thinker on abuse in religious communities, reflects on the power imbalance often inherent to religious settings, explaining that "those harmed within a religious institution—especially if abused by religious authorities—suffer trauma, shame, and guilt in a way that is different from the emotional, social, and physical injury of all abuse victims."[87] While Olivia did not use the language of abuse in relating her experience, the religious framework surrounding her experience at this particular church during the pandemic contributed to making her experience especially traumatic.

A Phenomenology of Disgust

Many underwent terrible and traumatic experiences during the COVID-19 pandemic. There was the trauma of a dying loved one, of course, but also trauma stemming from religious communities, an irresponsible presidential administration, and a wider society denying the pandemic's occurrence and/or disparaging its impact. Ideas like religious trauma and spiritual wounding seek to focus our attention on the emotions of the victims, but what do scholars and historians of religion do with this reality? How do we make sense of it?

Studying religion from an academic perspective can be a difficult and strange thing. Sometimes we are confronted with realities both loathsome and terrible, but we have to make sense of them. Part of the academic enterprise—in its platonic ideal—is limiting one's comments to explaining *why* something happened or enumerating *what* effect it had or is having on later developments, rather than saying *how* something should be. This is all fine and good when we are talking about the impact of a seventh-century Buddhist commentary on later doctrinal interpretations, or how early twentieth-century visions of the Virgin Mary among Catholic children inspired resistance to Communist forces. But when we are confronted with something traumatic like the COVID-19 pandemic—academic tools can fail us. Scholarship does not comfort; scholarship explains. And for that reason, it can often fall very, very short.

For these reasons, religion scholar Robert Orsi has encouraged nurturing what he calls a "phenomenology of disgust" when confronting religion's abuses and traumas. Based on his work with victims of clerical sex abuse in the Roman Catholic Church, he maintains that scholars have not adequately acknowledged religion's harm. By relying on an analytical tone that immediately attempts to historicize or relate phenomenon to larger cultural forces, they continue to treat missteps, abuse, and trauma as aberrations, rather than the rule. In contrast, a phenomenology of disgust centers such exploitations:

> Disgust is visceral and intimate; it is the power of revulsion in the body. Disgust lacks the cultivated reserve of the hermeneutics of suspicion that so easily slides into a posture of knowingness, with the accompanying reassurance of the scholar's superiority over religious practitioners. Disgust brings the scholar directly into the horror; it represents the force of his or her body refusing to allow him or her to step back. It signals arrival at a point where critical analysis, for the time being at least, is not adequate to the reality encountered. Disgust is not shame; it is the rejection of shame and a step toward agency.[88]

Orsi is explicitly calling on scholars to drop the bullshit, so to speak, and recognize the suffering that religions worldwide have caused as endemic, not secondary, to their operation. Rather than knee-jerk reactions to contextualize and analyze, Orsi urges scholars to acknowledge and sit with religion's injustice and misery. He elaborates, "on the other side of disgust is a clearer vision of how religion is actually lived in everyday life, with its intimate cruelties, its petty as well as profound humiliations, its sadism and its masochism, its abuses of power, and its impulses to destroy and dominate. We know there is more to religion than this. But we ought to know as well, and never forget, that there is nothing to religion without this."[89]

Orsi's essay is challenging and provocative, the product of years speaking to those abused when they were most vulnerable by a global system more interested in preserving power than limiting harm. We do not have to agree with all of it, nor perhaps should we. But when thinking about death during the COVID-19 pandemic, the churches who used doctrinal platitudes to give parishioners a false sense of security, the politicians who cared more for the economy than human lives, the society-wide disregard for millions of grieving Americans who lost loved ones to COVID-19, for simply all of it, Orsi's essay gives us permission to feel horror, anger, and disgust. Before we analyze or break apart, before we discuss the impact of this period on future generations, on future elections, on global perceptions of America, on whatever, we need to take a moment and feel disgusted. Those who lost loved ones to COVID-19, who confronted a tsunami of sick, dead, and dying, who tried to build whatever small memorials they could in the middle of a society actively obscuring their grief—they feel disgust. And as scholars, it is OK for us to feel that too.

Religion Post-COVID

Regardless of how we feel now or in the future, our ideas concerning spirituality and religious practice will be transformed by the COVID-19 pandemic. It may be too early to say anything with certainty about the post-pandemic world, but the experience revealed how interconnected we are and how easily death can affect all of us. As the COVID-19 virus becomes endemic as one among many annual respiratory illnesses that circulate, the crisis point of the pandemic is fading to reveal a new and transformed spiritual landscape. My conversations provide a hint of the nature and shape of post-pandemic religion.

Repeatedly, individuals spoke about the need for acknowledgment of grief in both public and religious settings. Leading the Episcopal Diocese of Texas, Bishop Kathryn Ryan reflected on her own efforts to grieve privately after her mother died, isolated by the pandemic:

> My mother died in November 2020. She was in an assisted living facility and got a bladder infection. She spent the last eight months of her life very lonely, and it still haunts me. I have all the privileges of someone who, under normal circumstances, could find a space to hold a service, could find a way to seek comfort in God. But there was no acknowledgment, no sharing of grief. When we deny the losses collectively that individuals know are real, we make them feel abandoned. It's why I am a big proponent of Longest Night Masses and plan to encourage them after the pandemic in the parishes I serve. We need to acknowledge the grief we have all suffered during this period, publicly and with each other.[90]

Sometimes called Blue Christmas or Solstice Masses, Longest Night Masses are held by several Christian denominations near Christmastime, often on the Winter Solstice marking the longest night of the year. Occurring during a time of family gathering and merriment—and near the feast day of St. Thomas the Apostle, who struggled with his own grief over Jesus's crucifixion and doubted the possibility for a joyful resolution—these Masses make space for those grieving a loss. Indeed, many of the religious professionals that I spoke with discussed a desire to make more space for grief in their future ministries. Swami Nikhilanand—a spiritual leader with the Radha Madhav Dham Hindu community—explained that the pandemic inspired him to speak more frequently about the state of suffering that Hindus believe is fundamental to the cycle of reincarnation.[91] Ordained in the Disciples of Christ tradition, Kristel hoped that a renewed focus on grief after the pandemic might lead to a more subtle and nuanced spirituality in the future. She said, "Grief must be the starting point for religious interpretation, rather than a doctrinal or historical overview. It is my hope that this moment will change that, and we can move to a more 'grief-centered' spirituality."[92]

Medical professionals also spoke about the ways in which the pandemic nurtured within them a greater sensitivity to the humanity and spirituality of their patients. Dr. Larry Kravitz explained how his time working as a doctor through the pandemic enriched his own spiritual contemplations: "I have never had need for the myths. Ever since I learned Santa Claus wasn't real, I have known I could never believe in God. But I do have the privilege and wonder of viewing the human condition. When I work with patients who are dying, who have come to me in their last days, I walk into the room and think, 'What am I going to learn today? What will this person teach me?' The pandemic highlighted for me how much I still have to learn."[93] Despite the trauma of working with so many dead and dying, other medical professionals described gaining a greater awareness for the role that spirituality could play in the medical process. Describing herself as "spiritual, but not religious," Mary explained that she came to value having dedicated space within the hospital to grieve or perform other spiritual practices while working as a COVID-19 nurse:

The pandemic highlighted the strength of the bond of humanity, and I am grateful for every day. I saw so many examples of people helping others simply because they were another person, another human. I work in a Catholic hospital and, while I am not Catholic and do not agree with everything the Catholic Church says or does, I appreciated the value of being able to gather as a community for prayer or a moment of silence to honor the person that was lost. In the middle of COVID, it is important to just recognize the humanity of the person who has died. In other hospitals I have worked at, where the staff weren't allowed to build a space for spirituality, it further traumatized them.[94]

As a hospital chaplain, Kristel agreed with the potential damage of making too firm a line between what some might see as the "secular" world of medicine and the "spiritual" world of religion during a high-mortality crisis like the COVID-19 pandemic. She felt the response to her work change during that time: "People in the hospital have been talking about religion more during the pandemic. No one has said the word 'prayer' with a tone of disdain—which they used to do quite regularly! I think the pandemic has brought some humility into the medical space."[95]

Despite these opportunities to deepen spiritual practice and to more concretely address grief, the politicized nature of the pandemic will fundamentally change American religion in ways we do not yet know. Based on working through her complex feelings concerning the death of her father, Olivia predicted a coming crisis of faith:

> Religion in this country is broken; American churches have misrepresented Jesus. I spent three years deployed in Japan and when I came back to America, I came to realize the gospel is watered

down here. It is all about being "blessed" and getting what you want materially. God is treated like a genie in a bottle, there to make you feel good. In other countries, they are literally risking their lives to be Christian, but it is the opposite here. I think there is going to be a widespread crisis of faith when the bottom falls out of American ideas of God as a gift-giving genie in a bottle.[96]

Olivia is referring to what scholars call the "Prosperity Gospel"—a belief that "God grants health and wealth to those with the right kind of faith."[97] While heavily criticized by other Christian leaders, the Prosperity Gospel remains prominent in the arena of American religion. During the pandemic, Christians attesting to Prosperity Gospel beliefs demonstrated a markedly greater disinterest in social isolation and other habits to prevent the coronavirus spread.[98] As one might expect of a faith system that understands illness as indicative of a weakened or faulted faith, Olivia foresees a future challenge to the Prosperity Gospel in America. Rev. Chuck Kuhlman from St. Austin Catholic Church describes a similar coming need for reevaluation: "I think religion is going to change from this, but we might not know how yet. The emphasis on politics and things like QAnon within conservative Evangelical Christian communities is going to make everyone question where their faith is at and what it means to be Christian. I hope there is a lot of soul-searching when this over."[99]

CONCLUSIONS: A FUTURE AFTER TRAUMA?

During the pandemic, there were many causes of trauma in what was an undoubtedly traumatic time—lost livelihoods and economic dreams, canceled celebrations, missed vacations, social isolation. But for those who lost loved ones to COVID-19, being isolated from loved ones in their final moments, only to have their loss ignored by a disinterested society, became the foundation for overwhelming trauma. These feelings often intersected with trauma caused by religious communities committed to a certain political agenda that told them the coronavirus was, at best, a minor inconvenience and, at worst, a government conspiracy. Harold Koenig has pointed out that religious traditions and beliefs represent an important tool for making sense of a crisis or disaster.[100] Therefore, those whose experience of death was doubted, minimized, or otherwise disparaged by their spiritual or religious communities lost an important tool for healing from their psychological tool kit. This ultimately had disastrous results for those who were, and are still, grieving.

The COVID-19 pandemic also revealed deep divisions within American society that have not yet been repaired. While it is unclear how this society-wide fracturing will be addressed in the future, the pain that it continues to cause speaks to our human need for connection with, and affirmation from, those around us. As Carmen explained, "This pandemic has not been a test of our faith; this has been a test of our humanity. I still have faith in God, but my faith in people—that is injured, that has been tested by this, and it may not come back."[101]

This chapter, therefore, does not have an easy or fitting conclusion. The experience of death during the pandemic left many with deep emotional scars that are still in the process of healing. Disasters like the 3/11 earthquake in Japan and the 9/11 terrorist attacks in America have demonstrated how society's ability to unite as a whole can be a major factor in ameliorating the initial trauma of a disaster.[102] Scholar Catherine Wessinger has shown how, in the aftermath of Hurricane Katrina, New Orleans's religious communities became important sources of solace and material support, even when some communities deployed punitive explanations for the disaster.[103] But due to many factors—the long and drawn-out nature of the COVID-19 pandemic, the arbitrary and uneven way that it affected families, the radicalizing political leadership—such unity was not present during the pandemic. In contrast to these other disasters, many felt ignored, neglected, and forgotten by the rest of America, even by the rest of the world. In this environment, divisive rhetoric transformed religious communities, undermined personal spiritual practice, and incubated significant trauma. The effects of this are still being felt and will continue to develop for years to come.

CONCLUSION
Taking the Book of Job Seriously

The tale of the COVID-19 pandemic is a story of victory. It took less than a year for pharmaceutical companies to produce a vaccine with novel technologies, which slashed the rate of severe disease and infection. Millions of people around the world canceled weddings, birthday parties, and other important life events to protect an unseen and unknown elderly population. Artists, musicians, and actors gave their work away for free to lift the spirits of a terrified country in crisis. And slowly, life returned to a new normal of (sometimes) public masking, endless at-home tests, and reoccurring booster shots. Indeed, *Silicon Republic* called 2020 the year of the triumph of STEM (science, technology, engineering, and mathematics) developments, where innovative medical treatments and virtual technologies were deployed to transform American life in a chaotic time.[1]

And yet, over a million Americans are still dead.

After World War II, Elie Wiesel said that he spent a lot of time thinking about the Book of Job—the narrative found in the Hebrew Bible and Old Testament where God, to win a bet with Satan, allows Satan to destroy Job's health and wealth, then kill his children, livestock, and wife. After Job's long-delayed crisis of faith and confrontation with God (where God provides no satisfactory answers to Job's accusations), Job meekly accepts God's power to act unjustly and is made whole in the end, when God gives him an even better wife, better children, and new livestock (all generally interpreted as different from the ones killed earlier in the story). It is a troubling story, and one about which rabbinical commentators have spent millennia trying to make sense. In Elie Wiesel's interpretation, Job's abdication in the face of unjustified suffering and his struggling forward in a new life, despite losing everything to a capricious God trying to win a bet, reveals an important truth: "It is given to man to transform divine injustice into human justice and compassion."[2]

Whether or not you believe in a divine figure (or figures) who controls the fate of the world, we can all acknowledge that the pandemic was a time of injustice. Some of these injustices were inherent to the structure of American society (the higher rates of COVID-19 mortality among people of color and those with disabilities); some reflected overwhelming fears about a swiftly transforming American landscape (the prevalence of COVID-19 denial and vaccine misinformation); and some were truly random (who survived a COVID-19 infection and who did not). In *Shattered Grief*, we have seen people answering those injustices with religious and spiritual innovation. As a society, we experienced novel and unexpected grief, and culture did essential work in responding to this very human problem with compassion and dignity. We might say that the pandemic was not only a triumph for STEM developments, but for cultural innovation as well.

Shattered Grief is also a snapshot of a particular period of human experience as individuals struggled to make sense of the pandemic. Scholars like me will be studying this period for decades to come, and the avenues for future research are endless. In many ways, however, this pandemic was not new at all. The Black Death that ravaged Europe in the fourteenth century lead to the rise of popular ecstatic religious movements based on self-mortification.[3] The Spanish Flu epidemic of 1918 prompted a variety of conspiratorial thinking across the world as to the virus's origins, spread, and impact.[4] The early twenty-first-century Ebola outbreak in West Africa was made worse, in part, by a resistance among local religious practitioners to transform traditional burial and mourning practices to prevent infection.[5] The realities of death and disease have always been part of the human condition, and grief accompanies us from the moment we are born. However, in this pandemic period we had the opportunity to observe such transformations firsthand, with an eye to how individuals spiritually responded in the immediate moment.

Not only is this not the end of our research into this period of history, but it is also not the end of my conversation partners' spiritual journeys. When, months later, I shared with my conversation partners their words from our original interviews, many were shocked to read what they had said. Some had forgotten the depth of their pain, while others found themselves in a very different place emotionally or spiritually than they had been at the time of our interview. Some had returned to religious communities and identities that they had previously rejected, while others had continued exploring and developing entirely new conceptions of their experience. A few had even gone on to do professional work with communities supporting political and social action for those impacted by COVID-19. It is important to remember that *Shattered Grief* captures a moment in time, not a timeless reality.

TOWARD A PHENOMENOLOGY OF HUMANNESS

In the bar where Arun and I used to drink beer, there is now a small plaque. Next to a picture of him smiling, it reads, "As your friend, I'm telling you to tell that imposter syndrome to fuck off and just start writing." Wise words for many professions, not just academics like me. Every now and then I still meet a few of my friends there to toast the photo, but our little group no longer meets quite so regularly. Some have moved away to jobs in different states, some have gotten married, had children, or transitioned into a different stage of life, and some never really returned to their pre-COVID socializing. Our university posthumously awarded Arun his doctorate degree in a small virtual ceremony, attended only by close friends and family. I found out about the event weeks after it happened, as I was only a small connection on the fringe of Arun's social group.

Some might say that we are all small connections on the fringe of each other's experiences. The weird truth about research such as that highlighted in *Shattered Grief* is that you are invited into the intimate tragedies and emotional lives of people—you embrace their pain, you cry along with them, you share your own fears—but at the end of it all, you are only a small connection on the edge of their lives. Weirder still was that, at some point, I had to take their words and work them into data; pull back and frame their experiences as evidence of this or that larger trend. I tried to do so with dignity and affection for those I spoke with, but the experience of being first so intimate, and then later so distant, remains uncomfortable. Like tracking down the profile of an ex-boyfriend on Facebook, I find myself sometimes looking through the social media presence of those I interviewed:

Oh, look, she got married! Her dress is so gorgeous!

His baby finally came! And look at those puffy little cheeks!

Her profile photo is still a photo of her mother—I hope she is doing all right.

I cannot find a social media profile for him anymore—I wonder if he is still alive.

In part, this is the nature of academic research. But I often find myself thinking back to Robert Orsi and his call to nurture a "phenomenology of disgust" that acknowledges our own visceral reaction to the content that we study. Perhaps there also needs to be room for a "phenomenology of humanness" that embraces you and I sitting together in a moment, not as scholar and subject, or author and reader, but as two people sharing a very human feeling of pain and loss. Confucian philosophers praise the virtue of *ren*, whose Chinese character is made up of the root radical for "person" and the character for "two." Sometimes translated as humaneness or benevolence, it is the essential acknowledgment that we live in society and cannot be separated from each other—my actions affect you, your pain affects me, and the decisions we make together will influence others. The truth of *ren* was made evident during the COVID-19 pandemic when we realized that it was our social connections, our I-and-you-being-together, that spread the virus. But I maintain that *ren* should also provide a model for doing research.

Returning to the story of Job. While he is sitting (miserably) on the ashes of his wealth, covered in boils and surrounded by the graves of his children, his friends come to see him. They offer advice, speak of God's ultimate justice, and interrogate what Job might have done to deserve this. They do anything and everything but simply sit with Job and his pain. Perhaps, a phenomenology of humanness would have served them better—to recognize, first and foremost, that this is a person experiencing something harrowing and heart-wrenching, and our first step should be to just share that with them. For those who train as academic researchers, it can sometimes feel as though we are like the three friends: immediately analyzing, interrogating, and explaining. Those are important tasks, to be sure. But so is being present with someone and dedicating all your focus and energy to understanding their experience, even if it is only for a two-hour interview. As Scott told me in our conversation about his work as a grief counselor, "A big part of meaning-making is nothing more than being really present with people. People are experiencing great loss, and many of us aren't listening to them fully with kind and compassionate curiosity. That makes people stop talking. We need to find ways to elicit their stories, and the best way is just to ask."[6]

Like the wisdom found in Scott's words, it was often the case that my conversation partners became my best teachers on how to do this research. Sabila, who experienced grief daily through her work with the COVID-19 Loss and Support for Family & Friends Facebook group, shared with me how to live with the constant state of grief that I felt when speaking to my interview subjects. Remembering her own mother's death, Amanda told me that, above all, those grieving just want to share their loved one with someone, to detail all the ways that they were incredible, and how the world seemed a little smaller for their loss. Based on her experience handling grieving loved ones while working as a spirit medium, Susan explained that "Instead of trying to control grief, we need to allow it. When we express sorrow or pain, there is a real effort to quickly dismiss it and make it go away. But that doesn't actually inspire healing. We need to sit with our pain and help guide each other in our grief. Because grief always is, always was, and always will be."[7] This is not what I was trained for as an academic, but it has been crucial to this project. Indeed, people in many fields find that the job they train for and the job that they actually do are quite different. Dr. Paul Tatum described learning how to do his job as a young hospice doctor, not from a classroom, but from the nurses around him:

> We didn't have great teaching about death and dying in medical school. We were trained to save lives at all costs, but no one prepared me as a young doctor for encountering death. I had to learn from the hospice nurses how to do that. If a fundamental part of medicine is healing suffering, how do you heal what you cannot cure? There's an old saying in medicine: "To cure sometimes, to heal often, to comfort always." We're constantly blasted with "Cure. Cure. Cure. Cure. Heal. Heal. Heal. Heal." But we never learn how to comfort.[8]

Through my conversation partners, I learned how to open myself up fully to their grief, not only as a researcher, but even more so as a fellow human. It is this skill that became the foundation for documenting their voices during a painful and traumatic time, and it is in that way I hope *Shattered Grief* is received.

We can all learn from each other if we just allow ourselves to listen first.

Appendix

NOTES ON METHODOLOGY

Doing ethnography during a global pandemic is a tricky thing. Robert Orsi, a leading theorist on how scholars should study lived religious cultures in America wrote, "Religious cultures are local and to study religion is to study local worlds."[1] But what happens when those local worlds have shifted into digital spaces or are emptied entirely by social distancing? The "thick description" approach to ethnography, described by anthropologist Clifford Geertz and endorsed by so many scholars of "lived religion," had to be radically retooled and adapted to study religious worlds that were now mostly digital.

The foundation of this study is intimate interviews with those who encountered death—either professionally or personally—during the COVID-19 pandemic. These interviews lasted from one to two hours and generally occurred via Zoom, although some interlocutors felt more comfortable with a telephone call.[2] I often began my interviews with a set of questions about their deceased loved one, the state of their religious community, or what their work experience was like during the worst parts of the pandemic. However, the conversations quickly became wide-ranging discussions, and I let my conversation partners direct our exchanges into the topics that were important to them. This meant that I sometimes learned detailed, but seemingly extraneous, information: the subject's dad had never liked their fiancé; their wife had a frustrating inability to pick a restaurant for dinner; there were endless arguments about naming the family's new dog. Yet, as I discussed in *Shattered Grief*'s Conclusion, when describing a phenomenology of humanness, all of these details matter because they provide glimpses into the "local world" that the subject inhabits. If every person is a universe unto themselves, my role as a researcher is to listen intently with my entire being as they unfold themselves. Doing so in this study allowed me to gain a deep and emotionally nuanced picture of an individual at one specific moment in their life. Listening is a two-way street, and the interviews affected my interlocutors as well. Many of them emailed me afterward to thank me for listening to them, noting that they often felt unable to speak without judgment among friends and family. My interviews were augmented by virtual ethnography, conducted in various social media groups on Instagram, Reddit, and Facebook. While dozens of such groups exist, membership is often limited to those that share specific forms of grief—mourning a child, a spouse, and so forth. As a result, I was restricted to those groups that allowed outside observers to join.

Locating individuals willing to be interviewed during a global pandemic presented some challenges as well. Most religious and funerary professionals were contacted via email with little to no introduction, resulting in a thirty to forty percent response rate. Reflecting this low response rate, it was often only religious and funerary professionals in Texas who answered my emails—possibly because they were familiar with the name of my academic institution, Texas State University. Among religious professionals, I aimed to get a swath of different religious traditions or denominations, but my results were limited, in large part, to who would answer my unsolicited emails. As noted in the body of this work, many leaders of conservative or reactionary religious communities—especially Evangelical Christian—refused to answer my request for an interview. I had similar experiences with the miscellaneous other professionals from whom I requested interviews—spirit mediums, death doulas, and grief counselors. My response rate from this group was exceptionally low (ten to twenty percent) as many were likely busy, uncertain as to my professional goals, or otherwise suspicious of my intent. My research contacts in the medical field came about largely through social media posts and word of mouth among my larger social and research network, although a handful were referred to me through their personal religious leaders.

While most of my religious, funerary, and medical professional interlocutors were based in Texas, those who lost loved ones to COVID-19 came from all across the country. COVID-19 affected everyone in America, and due to the personal nature of a COVID loss, I was limited in speaking to those who were willing to share their stories. I posted requests for interviews in two social media communities on Reddit and on Facebook's COVID-19 Loss Support Group for Family & Friends. All my interlocutors sought me out, although some declined to sit for an interview after learning that the work would be published. A handful were contacted via word of mouth after the positive interview experience had by other mourners. The fact that my conversation partners who lost loved ones to COVID-19 were, by and large, contacted via social media groups specifically dedicated to addressing COVID-19 grief does curve the data somewhat to privilege the voices of those who struggled with their loved ones' deaths. *Shattered Grief*, however, is not presented as the final or definitive statement on the experience of losing someone to COVID-19 and its impact on religious identity.

Rather, by focusing on those who struggled with the death of their loved ones in the larger framework of a transforming American society, this study examines one set of intimate experiences collected during the pandemic to suggest how this national and international disaster might shape the religious landscape in the future. As discussed in *Shattered Grief*'s Introduction and in the glossary of research interlocutors and conversation partners, I anonymized or used first names only to refer to those individuals who lost loved ones to COVID-19, while professionals, whose leadership role in a religious or medical community had some bearing on contextualizing their words, were referred to by their full titles unless requested otherwise.

In a similar fashion, rather than looking at a phenomenon over a period of time, *Shattered Grief* has sought to capture a snapshot of professional and personal encounters with death in a highly chaotic and transformative time. In this way, it is not a story of change, but rather a reflection of a single moment, and it is my hope that future work in this area continues to flesh out the intersection of death, grief, and spirituality during the COVID-19 pandemic period. The present study is, essentially, a microhistory, a genre that has its own merits and weaknesses. Historian István Szijàrtó notes that small, limited microstudies are important to "convey the lived experience to readers directly on the micro-level of everyday life."[3] American Historian Jill Lepore has herself defended studies that capture the sheer ordinariness of an individual's experience, arguing that they can ultimately reveal larger, ineffable trends.[4] While *Shattered Grief* is not a replacement for the more systematic work that remains to be performed, it captures an important moment in the process of meaning-making undergone by everyone during the COVID-19 pandemic.

In her work on myth, Wendy Doniger has described the contrasting research modes of, on one hand, the telescope that zooms out to the bigger picture and, on the other hand, the microscope that zooms in to the deeply-felt individual experience.[5] I consider *Shattered Grief* as something of a microscope, suggesting broader trends that a telescope might one day reveal. While I look forward to seeing what the telescope researchers one day reveal, there is indispensable value in the sustained study of a limited group in the middle of a globally transformative event as a means to understand how humans construct their worlds, values, and lives.

NOTES

INTRODUCTION: IN A BARBECUE PARKING LOT

1. Centers for Disease Control and Prevention (CDC), "COVID Data Tracker," https://www.cdc.gov/coronavirus/2019-ncov/covid-data/covidview/index.html.
2. World Health Organization, "14.9 Million Excess Deaths Associated with the COVID-19 Pandemic in 2020 and 2021," May 5, 2022, https://www.who.int/news/item/05-05-2022-14.9-million-excess-deaths-were-associated-with-the-covid-19-pandemic-in-2020-and-2021.
3. World Health Organization, "WHO Coronavirus (COVID-19) Dashboard," https://covid19.who.int/.
4. Gary Laderman, *Rest in Peace: A Cultural History of Death and the Funeral Home in Twentieth-Century America* (Oxford: Oxford University Press, 2003).
5. Austra Reinis, *Reforming the Art of Dying: The Ars Moriendi in the German Reformation (1519–1528)* (New York: Routledge, 2007).
6. Leor Halevi, *Muhammad's Grave: Death Rites and the Making of Islamic Society* (New York: Columbia University Press, 2007).
7. Jacqueline Stone, *Right Thoughts at the Last Moment* (Honolulu: University of Hawai'i Press, 2013).
8. Kiri Walsh, et al., "Spiritual Beliefs May Affect Outcome of Bereavement: Prospective Study," *British Medical Journal* 324, no. 7353 (2002): 1551; Scott J. Fitzpatrick, et al., "Religious Perspectives on Human Suffering: Implications for Medicine and Bioethics," *Journal of Religion and Health* 55 (2016): 159–73.

9. Kristel Clayville, personal interview with author, March 8, 2021.
10. Thomas Tweed, *Crossing and Dwelling: A Theory of Religion* (Cambridge, MA: Harvard University Press, 2008), 54.
11. Friederich Schleiermacher, *On Religion: Speeches to Its Cultured Despisers*, trans. John Oman (New York: Harper & Brothers, [1799] 1958).
12. Émile Durkheim, *The Elementary Forms of Religious Life*, trans. Karen Fields (New York: Free Press, [1912] 1995).
13. Karl Marx and Friederich Engels, *On Religion* (Mineola, NY: Dover, [1955] 2008).
14. William James, *The Varieties of Religious Experience* (Oxford: Oxford University Press, [1902] 2012).
15. Tomoko Masuzawa, *The Invention of World Religions* (Chicago: University of Chicago Press, 2005).
16. Catherine Albanese, *America: Religions and Religion* (New York: Wadsworth, [1981] 2012).

1. RITUAL

1. Jonathan Z. Smith notes that "religion" is discussed as having something to do with ritual as early as the 1600s. See "Religion, Religions, Religious," in *Critical Terms for Religious Studies*, ed. Mark C. Taylor (Chicago: University of Chicago Press, 1998), 270–71.
2. Sigmund Freud, "Obsessive Actions and Religious Practices," in *The Freud Reader*, ed. Peter Gay (New York: Norton, [1907] 1995), 429–35.
3. Bronislaw Malinowski, *Magic, Science, and Religion and Other Essays* (Long Grove, IL: Waveland Press, [1925] 1992); A. R. Radcliffe-Brown, *The Andaman Islanders* (New York: Free Press, [1933] 1964).
4. Andrew Henry, "What Is Ritual?," *Religion for Breakfast*, July 5, 2016, https://www.youtube.com/watch?v=F_URgZfo1hU.
5. Ann Taves, *Religious Experience Reconsidered: A Building-Block Approach to the Study of Religion and Other Special Things* (Princeton, NJ: Princeton University Press, 2009).
6. Dennis W. Rook, "The Ritual Dimension of Consumer Behavior," *Journal of Consumer Research* 12 (1985): 251-64.
7. Qing Lan, "Does Ritual Exist? Defining and Classifying Ritual Based on Belief Theory," *Journal of Chinese Sociology* 5, no. 5 (2018),

https://journalofchinesesociology.springeropen.com/articles/10.1186/s40711-018-0073-x.

8. Catherine Bell, "Performance," in *Critical Terms for the Study of Religion*, ed. Mark Taylor (Chicago: University of Chicago Press, 1998).
9. Jacobellis v. Ohio (1964).
10. Richard Sosis, et al., "Psalms and Coping with Uncertainty: Religious Israeli Women's Responses to the 2006 Lebanon War," *American Anthropologist* 113, no. 1 (2011): 40–55; Martin Lang, et al., "Effects of Anxiety on Spontaneous Ritualized Behavior," *Current Biology* 25, no. 14 (2015): 1892–97.
11. Catherine Bell, *Ritual: Perspectives and Dimensions* (Oxford: Oxford University Press, 1997).
12. Erik Seeman, *Death in the New World: Cross-Cultural Encounters, 1492–1800* (Philadelphia: University of Pennsylvania Press, 2010), 49–50.
13. There is some disagreement over when exactly William Gladstone said this quote, or whether it was ever said at all. Nevertheless, the quote remains popular among funeral directors and death historians.
14. Gary Laderman, *Rest in Peace: A Cultural History of Death and the Funeral Home in Twentieth-Century America* (Oxford: Oxford University Press, 2005).
15. Jue Ji, personal interview with author, January 27, 2021.
16. Shannon Lee Dawdy, *American Afterlives: Reinventing Death in the 21st Century* (Princeton, NJ: Princeton University Press, 2021).
17. Sofie, personal interview with author, March 7, 2021.
18. Mitzi Chafetz, personal interview with author, March 7, 2021.
19. "Funeral Guidance for Individuals and Families," https://stacks.cdc.gov/view/cdc/88415/cdc_88415_DS1.pdf?
20. Richard Davis, personal interview with author, February 12, 2021.
21. Kay, personal interview with author, February 9, 2021.
22. Andie MacNeil, et al., "Exploring the Use of Virtual Funerals during the COVID-19 Pandemic: A Scoping Review," *OMEGA—Journal of Death and Dying* (2021): 1–24.
23. Adam Seligman, et al., *Ritual and Its Consequences: An Essay on the Limits of Sincerity* (Oxford: Oxford University Press, 2008), 5.
24. Jue Ji, personal interview with author, January 27, 2021.
25. Chuck Treadwell, personal interview with author, February 1, 2021.

26. Amanda, personal interview with author, February 16, 2021.
27. Jonathan Z. Smith, *To Take Place: Toward Theory in Ritual* (Chicago: University of Chicago Press, 1987), 109.
28. Cristine Legare and André Souza, "Evaluating Ritual Efficacy: Evidence from the Supernatural," *Cognition* 124, no. 1 (2021): 1–15.
29. Rich Andre, personal interview with author, February 18, 2021.
30. Neil Blumofe, personal interview with author, February 10, 2021.
31. Gurpreet, personal interview with author, March 1, 2021.
32. Jue Ji, personal interview with author, January 27, 2021.
33. Craig Taylor, personal interview with author, February 25, 2021.
34. Rich Andre, personal interview with author, February 18, 2021.
35. Chuck Treadwell, personal interview with author, February 1, 2021.
36. Amanda, personal interview with author, February 16, 2021.
37. Dulce Torres Guzman, "Immigrant Communities Suffer as Funeral Traditions Upended in Pandemic," *Tennessee Lookout*, October 22, 2020, https://tennesseelookout.com/2020/10/22/immigrant-communities-suffer-as-funeral-traditions-upended-in-pandemic/.
38. Manpreet, personal interview with author, February 25, 2021.
39. Dan, personal interview with author, February 4, 2021.
40. Carmen, personal interview with author, February 9, 2021.
41. Yoon Tae, personal interview with author, February 23, 2021.
42. Craig Taylor, personal interview with author, February 25, 2021.
43. Craig Taylor, personal interview with author, February 25, 2021.
44. Julia, personal interview with author, February 19, 2021.
45. Sabila, personal interview with author, February 10, 2021.
46. Attia Omara, personal interview with author, February 8, 2021.
47. Attia Omara, personal interview with author, February 8, 2021.
48. Attia Omara, personal interview with author, February 8, 2021.
49. Neil Blumofe, personal interview with author, February 10, 2021.
50. Mitzi Chafetz, personal interview with author, March 7, 2021.
51. Mitzi Chafetz, personal interview with author, March 7, 2021.
52. Neil Blumofe, personal interview with author, February 10, 2021.
53. Mary Barton, personal interview with author March 3, 2021.
54. Mary Barton, personal interview with author March 3, 2021.
55. Kristel Clayville, personal interview with author, March 8, 2021.
56. Kristel Clayville, personal interview with author, March 8, 2021.

57. Paul Tatum, personal interview with author, February 16, 2021.
58. Christine Celio, personal interview with author, March 3, 2021.
59. Mary Barton, personal interview with author, March 3, 2021.
60. Carmen, personal interview with author, February 9, 2021.
61. Amanda, personal interview with author, February 16, 2021.
62. Martha Heymann, personal interview with author, June 16, 2021.
63. Martha Heymann, personal interview with author, June 16, 2021.
64. Martha Heymann, personal interview with author, June 16, 2021.
65. Sabila, Personal interview with author, February 10, 2021.
66. John Lagerway and Marc Kalinowski, eds., *Early Chinese Religion: Part One: Shang through Han (1250 BC–220 AD)* (Amsterdam: Brill, 2008).
67. Stephen Teiser, *The Scripture on the Ten Kings and the Making of Purgatory in Medieval Chinese Buddhism* (Honolulu: University of Hawai'i Press, 1994).
68. Lalita P. Vidyarthi, *The Sacred Complex in Hindu Gaya* (New York: Asia Publishing House, 1961).
69. Maurice Lamm, *The Jewish Way in Death and Mourning* (Middle Village, NY: Jonathan David Publishers, [1969] 2000).
70. Carmen, personal interview with author, February 9, 2021.
71. Linda Pershing and Margaret R. Yocom, "The Yellow Ribboning of the USA: Contested Meanings in the Construction of a Political Symbol," *Western Folklore* 55, no. 1 (1996): 41–85.
72. Robert Bellah, *Religion in Human Evolution: From the Paleolithic to the Axial Age* (Cambridge, MA: Harvard University Press, 2011).
73. Jeffrey Kluger, "Accidental Poisonings Increased After President Trump's Disinfectant Comments," *Time*, May 12, 2020, https://time.com/5835244/accidental-poisonings-trump/.

2. COMMUNITY

1. Mark Chaves, "Family Structure and Protestant Church Attendance: The Sociological Basis of Cohort and Age Effects," *Journal for the Scientific Study of Religion* 30, no. 4 (1991): 501–14.
2. Karen McCarthy Brown, *Mama Lola: A Vodou Priestess in Brooklyn* (Berkeley: University of California Press, 2001).

3. Joseph Laycock, *Speak of the Devil: How the Satanic Temple Is Changing the Way We Talk About Religion* (Oxford: Oxford University Press, 2020).
4. Erik Braun, *The Birth of Insight: Meditation, Modern Buddhism, and the Burmese Monk Ledi Sayadaw* (Chicago: University of Chicago Press, 2016).
5. On this problem, see Kevin Schilbrack, "What *Isn't* Religion?," *Journal of Religion* 93, no. 3 (2013): 291–318.
6. Durkheim does refer to the tribes as "inferior" (*inférieure*), although it is unclear whether by this he meant "lesser" or simply less complicated, as the word can mean both in French.
7. Émile Durkheim, *The Elementary Forms of Religious Life*, trans. Karen E. Fields (New York: Free Press, 1995), 10.
8. Durkheim, *Elementary Forms*, 238.
9. Jennifer, personal interview with author, March 17, 2021.
10. Yoon Tae, personal interview with author, February 23, 2021.
11. Durkheim, *Elementary Forms*, 400–401.
12. Kay, personal interview with author, February 9, 2021.
13. Charles Kuhlman, personal interview with author, February 8, 2021.
14. Kathryn Ryan, personal interview with author, April 7, 2021.
15. Craig Taylor, personal interview with author, February 25, 2021.
16. Craig Taylor, personal interview with author, February 25, 2021.
17. John Scott and Gordon Marshall, eds. "Moral Communities," in *A Dictionary of Sociology*, 3rd ed. (Oxford: Oxford University Press, 2009), 488.
18. Khursheed Dastur, personal interview with author, March 10, 2021.
19. Bahá'í has no ordained leadership and, therefore, local community leaders have no rank or title. Ajit Giani was introduced to me as a leading voice in organizing the community, but he explained that because Bahá'í practitioners utilize radical democratic governance, he was only one leader among many.
20. Ajit Giani, personal interview with author, March 1, 2021.
21. Richard Andre, personal interview with author, February 18, 2021.
22. Richard Andre, personal interview with author, February 18, 2021.
23. Jennifer, personal interview with author, March 17, 2021.
24. Bruce Baillio, personal interview with author, March 12, 2021.

2. COMMUNITY ᑫ 215

25. David Feltmate, "Rethinking New Religious Movements beyond a Social Problems Paradigm," *Nova Religio* 20, no. 2 (2016): 82–96.
26. Attia Omara, personal interview with author, February 8, 2021.
27. Neil Blumofe, personal interview with author, February 10, 2021.
28. Lou McElroy, personal interview with author, June 2, 2021.
29. E. Eric Lincoln and Lawrence Mamiya, *The Black Church in the African American Experience* (Durham, NC: Duke University Press, 1990), 17.
30. Nambi Ndugga, et al., "Latest Data on COVID-19 Vaccinations by Race/Ethnicity," *KFF*, July 14, 2022, https://www.kff.org/coronavirus-covid-19/issue-brief/latest-data-on-covid-19-vaccinations-by-race-ethnicity/.
31. Amanda, personal interview with author, February 16, 2021.
32. Durkheim, *Elementary Forms*, 403.
33. Durkheim, *Elementary Forms*, 403.
34. Kathryn Ryan, personal interview with author, April 7, 2021.
35. Paul, personal interview with author, February 19, 2021.
36. Yoon Tae, personal interview with author, February 23, 2021.
37. Richard Andre, personal interview with author, February 18, 2021.
38. Khursheed Dastur, personal interview with author, March 10, 2021.
39. Jeremy Brown, *The Eleventh Plague: Jews and Pandemics from the Bible to COVID-19* (Oxford: Oxford University Press, 2022), 313
40. Neil Blumofe, personal interview with author, February 10, 2021.
41. Neil Blumofe, personal interview with author, February 10, 2021.
42. Mary Findling, et al., "COVID-19 Has Driven Racism and Violence Against Asian Americans: Perspectives from 12 National Polls," *Health Affairs Forefront*, April 12, 2022, https://www.healthaffairs.org/do/10.1377/forefront.20220411.655787/.
43. Arla, personal interview with author, April 27, 2021.
44. Arla, personal interview with author, April 27, 2021. Arla is referencing the March 2021 shooting of six women of Asian descent working in spas in Atlanta that authorities believe was racially motivated.
45. Jue Ji, personal interview with author, January 27, 2021.
46. Elisabeth Gawthrop, "The Color of Coronavirus: COVID-19 Deaths by Race and Ethnicity in the U.S.," *APM Research Lab*, December 14, 2022, https://www.apmresearchlab.org/covid/deaths-by-race.

47. Manpreet, personal interview with author, February 25, 2021.
48. Manpreet, personal interview with author, February 25, 2021.
49. Amanda, personal interview with author, February 16, 2021.
50. Irawaty Djaharuddin, et al., "Comorbidities and Mortality in COVID-19 Patients," *Gaceta Sanitaria* 35, no. 2 (2021): S530–S532.
51. Amanda, personal interview with author, February 16, 2021.
52. Carmen, personal interview with author, February 9, 2021.
53. Maggie Astor, "The C.D.C. Chief's Remark About Covid Deaths Continues to Anger Advocates for the Disabled," *New York Times*, January 13, 2022, https://www.nytimes.com/live/2022/01/13/world/biden-covid-19-speech#walenskys-remark-about-covid-deaths-continues-to-anger-advocates-for-the-disabled.
54. Paula Span. "For Older Americans, the Pandemic Is Not Over," *New York Times*, February 11, 2023, https://www.nytimes.com/2023/02/11/health/covid-pandemic-seniors.html.
55. Sabila, personal interview with author, February 10, 2021.
56. Julia, personal interview with author, February 19, 2021.
57. Olivia, personal interview with author, February 8, 2021.
58. Bianca, personal interview with author, June 17, 2021.
59. Mary Barton, personal interview with author March 3, 2021.
60. Arla, personal interview with author, April 27, 2021.
61. Sabila, personal interview with author, February 10, 2021.
62. Yoon Tae, personal interview with author, February 23, 2021.
63. Arla, personal interview with author, April 27, 2021.
64. Manpreet, personal interview with author, February 25, 2021.
65. Paul, personal interview with author, February 19, 2021.
66. Heidi Campbell, "Understanding the Relationship Between Religion Online and Offline in a Networked Society," *Journal of the American Academy of Religion* 80, no. 1 (2012): 64–93: 71.
67. Chuck Treadwell, personal interview with author, February 1, 2021.
68. Kathryn Ryan, personal interview with author, April 7, 2021.
69. Jason Tveten, personal interview with author, March 22, 2021.
70. Charles Kuhlman, personal interview with author, February 8, 2021.
71. Lou McElroy, personal interview with author, June 2, 2021.
72. Richard Andre, personal interview with author, February 18, 2021.
73. Richard Andre, personal interview with author, February 18, 2021.

74. Craig Taylor, personal interview with author, February 25, 2021.
75. Yoon Tae, personal interview with author, February 23, 2021.
76. Arla, personal interview with author, April 27, 2021.
77. Robert Wuthnow, *The Restructuring of American Religion: Society and Faith Since World War II* (Princeton, NJ: Princeton University Press, 1988).
78. "Political Polarization in the American Public," *Pew Research Center*, June 12, 2014, https://www.pewresearch.org/politics/2014/06/12/political-polarization-in-the-american-public/; "A Sore Subject: Almost Half of Americans Have Stopped Talking Politics with Someone," *Pew Research Center*, February 5, 2020, https://www.pewresearch.org/journalism/2020/02/05/a-sore-subject-almost-half-of-americans-have-stopped-talking-politics-with-someone/.
79. Cass Sunstein, *#republic: Divided Democracy in the Age of Social Media* (Princeton, NJ: Princeton University Press, 2017).
80. Keith O'Brian, "Amid Horror, 2 Officers Commit Suicide," *Boston Globe*, September 5, 2005.

3. NARRATIVE

1. Stephen Prothero, *Religion Matters* (New York: Norton, 2020).
2. Mircea Eliade, *Myth and Reality* (New York: Harper & Row, 1963).
3. Casey Delehanty and Erin Kearns, "Wait, There's Torture in Zootopia? Examining the Prevalence of Torture in Popular Movies," *Perspectives on Politics* 18, no. 3 (2020): 838–50.
4. Thomas Johnson, *Taliban Narratives: The Use and Power of Stories in the Afghanistan Conflict* (Oxford: Oxford University Press, 2018).
5. Reiko Ohnuma, *Unfortunate Destiny; Animals in the Indian Buddhist Imagination* (Oxford: Oxford University Press, 2017).
6. Laura Beth Nielsen, et al., "'Ahead of the Lawmen': Law and Morality in Disney Animated Films, 1960–1998," *Law, Culture, and the Humanities* 13, no. 1 (2017): 104–22.
7. Paul Ricoeur, "Narrative Identity," *Philosophy Today* 35, no. 1 (1991): 73–81:73.
8. Hayden White, *Metahistory: The Historical Imagination in Nineteenth-Century Europe* (Baltimore, MD: Johns Hopkins University, 1973).

9. Dr. Black, personal interview with author, February 13, 2021.
10. Jack Kravitz, personal interview with author, February 17, 2021.
11. Larry Kravitz, personal interview with author, February 14, 2021.
12. Arto Laitninen, "Charles Taylor and Paul Ricoeur on Self-Interpretations and Narrative Identity," in *Narrative Research: Voices of Teachers and Philosophers*, ed. Rauno Huttunen, Hannu Heikkinen, and Leene Syrjälä (Jyväskylä, Finland: SoPhi, 2002), 58.
13. Kay, personal interview with author, February 9, 2021.
14. Olivia, personal interview with author, February 8, 2021.
15. Sabila, personal interview with author, February 10, 2021.
16. Sahih al-Bukhari, "What Has Been Mentioned About the Plague," vol. 7, book 71, no. 624, https://sunnah.com/bukhari:5728.
17. Sahih al-Bukhari, vol. 7, book 11, no. 688.
18. Sabila, personal interview with author, February 10, 2021.
19. Bianca, personal interview with author, June 17, 2021.
20. Bianca, personal interview with author, June 17, 2021.
21. Lou McElroy, personal interview with author, June 2, 2021.
22. Jason Tveten, personal interview with author, March 22, 2021.
23. Jue Ji, personal interview with author, January 27, 2021.
24. Jue Ji, personal interview with author, January 27, 2021.
25. Carmen, personal interview with author, February 9, 2021.
26. Carmen, personal interview with author, February 9, 2021.
27. Leslie Kean, *Surviving Death: A Journalist Investigates Evidence for an Afterlife* (New York: Crown Archetype. 2017).
28. Name redacted. Facebook post, April 3, 2021.
29. Manpreet, personal interview with author, February 25, 2021.
30. Julia, personal interview with author, February 19, 2021.
31. Sabila, personal interview with author, February 10, 2021.
32. Amanda, personal interview with author, February 16, 2021.
33. Danièle Hervieu-Léger, *Religion as a Chain of Memory* (New Brunswick, N.J.: Rutgers University Press, 2000).
34. Greg Neuberger, personal interview with author, March 9, 2021.
35. Lou McElroy, personal interview with author, June 2, 2021.
36. Neil Blumofe, personal interview with author, February 10, 2021.
37. Stephen Prothero, *God Is Not One: The Eight Rival Religions that Run the World* (New York: HarperOne, 2010).

3. NARRATIVE ❧ 219

38. Attia Omara, personal interview with author, February 8, 2021.
39. Ajit Giani, personal interview with author, March 1, 2021.
40. Chuck Treadwell, personal interview with author, February 1, 2021.
41. Kathryn Ryan, personal interview with author, April 7, 2021.
42. Kathryn Ryan, personal interview with author, April 7, 2021.
43. Dr. Black, personal interview with author, February 13, 2021.
44. Elisha Friedman, "How One 19th-Century Rabbi Responded to a Worldwide Cholera Epidemic," *My Jewish Learning*, https://www.myjewishlearning.com/article/how-one-19th-century-rabbi-responded-to-a-worldwide-cholera-epidemic/.
45. Name Redacted, Facebook post, March 24, 2020.
46. Manpreet, personal interview with author, February 25, 2021.
47. Amanda, personal interview with author, February 16, 2021.
48. Amanda, personal interview with author, February 16, 2021.
49. Dan, personal interview with author, February 4, 2021.
50. Craig Taylor, personal interview with author, February 25, 2021.
51. Robert Bellah et al., *Habits of the Heart: Individualism and Commitment in American Life* (Berkeley: University of California Press, 1985), 221.
52. Thomas Tweed, *Crossing and Dwelling: A Theory of Religion* (Cambridge, MA: Harvard University Press, 2008), 59–60.
53. Leonard Primiano, "Vernacular Religion and the Search for Method in Religious Folklife," *Western Folklore* 54, no. 1 (1995): 37–56.
54. Julia, personal interview with author, February 19, 2021.
55. Julia, personal interview with author, February 19, 2021.
56. According to my research, most mediums in 2021 charge $150 an hour, but many mediums will offer much higher "emergency" rates for faster booking.
57. Carla, personal interview with author, March 30, 2021.
58. Carla, personal interview with author, March 30, 2021.
59. Susan, personal interview with author, March 29, 2021.
60. Susan, personal interview with author, March 29, 2021.
61. Maria, personal interview with author, March 24, 2021. For a more detailed case study on the role of spirit mediumship during the pandemic, please see Natasha L. Mikles, "Three Spirit Mediums: A Case Study on Grief, Death, and Alternative Religious Traditions During

the COVID-19 Pandemic," *Nova Religio: The Journal of Alternative and Emergent Religions* 27, no. 2 (2023): 86–100.
62. Joseph Friedman, "Overdose-Related Cardiac Arrests Observed by Emergency Medical Services During the US COVID-19 Epidemic," *JAMA, Psychiatry* 78, no. 5 (2021): 562–64.
63. Yoon Tae, personal interview with author, February 23, 2021.
64. Gurpreet, personal interview with author, March 1, 2021.
65. Gurpreet, personal interview with author, March 1, 2021.
66. Sofia, personal interview with author, February 5, 2021.
67. Sofia, personal interview with author, February 5, 2021.
68. Susan, personal interview with author, March 29, 2021. [Following guidance from the spirit mediums I interviewed, Spirit is capitalized when referenced as a singular, transpersonal entity].
69. Carla, personal interview with author, March 30, 2021.
70. Charlotte Ward, "The Emergence of Conspirituality," *Journal of Contemporary Religion* 26, no. 1 (2011): 103–21.
71. Lou McElroy, personal interview with author, June 2, 2021.
72. Lou McElroy, personal interview with author, June 2, 2021.
73. Bruce Baillio, personal interview with author, March 12, 2021
74. Manpreet, personal interview with author, February 25, 2021.

4. TRAUMA

1. Kenneth E. Vail III, et al., "Terror Management Theory and Religious Belief," in *Handbook of Terror Management Theory*, ed. Clay Routledge and Matthew Vess (London: Elsevier, 2019), 259–85.
2. Simona Petru, "Identity and Fear—Burials in the Upper Palaeolithic," *Documenta Praehistorica* 45 (2018): 6–13.
3. Dimitri Tsintjilonis, "Death and the Sacrifice of Signs: 'Measuring' the Dead in Tana Toraja," *Oceania* 71, no. 1 (2000): 1–17; Myriam Lamrani, "The Ultimate Intimacy: Death and Mexico, an Anthropological Relation in Images," *American Ethnologist* 49, no. 2 (2022): 204–20.
4. Wallace Maison, "Death and Destruction in Spinoza's *Ethics*," *Inquiry* 20, nos. 1–4 (1977): 403–17.
5. Nancy J. Smyth and Laura Greybur, "Trauma," *Oxford Bibliographies* (Oxford University Press), September 29, 2015, https://www

.oxfordbibliographies.com/display/document/obo-9780195389678/obo-9780195389678-0229.xml.
6. American Psychiatric Association, *Diagnostic and Statistical Manual of Mental Disorders*, 5th ed. (Arlington, VA: American Psychological Association, 2013), 271.
7. Martha Heymann, personal interview with author, June 16, 2021.
8. Sabila, personal interview with author, February 10, 2021.
9. Lou McElroy, personal interview with author, June 2, 2021.
10. Bianca, personal interview with author, June 17, 2021.
11. Mary Barton, personal interview with author March 3, 2021.
12. Jack Kravitz, personal interview with author, February 17, 2021.
13. Julia, personal interview with author, February 19, 2021.
14. Paul, personal interview with author, February 19, 2021.
15. Scott van Camp, personal interview with author, February 24, 2021.
16. Carmen, personal interview with author, February 9, 2021.
17. Jack Kravitz, personal interview with author, February 17, 2021.
18. Yoon Tae, personal interview with author, February 23, 2021.
19. Julia, personal interview with author, February 19, 2021.
20. Larry Kravitz, personal interview with author, February 14, 2021.
21. Kristel Clayville, personal interview with author, March 8, 2021.
22. Paul Tatum, personal interview with author, February 16, 2021.
23. Christine Celio, personal interview with author, March 3, 2021.
24. Jennifer, personal interview with author, March 17, 2021.
25. Thomas R. Kopfensteiner, "Death with Dignity: A Roman Catholic Perspective," *Linacre Quarterly* 63, no. 4 (1996): 64–75.
26. Alineh Haidery, "FAQ: A Good Death for Muslims," *CBC*, May 17, 2011, https://www.cbc.ca/news/health/faq-a-good-death-for-muslims-1.1090815.
27. Patricia Anderson, "Good Death: Mercy, Deliverance, and the Nature of Suffering," *Tricycle* (Winter 1992), https://tricycle.org/magazine/good-death/.
28. Sabila, personal interview with author, February 10, 2021.
29. Julia, personal interview with author, February 19, 2021.
30. Richard Andre, personal interview with author, February 18, 2021.
31. Jackie Roman, "First Permanent National Memorial for COVID-19 Victims Unveiled at N.J. Farm," *NJ Advance Media*, September 22, 2021,

www.nj.com/coronavirus/2021/09/first-permanent-national-memorial-for-covid-19-victims-unveiled-at-nj-farm.html. This memorial eventually became a permanent installation.

32. Jeff Bell and Mike Marut, "Pop-up Memorial Honors COVID-9 Victims with Ribbons, Slideshow Outside Governor's Mansion," *KVUE*, May 9, 2020, https://www.kvue.com/article/news/health/coronavirus/austin-pop-up-covid-memorial-governors-mansion-ribbons/269-ed8851e9-4446-42aa-aaf2-673fea37e5ec.

33. Marco Torrez, "Additional Names Added to Local COVID-19 Memorial," *KGET*, October 8, 2022, https://www.kget.com/health/coronavirus/additional-names-added-to-local-covid-19-memorial/.

34. For more information, see Christine Hauser, "How We Mourn Covid's Victims," *New York Times*, August 9, 2022, https://www.nytimes.com/2022/08/09/us/covid-deaths-memorials.html.

35. Jonathan Franklin, "More Than 600,000 White Flags on the National Mall Honor Lives Lost to COVID," *NPR*, September 17, 2021, https://www.npr.org/sections/coronavirus-live-updates/2021/09/17/1037011493/covid-national-mall-white-flags-art-exhibit-memorial-pandemic-dead.

36. Carmen, personal interview with author, February 9, 2021.
37. Jack Kravitz, personal interview with author, February 17, 2021.
38. Jack Kravitz, personal interview with author, February 17, 2021.
39. Mitzi Chafetz, personal interview with author, March 7, 2021.
40. Kristel Clayville, personal interview with author, March 8, 2021.
41. Kevin, personal interview with author, May 14, 2021.
42. Dr. Black, personal interview with author, February 13, 2021.
43. Paul Tatum, personal interview with author, February 16, 2021.
44. Mary Barton, personal interview with author, March 3, 2021.
45. Paul, personal interview with author, February 19, 2021.
46. Larry Kravitz, personal interview with author, February 14, 2021.
47. Dr. Black, personal interview with author, February 13, 2021.
48. Governor Greg Abbott, Executive Order 36, May 18, 2021.
49. Mary Barton, personal interview with author, March 3, 2021.
50. Arla, personal interview with author, April 27, 2021.
51. Olivia, personal interview with author, February 8, 2021.
52. Kathryn Ryan, personal interview with author, April 7, 2021.

4. TRAUMA ○₰ 223

53. Arla, personal interview with author, April 27, 2021.
54. Arla, personal interview with author, April 27, 2021.
55. Dan, personal interview with author, February 4, 2021.
56. David Hayword, "Deconstruction," *The Naked Pastor*, https://nakedpastor.com/pages/deconstruction.
57. David Hayword, "The Stages of Deconstruction," *YouTube*, https://www.youtube.com/watch?v=HJk9aKGP2tI&t=1s.
58. Olivia, personal interview with author, February 8, 2021.
59. Olivia, personal interview with author, February 8, 2021.
60. Dr. Black, personal interview with author, February 13, 2021.
61. Jennifer, personal interview with author, March 17, 2021.
62. Amanda, personal interview with author, February 16, 2021.
63. Yoon Tae, personal interview with author, February 23, 2021.
64. Carmen, personal interview with author, February 9, 2021.
65. Gurpreet, personal interview with author, March 1, 2021.
66. Kirpal Singh, "When Does Waheguru (God) Answer Our Prayer?," *Gurmat Saachi Saacha Vichaar*, November 19, 2018, https://gurmatvichaar.home.blog/2018/11/19/27/.
67. Amanda, personal interview with author, February 16, 2021.
68. Olivia, personal interview with author, February 8, 2021.
69. Olivia, personal interview with author, February 8, 2021.
70. Wayne Proudfoot, "William James on an Unseen Order," *Harvard Theological Review* 93, no. 1 (2000): 51–66.
71. See Mark S. M. Scott, *Pathways in Theodicy: An Introduction to the Problem of Evil* (Minneapolis: Fortress Press, 2015).
72. Elie Wiesel, *The Trial of God: (as it was held on February 25, 1649, in Shamgorod)* (New York: Schocken Books, 1995 [1979]).
73. Robert McAfee Brown, "Introduction," *The Trial of God*, vii.
74. Jeffrey Jones, "U.S. Church Membership Falls Below Majority for First Time," *Gallup*, March 29, 2021, https://news.gallup.com/poll/341963/church-membership-falls-below-majority-first-time.aspx. It is important to not mistake a decline in church attendance with a decline in theistic beliefs. While there has been a decline in those who say they believe in God, it has not been as dramatic as seen with membership to a religious institution, indicating that many people are simply abandoning organized religion, not belief in God. See further, Jeffrey

Jones, "Belief in God in U.S. Dips to 81%, a New Low," *Gallup*, June 17, 2022, https://news.gallup.com/poll/393737/belief-god-dips-new-low.aspx.

75. Marlene Winnell, "Religious Trauma Syndrome: It's Time to Recognize It," *Cognitive Behavioral Therapy Today* 39, no. 2 (2011): 16–18.
76. Alyson M. Stone, "Thou Shalt Not: Treating Religious Trauma and Spiritual Harm with Combined Therapy," *Eastern Group Psychotherapy Society* 37 (2013): 323–37: 326.
77. Alison Downie, "Christian Shame and Religious Trauma," *Religions* 13, no. 925 (2022), Special Issue editor: Dyron B. Daughrity.
78. Michelle Panchuk, "The Shattered Spiritual Self: A Philosophical Exploration of Religious Trauma," *Res Philosphica* 95 (2018): 505–30; Michelle Panchuk, "What is Religious Trauma?," Center for Philosophy of Religion, University of Notre Dame, October 31, 2018. https://www.youtube.com/watch?v=1BQF7qvtkGQ.
79. Palwasha A., "What is Religious Trauma?," *The Pvblication*, August 9, 2021.
80. "Judaism," *Dare to Doubt*, 2019, https://www.daretodoubt.org/judaism.
81. Claudine Foudray, "Religious Trauma: What No One Tells You at Church," *Post-Mormon Coaching*, May 1, 2018, https://postmormoncoaching.com/blog/religious-trauma-at-church/.
82. Julia, personal interview with author, February 19, 2021.
83. Manpreet, personal interview with author, February 25, 2021.
84. Yoon Tae, personal interview with author, February 23, 2021.
85. Dan, personal interview with author, February 4, 2021.
86. Olivia, personal interview with author, February 8, 2021.
87. Kibbie Ruth, "Risk of Abuse in Faith Communities," *Child Maltreatment: A Clinical Guide and Reference*, ed. Angelo P. Giardino and Randell Alexander (St. Louis, MO: G. W. Medical, 2005), 539.
88. Robert Orsi, "The Study of Religion on the Other Side of Disgust: Modern Catholic Sexuality Is a Dark and Troubled Landscape," *Harvard Divinity Bulletin*, Spring/Summer 2019, https://bulletin.hds.harvard.edu/the-study-of-religion-on-the-other-side-of-disgust/.
89. Orsi, "The Study of Religion on the Other Side of Disgust."
90. Kathryn Ryan, personal interview with author, April 7, 2021.
91. Swami Nikhilanand, personal interview with author, January 28, 2021.

92. Kristel Clayville, personal interview with author, March 8, 2021.
93. Larry Kravitz, personal interview with author, February 14, 2021.
94. Mary Barton, personal interview with author, March 3, 2021
95. Kristel Clayville, personal interview with author, March 8, 2021.
96. Olivia, personal interview with author, February 8, 2021.
97. Kate Bowler, "Death, the Prosperity Gospel and Me," *New York Times*, February 13, 2016, https://www.nytimes.com/2016/02/14/opinion/sunday/death-the-prosperity-gospel-and-me.html.
98. Paul A. Djupe and Ryan P. Burge, "The Prosperity Gospel of Coronavirus Response," *Politics and Religion* 14, no. 3 (2021): 552–73.
99. Charles Kuhlman, personal interview with author, February 8, 2021.
100. Harold Koenig, *In the Wake of Disaster: Religious Responses to Terrorism & Catastrophe* (Philadelphia: Templeton Press, 2006).
101. Carmen, personal interview with author, February 9, 2021.
102. Kazunori Matsumoto, "Psychological Trauma After the Great East Japan Earthquake," *Psychiatry Clinical Neurosciences* 70, no. 8 (2016): 318–31; Marc Fisher, "After Pearl Harbor and 9/11, Americans Came Together. Have We Lost That Capacity?," *Washington Post*, September 27, 2021, https://www.washingtonpost.com/politics/after-pearl-harbor-and-911-americans-came-together-have-we-lost-that-capacity/2021/09/26/1246b22e-1492-11ec-9589-31ac3173c2e5_story.html.
103. Catherine Wessinger, "Religious Responses to the Katrina Disaster in New Orleans and the American Gulf Coast," *Journal of Religious Studies* (Japanese Association for Religious Studies) 86–2, no. 373 (2012): 53–83.

CONCLUSION: TAKING THE BOOK OF JOB SERIOUSLY

1. "2020: The Triumph of Science," *Silicon Republic*, January 21, 2022, https://www.siliconrepublic.com/innovation/2020-20-years-of-stem-science-technology.
2. Elie Wiesel, "Job: Our Contemporary," *Messengers of God: Biblical Portraits and Legends*, trans. Marion Wiesel (New York: Random House, 1976), 211–35, 235.
3. John Aberth, *From the Brink of the Apocalypse: Confronting Famine, War, Plague, and Death in the Later Middle Ages* (London: Routledge, 2009).

4. Vanessa Northington Gamble, "'There Wasn't a Lot of Comfort in Those Days': African Americans, Public Health, and the 1918 Influenza Epidemic," *Public Health Reports* 125, no. 3 (2010): 114–22; Howard Phillips, "Why Did it Happen? Religious and Lay Explanations of the Spanish Flu Epidemic of 1918 in South Africa," *Kronos* 12 (1987): 79–92; Siniša Malešević, "Imagined Communities and Imaginary Plots: Nationalisms, Conspiracies, and Pandemics in the Longue Durée," *Nationalities Papers* 50 (2022): 45–60.
5. John B. Blevins, et al., "Faith and Global Health Practice in Ebola and HIV Emergencies," *American Journal of Public Health* 109, no. 3 (2019): 379–84.
6. Scott van Camp, personal interview with author, February 24, 2021.
7. Susan, personal interview with author, March 29, 2021.
8. Paul Tatum, personal interview with author, February 16, 2021.

APPENDIX: NOTES ON METHODOLOGY

1. Robert Orsi, *Between Heaven and Earth: The Religious Worlds People Make and the Scholars Who Study Them* (Princeton, NJ: Princeton University Press, 2004), 167.
2. Debates about what to call the individuals that one interviews have existed almost as long as the formal practice of ethnography itself. In methodological writing, I prefer to use the term "interlocuter" or "conversation partner" to reflect the dialogic nature of ethnographic fieldwork. I predominantly used the term "conversation partner" in the body of this work, although I was sometimes forced to rely on other terminology due to sheer syntactic repetition.
3. István Szijátó, "Four Arguments for Microhistory," *Rethinking History* 6, no. 2 (2002): 209–15: 210.
4. Jill Lepore, "Historians Who Love Too Much: Reflections on Microhistory and Biography," *Journal of American History* 88, no. 1 (2001): 129–44.
5. Wendy Doniger, *The Implied Spider: Politics and Theology in Myth* (New York: Columbia University Press, 1999).

BIBLIOGRAPHY

"2020: The Triumph of Science." *Silicon Republic*, January 21, 2022. https://www.siliconrepublic.com/innovation/2020-20-years-of-stem-science-technology.

Aberth, John. *From the Brink of the Apocalypse: Confronting Famine, War, Plague, and Death in the Later Middle Ages*. London: Routledge, 2009.

Albanese, Catherine. *America: Religions and Religion*. New York: Wadsworth, [1981] 2012.

American Psychiatric Association. *Diagnostic and Statistical Manual of Mental Disorders*, 5th edition. Arlington, VA: American Psychological Association, 2013.

Anderson, Patricia. "Good Death: Mercy, Deliverance, and the Nature of Suffering." *Tricycle*, Winter 1992. https://tricycle.org/magazine/good-death/.

Astor, Maggie. "The C.D.C. Chief's Remark About Covid Deaths Continues to Anger Advocates for the Disabled." *New York Times*, January 13, 2022. https://www.nytimes.com/live/2022/01/13/world/biden-covid-19-speech#walenskys-remark-about-covid-deaths-continues-to-anger-advocates-for-the-disabled.

Bell, Catherine. "Performance." In *Critical Terms for the Study of Religion*, ed. Mark Taylor. Chicago: University of Chicago Press, 1998.

——. *Ritual: Perspectives and Dimensions*. Oxford: Oxford University Press, 1997.

Bell, Jeff, and Mike Marut. "Pop-up Memorial Honors COVID-19 Victims with Ribbons, Slideshow Outside Governor's Mansion." *KVUE*, May 9,

2020. https://www.kvue.com/article/news/health/coronavirus/austin-pop-up-covid-memorial-governors-mansion-ribbons/269-ed88s1e9-4446-42aa-aaf2-673fea37e5ec.

Bellah, Robert. *Religion in Human Evolution: From the Paleolithic to the Axial Age*. Cambridge, MA: Harvard University Press, 2011.

Bellah, Robert, Richard Madsen, William Sullivan, Ann Swidler, and Steven M. Tipton. *Habits of the Heart: Individualism and Commitment in American Life*. Berkeley: University of California Press, 1985.

Blevins, John B., et al. "Faith and Global Health Practice in Ebola and HIV Emergencies." *American Journal of Public Health* 109, no. 3 (2019): 379–84.

Bowler, Kate. "Death, the Prosperity Gospel and Me." *New York Times*, February 13, 2016. https://www.nytimes.com/2016/02/14/opinion/sunday/death-the-prosperity-gospel-and-me.html.

Braun, Erik. *The Birth of Insight: Meditation, Modern Buddhism, and the Burmese Monk Ledi Sayadaw*. Chicago: University of Chicago Press, 2016.

Brown, Jeremy. *The Eleventh Plague: Jews and Pandemics from the Bible to COVID-19*. Oxford: Oxford University Press, 2022.

Brown, Karen McCarthy. *Mama Lola: A Vodou Priestess in Brooklyn*. Berkeley: University of California Press, 2001.

Campbell, Heidi. "Understanding the Relationship Between Religion Online and Offline in a Networked Society." *Journal of the American Academy of Religion* 80, no. 1 (2012): 64–93.

Centers for Disease Control and Prevention (CDC). "COVID Data Tracker," February 21, 2023. https://www.cdc.gov/coronavirus/2019-ncov/covid-data/covidview/index.html.

Chaves, Mark. "Family Structure and Protestant Church Attendance: The Sociological Basis of Cohort and Age Effects." *Journal for the Scientific Study of Religion* 30, no. 4 (1991): 501–14.

Dawdy, Shannon Lee. *American Afterlives: Reinventing Death in the 21st Century*. Princeton, NJ: Princeton University Press, 2021.

Delehanty, Casey, and Erin Kearns. "Wait, There's Torture in *Zootopia*? Examining the Prevalence of Torture in Popular Movies." *Perspectives on Politics* 18, no. 3 (2020): 838–50.

Djaharuddin, Irawaty, et al. "Comorbidities and Mortality in COVID-19 Patients." *Gaceta Sanitaria* 35, no. 2 (2021): S530–S532.

Djupe, Paul A., and Ryan P. Burge. "The Prosperity Gospel of Coronavirus Response." *Politics and Religion* 14, no. 3 (2021): 552–73.

Doniger, Wendy. *The Implied Spider: Politics and Theology in Myth*. New York: Columbia University Press, 1999.

Downie, Alison. "Christian Shame and Religious Trauma." *Religions* 13, no. 925 (2022). Special Issue editor, Dyron B. Daughrity.

Durkheim, Émile. *The Elementary Forms of Religious Life*. Translated by Karen Fields. New York: Free Press, [1912] 1995.

Eliade, Mircea. *Myth and Reality*. New York: Harper & Row, 1963.

Feltmate, David. "Rethinking New Religious Movements Beyond a Social Problems Paradigm." *Nova Religio* 20, no. 2 (2016): 82–96.

Findling, Mary, et. al. "COVID-19 Has Driven Racism and Violence Against Asian Americans: Perspectives from 12 National Polls." *Health Affairs Forefront*, April 12, 2022. https://www.healthaffairs.org/do/10.1377/forefront.20220411.655787/.

Fisher, Marc. "After Pearl Harbor and 9/11, Americans Came Together. Have We Lost That Capacity?" *Washington Post*, September 27, 2021. https://www.washingtonpost.com/politics/after-pearl-harbor-and-911-americans-came-together-have-we-lost-that-capacity/2021/09/26/1246b22e-1492-11ec-9589-31ac3173c2e5_story.html.

Fitzpatrick, Scott J., et al. "Religious Perspectives on Human Suffering: Implications for Medicine and Bioethics." *Journal of Religion and Health* 55 (2016): 159–73.

Foudray, Claudine. "Religious Trauma: What No One Tells You at Church." *Post-Mormon Coaching*, May 1, 2018. https://postmormoncoaching.com/blog/religious-trauma-at-church/.

Franklin, Jonathan. "More Than 600,000 White Flags on the National Mall Honor Lives Lost to COVID." *NPR*, September 17, 2021. https://www.npr.org/sections/coronavirus-live-updates/2021/09/17/1037011493/covid-national-mall-white-flags-art-exhibit-memorial-pandemic-dead.

Freud, Sigmund. "Obsessive Actions and Religious Practices." In *The Freud Reader*, ed. Peter Gay, 429–35. New York: Norton, [1907] 1995.

Friedman, Elisha. "How One 19th-Century Rabbi Responded to a Worldwide Cholera Epidemic." *My Jewish Learning*. https://www.myjewishlearning.com/article/how-one-19th-century-rabbi-responded-to-a-worldwide-cholera-epidemic/.

Friedman, Joseph. "Overdose-Related Cardiac Arrests Observed by Emergency Medical Services During the US COVID-19 Epidemic," *JAMA, Psychiatry* 78, no. 5 (2021): 562–64.

Gamble, Vanessa Northington. "'There Wasn't a Lot of Comfort in Those Days': African Americans, Public Health, and the 1918 Influenza Epidemic." *Public Health Reports* 125, no. 3 (2010): 114–22.

Gawthrop, Elisabeth. "The Color of Coronavirus: COVID-19 Deaths by Race and Ethnicity in the U.S." *APM Research Lab*, December 14, 2022. https://www.apmresearchlab.org/covid/deaths-by-race.

Guzman, Dulce Torres. "Immigrant Communities Suffer as Funeral Traditions Upended in Pandemic." *Tennessee Lookout*, October 22, 2020. https://tennesseelookout.com/2020/10/22/immigrant-communities-suffer-as-funeral-traditions-upended-in-pandemic/.

Haidery, Alineh. "FAQ: A Good Death for Muslims." *CBC*, May 17, 2011. https://www.cbc.ca/news/health/faq-a-good-death-for-muslims-1.1090815-.

Halevi, Leor. *Muhammad's Grave: Death Rites and the Making of Islamic Society.* New York: Columbia University Press, 2007.

Hauser, Christine. "How We Mourn Covid's Victims." *New York Times*, August 9, 2022. https://www.nytimes.com/2022/08/09/us/covid-deaths-memorials.html.

Hayword, David. "Deconstruction." *The Naked Pastor*. https://nakedpastor.com/pages/deconstruction.

———. "The Stages of Deconstruction." *YouTube*. https://www.youtube.com/watch?v=HJk9aKGP2tI&t=1s.

Henry, Andrew. "What Is Ritual?" *Religion for Breakfast*, July 5, 2016. https://www.youtube.com/watch?v=F_URgZfo1hU.

Hervieu-Léger, Danièle. *Religion as a Chain of Memory.* New Brunswick, NJ: Rutgers University Press, 2000.

James, William. *The Varieties of Religious Experience.* Oxford: Oxford University Press, [1902], 2012.

Johnson, Thomas. *Taliban Narratives: The Use and Power of Stories in the Afghanistan Conflict.* Oxford: Oxford University Press, 2018.

Jones, Jeffrey. "U.S. Church Membership Falls Below Majority for First Time." *Gallup*, March 29, 2021. https://news.gallup.com/poll/341963/church-membership-falls-below-majority-first-time.aspx.

———. "Belief in God in U.S. Dips to 81%, a New Low," *Gallup*, June 17, 2022. https://news.gallup.com/poll/393737/belief-god-dips-new-low.aspx.

"Judaism." *Dare to Doubt*, 2019. https://www.daretodoubt.org/judaism.

Kean, Leslie. *Surviving Death: A Journalist Investigates Evidence for an Afterlife*. New York: Crown Archetype. 2017.

Kluger, Jeffrey. "Accidental Poisonings Increased After President Trump's Disinfectant Comments." *Time*, May 12, 2020. https://time.com/5835244/accidental-poisonings-trump/.

Koenig, Harold. *In the Wake of Disaster: Religious Responses to Terrorism & Catastrophe*. Philadelphia: Templeton Press, 2006.

Kopfensteiner, Thomas R. "Death with Dignity: A Roman Catholic Perspective." *Linacre Quarterly* 63, no. 4 (1996): 64–75.

Laderman, Gary. *Rest in Peace: A Cultural History of Death and the Funeral Home in the Twentieth-Century America*. Oxford: Oxford University Press, 2003.

Lagerway, John, and Marc Kalinowski, eds. *Early Chinese Religion: Part One: Shang Through Han (1250 BC–220 AD)*. Amsterdam: Brill, 2008.

Laitninen, Arto. "Charles Taylor and Paul Ricoeur on Self-Interpretations and Narrative Identity." In *Narrative Research: Voices of Teachers and Philosophers*, ed. Rauno Huttunen, Hannu Heikkinen, and Leene Syrjälä, 57–71. Jyväskylä, Finland: SoPhi, 2002.

Lamm, Maurice. *The Jewish Way in Death and Mourning*. Middle Village, NY: Jonathan David Publishers, [1969] 2000.

Lamrani, Myriam. "The Ultimate Intimacy: Death and Mexico, an Anthropological Relation in Images." *American Ethnologist* 49, no. 2 (2022): 204–20.

Lan, Qing. "Does Ritual Exist? Defining and Classifying Ritual Based on Belief Theory." *Journal of Chinese Sociology* 5. no. 5 (2018). https://journalofchinesesociology.springeropen.com/articles/10.1186/s40711-018-0073-x.

Lang, Martin, et al. "Effects of Anxiety on Spontaneous Ritualized Behavior." *Current Biology* 25, no. 14 (2015): 1892–97.

Laycock, Joseph. *Speak of the Devil: How the Satanic Temple is Changing the Way We Talk About Religion*. Oxford: Oxford University Press, 2020.

Legare, Cristine, and André Souza. "Evaluating Ritual Efficacy: Evidence from the Supernatural." *Cognition* 124, no. 1 (2021): 1–15.

Lepore, Jill. "Historians Who Love Too Much: Reflections on Microhistory and Biography." *Journal of American History* 88, no. 1 (2001): 129–44.

Lincoln, E. Eric, and Lawrence Mamiya. *The Black Church in the African American Experience*. Durham, NC: Duke University Press, 1990.

MacNeil, Andie, et al. "Exploring the Use of Virtual Funerals During the COVID-19 Pandemic: A Scoping Review." *OMEGA—Journal of Death and Dying* (2021): 1–24.

Maison, Wallace. "Death and Destruction in Spinoza's *Ethics*." *Inquiry* 20, nos. 1–4 (1977): 403–17.

Malešević, Siniša. "Imagined Communities and Imaginary Plots: Nationalisms, Conspiracies, and Pandemics in the Longue Durée." *Nationalities Papers* 50 (2022): 45–60.

Malinowski, Bronislaw Malinowski. *Magic, Science, and Religion and Other Essays*. Long Grove, IL: Waveland Press, [1925] 1992.

Marx, Karl, and Friederich Engels. *On Religion*. Mineola, NY: Dover, [1955] 2008.

Masuzawa, Tomoko. *The Invention of World Religions*. Chicago: University of Chicago Press, 2005.

Matsumoto, Kazunori. "Psychological Trauma After the Great East Japan Earthquake." *Psychiatry Clinical Neurosciences* 70, no. 8 (2016): 318–31.

Mikles, Natasha L. "Three Spirit Mediums: A Case Study on Grief, Death, and Alternative Religious Traditions During the COVID-19 Pandemic." *Nova Religio: The Journal of Alternative and Emergent Religions* 27, no. 2 (2023): 86–100.

Ndugga, Nambi, et al. "Latest Data on COVID-19 Vaccinations by Race/Ethnicity." *KFF*, July 14, 2022. https://www.kff.org/coronavirus-covid-19/issue-brief/latest-data-on-covid-19-vaccinations-by-race-ethnicity/.

Nielsen, Laura Beth, et al. "'Ahead of the Lawmen': Law and Morality in Disney Animated Films, 1960–1998." *Law, Culture, and the Humanities* 13, no. 1 (2017): 104–22.

O'Brian, Keith. "Amid Horror, 2 Officers Commit Suicide." *Boston Globe*, September 5, 2005.

Ohnuma, Reiko. *Unfortunate Destiny; Animals in the Indian Buddhist Imagination*. Oxford: Oxford University Press, 2017.

Orsi, Robert. *Between Heaven and Earth: The Religious Worlds People Make and the Scholars Who Study Them.* Princeton, NJ: Princeton University Press, 2004.

———. "The Study of Religion on the Other Side of Disgust: Modern Catholic Sexuality Is a Dark and Troubled Landscape." *Harvard Divinity Bulletin,* Spring/Summer 2019. https://bulletin.hds.harvard.edu/the-study-of-religion-on-the-other-side-of-disgust/.

Palwasha A. "What Is Religious Trauma?" *The Pvblication,* August 9, 2021.

Panchuk, Michelle. "The Shattered Spiritual Self: A Philosophical Exploration of Religious Trauma." *Res Philosphica* 95 (2018): 505–30.

———. "What is Religious Trauma?" Center for Philosophy of Religion, University of Notre Dame. October 31, 2018.

Pershing, Linda, and Margaret R. Yocom. "The Yellow Ribboning of the USA: Contested Meanings in the Construction of a Political Symbol." *Western Folklore* 55, no. 1 (1996): 41–85.

Petru, Simona. "Identity and Fear—Burials in the Upper Palaeolithic." *Documenta Praehistorica* 45 (2018): 6–13.

Phillips, Howard. "Why Did It Happen? Religious and Lay Explanations of the Spanish Flu Epidemic of 1918 in South Africa." *Kronos* 12 (1987): 79–92.

Primiano, Leonard. "Vernacular Religion and the Search for Method in Religious Folklife." *Western Folklore* 54, no. 1 (1995): 37–56.

Prothero, Stephen. *God Is Not One: The Eight Rival Religions That Run the World.* New York: HarperOne, 2010.

———. *Religion Matters.* New York: Norton, 2020.

Proudfoot, Wayne. "William James on an Unseen Order." *Harvard Theological Review* 93, no. 1 (2000): 51–66.

Radcliffe-Brown, A. R. *The Andaman Islanders.* New York: Free Press, [1933] 1964.

Reinis, Austra. *Reforming the Art of Dying: The Ars Moriendi in the German Reformation (1519–1528).* New York: Routledge, 2007.

Ricoeur, Paul. "Narrative Identity." *Philosophy Today* 35, no. 1 (1991): 73–81.

Roman, Jackie. "First Permanent National Memorial for COVID-19 Victims Unveiled at N.J. Farm." *NJ Advance Media,* September 22, 2021. www.nj.com/coronavirus/2021/09/first-permanent-national-memorial-for-covid-19-victims-unveiled-at-nj-farm.html. This memorial eventually became a permanent installation.

Rook, Dennis W. "The Ritual Dimension of Consumer Behavior." *Journal of Consumer Research* 12 (1985): 251–64.

Ruth, Kibbie. "Risk of Abuse in Faith Communities." In *Child Maltreatment: A Clinical Guide and Reference*, ed. Angelo P. Giardino and Randell Alexander, 539–55. St. Louis, MO: G. W. Medical, 2005.

Schilbrack, Kevin. "What *Isn't* Religion?" *Journal of Religion* 93, no. 3 (2013): 291–318.

Schleiermacher, Friedrich. *On Religion: Speeches to Its Cultured Despisers*. Trans. John Oman. New York: Harper & Brothers, [1799] 1958.

Scott, John, and Gordon Marshall, eds. "Moral Communities." In *A Dictionary of Sociology, 3rd ed*. Oxford: Oxford University Press, 2009.

Scott, Mark S. M. *Pathways in Theodicy: An Introduction to the Problem of Evil*. Minneapolis: Fortress Press, 2015.

Seeman, Erik. *Death in the New World: Cross-Cultural Encounters, 1492–1800*. Philadelphia: University of Pennsylvania Press, 2010.

Seligman, Adam, et al. *Ritual and Its Consequences: An Essay on the Limits of Sincerity*. Oxford: Oxford University Press, 2008.

Singh, Kirpal. "When Does Waheguru (God) Answer Our Prayer?" *Gurmat Saachi Saacha Vichaar*, November 19, 2018. https://gurmatvichaar.home.blog/2018/11/19/27/.

Smith, Jonathan Z. "Religion, Religions, Religious." In *Critical Terms for Religious Studies*, ed. Mark C. Taylor, 269–84. Chicago: University of Chicago Press, 1998.

———. *To Take Place: Toward Theory in Ritual*. Chicago: University of Chicago Press, 1987.

Smyth, Nancy J., and Laura Greybur. "Trauma." *Oxford Bibliographies* (Oxford University Press) September 29, 2015. https://www.oxfordbibliographies.com/display/document/obo-9780195389678/obo-9780195389678-0229.xml.

Sosis, Richard, et al. "Psalms and Coping with Uncertainty: Religious Israeli Women's Responses to the 2006 Lebanon War." *American Anthropologist* 113, no. 1 (2011): 40–55.

Span, Paula. "For Older Americans, the Pandemic Is Not Over." *New York Times*, February 11, 2023. https://www.nytimes.com/2023/02/11/health/covid-pandemic-seniors.html.

Stone, Alyson M. "Thou Shalt Not: Treating Religious Trauma and Spiritual Harm with Combined Therapy." *Eastern Group Psychotherapy Society* 37 (2013): 323–37.

Stone, Jacqueline. *Right Thoughts at the Last Moment.* Honolulu: University of Hawai'i Press, 2013.

Sunstein, Cass. *#republic: Divided Democracy in the Age of Social Media.* Princeton, NJ: Princeton University Press, 2017.

Szijátó, István. "Four Arguments for Microhistory." *Rethinking History* 6, no. 2 (2002): 209–15.

Taves, Ann. *Religious Experience Reconsidered: A Building-Block Approach to the Study of Religion and Other Special Things.* Princeton, NJ: Princeton University Press, 2009.

Teiser, Stephen. *The Scripture on the Ten Kings and the Making of Purgatory in Medieval Chinese Buddhism.* Honolulu: University of Hawai'i Press, 1994.

Torrez, Marco. "Additional Names Added to Local COVID-19 Memorial." *KGET*, October 8, 2022. https://www.kget.com/health/coronavirus/additional-names-added-to-local-covid-19-memorial/.

Tsintjilonis, Dimitri. "Death and the Sacrifice of Signs: 'Measuring' the Dead in Tana Toraja." *Oceania* 71, no. 1 (2000): 1–17.

Tweed, Thomas. *Crossing and Dwelling: A Theory of Religion.* Cambridge, MA: Harvard University Press, 2008.

Vail, Kenneth E., III, et al. "Terror Management Theory and Religious Belief." In *Handbook of Terror Management Theory*, ed. Clay Routledge and Matthew Vess, 259–85. London: Elsevier, 2019.

Vidyarthi, Lalita P. *The Sacred Complex in Hindu Gaya.* New York: Asia Publishing House, 1961.

Walsh, Kiri, et al. "Spiritual Beliefs May Affect Outcome of Bereavement: Prospective Study." *British Medical Journal* 324, no. 7353 (2002): 1551.

Ward, Charlotte. "The Emergence of Conspirituality." *Journal of Contemporary Religion* 26, no. 1 (2011): 103–21.

Wessinger, Catherine. "Religious Responses to the Katrina Disaster in New Orleans and the American Gulf Coast." *Journal of Religious Studies (Japanese Association for Religious Studies)* 86-2, no. 373 (2012): 53–83.

White, Hayden. *Metahistory: The Historical Imagination in Nineteenth-Century Europe.* Baltimore, MD: Johns Hopkins University, 1973.

Wiesel, Elie. "Job: Our Contemporary." In *Messengers of God: Biblical Portraits and Legends*, trans. Marion Wiesel, 211–35. New York: Random House, 1976.

———. *The Trial of God: (as it was held on February 25, 1649, in Shamgorod)*. New York City: Schocken Books, 1995 [1979].

Winnell, Marlene. "Religious Trauma Syndrome: It's Time to Recognize It." *Cognitive Behavioral Therapy Today* 39, no. 2 (2011): 16–18.

World Health Organization. "14.9 Million Excess Deaths Associated with the COVID-19 Pandemic in 2020 and 2021," May 5, 2022. https://www.who.int/news/item/05-05-2022-14.9-million-excess-deaths-were-associated-with-the-covid-19-pandemic-in-2020-and-2021.

———. "WHO Coronavirus (COVID-19) Dashboard." February 21, 2023. https://covid19.who.int/.

Wuthnow, Robert. *The Restructuring of American Religion: Society and Faith Since World War II*. Princeton, NJ: Princeton University Press, 1988.

INDEX

3/11, 193
9/11, 23, 161, 193, 177

Abbott, Greg, 102, 169. *See also* Republican Party
ableism, 88–89
Aboriginal Tribes, 61–62, 78
Abraham (prophet), 129
addiction, 71, 141
Afghanistan, 106
African Americans, 75–76, 102, 126–27, 146. *See also* Black community
Albaense, Catherine, 12
Amanda (research informant), 29, 37, 51–52, 76–77, 88, 124, 135–36, 176, 178, 200
Amida Buddha, 7
Andre, Rich R. (research informant), 32–33, 36–37, 70–71, 81, 100, 162
anomic suicide, 104

Apache Indians, 29–30, 37, 77, 136. *See also* Amanda (research informant); Native Americans
Arla (research informant), 86–87, 94, 97, 102, 169, 171–72, 175
Ars Moriendi, 6
Asian Americans, 86–87, 215n44. *See also* racism
atheism, 109–111, 137
Atlanta, 87, 215n44
Austin, 43, 47, 66, 100,
Australia, 61–62

Bahá'í, 70, 129–130, 214n19. *See also* Giani, Ajit (research informant); Bahá'u'lláh
Bahá'u'lláh, 129–130
Baillio, Bruce (research informant), 72–74, 147–148
Baptists, 4, 35, 67, 75, 100–101, 115, 137, 147, 154. *See also* McElroy, Lou (research informant); Taylor, Craig (research informant)

Bellah, Robert, 138
Bianca (research informant), 91–92, 114–15, 155
Bible, 94, 131
Biden, Joseph, 163, 185
Black, Dr. (research informant), 109–10, 131, 165, 169, 175
Black community, 75–76, 147, 174
Black Death, 197
Blumofe, Neil (research informant), 32–33, 45–46, 75, 83–85, 128, 133
Braun, Erik, 59
Brazil, 162
Britain, 2, 55, 60
Brown, Karen McCarthy, 59
Brown, Robert McAfee, 179
Buddha, 27, 35, 118
Buddhism, 6–7, 11, 27, 34, 54, 60, 87, 117–19, 142, 160, 186. *See also* Amida Buddha; Buddha; Ji, Jue (research informant); karma
Burma, 60

California, 86, 92, 100, 118, 136
Camp, Scott van (research informant), 200
Campbell, Heidi, 98
Carla (research informant), 140, 145
Carmen (research informant), 40, 51–52, 55, 89, 120–21, 158, 163, 177, 193
Carpenter, John, 149
cemetery, 41–43
Centers for Disease Control (CDC), 3, 23, 89, 169

Chafetz, Mitzi (research informant), 23, 45, 164
chanting, 2, 34–35
Chevra Kadisha, 45
Chicago, 24, 48, 102, 111, 159
China, 54, 86, 87, 98, 170, 199. *See also* Wuhan
cholera, 132
Christianity, 4, 6, 141–42, 189; anger at Christian communities, 169–70, 172–75, 178; deconstruction, 173, 181; difficulties with virtual practice, 80–81, 84–85; loss of faith in, 135–37, 141–42, 184–86; moral communities, 63–64, 77–78; narratives in, 110–12, 116, 131; Prosperity Gospel, 191–92; sacraments in, 28–29, 81–82, 99; and spirit mediums, 138–39. *See also* Baptists; Bible; Episcopal Church; Evangelicals; Exodus, Book of; Genesis, Book of; Jesus of Nazareth; Job, Book of; John the Baptist; Last Rites; Lazarus; Leviticus, Book of; Mass; Old Testament; New Testament; Roman Catholic Church
Christian Right, 137, 169–70, 188, 205. *See also* Evangelicals
Christine (research informant), 49, 159
Church of Jesus Christ of Latter-Day Saints, 63, 72–74, 99, 116–17, 125–26, 147–48, 182. *See also* Baillio, Bruce (research

informant); Jennifer (research
informant); Mormon;
Neuberger, Greg (research
informant); Tveten, Jason
(research informant)
Civil War, U.S., 23, 126, 163
Clayville, Kristel (research
informant), 8, 48–49, 159, 164,
190, 191
community, virtual, 9, 101–3;
failure of, 79–85; invented ritual
and, 53–56; moral communities
and, 67–69; social media and,
93–98
comorbidities, 88
complicated grief, 157
Confucianism, 11, 199
conspiracy theory, 57, 145–48,
165, 192–93, 197. See also
QAnon
conspirituality, 146
Council of Trent, 100
COVID-19 Loss Support for
Family & Friends (Facebook
group), 15, 53–54, 94–98, 103,
139–40, 161, 200, 205
CPR, 135
cremation, 2, 23, 97
crisis actor, 92, 162. See also
conspiracy theory
cybercascades, 103
Czech Republic, 162

Dan (research informant), 39–41,
136–37, 172, 184–85
Dastur, Khursheed (research
informant), 69, 83

Davis, Richard (research
informant), 24, 39
Dawdy, Shannon Lee, 23
death doula, 4, 50, 52, 153, 205.
See also Heymann, Martha B.
(research informant)
Democratic Party, 171
Detroit, 50, 166
disability, 68, 196
Disciples of Christ, 190
Divino Niño, 51
doctors, 108, 131, 134, 149, 156, 159,
166–167, 201. See also Black,
Dr. (research informant);
Kravitz, Jack (research
informant); Kravitz, Larry
(research informant); medical
professionals; Tatum, Paul E.
(research informant)
Doniger, Wendy, 207
Downie, Alison, 181
Durkheim, Émile, 10, 61, 64–65,
68–69, 71, 78–79, 81, 85, 91, 104

ebola, 197
Eliade, Mircea, 105–6
Elijah, prophet, 129
embalming, 21–23
emplotment, 108, 115, 117, 119, 121,
134, 162. See also
phenomenological time
England, 162
Episcopal Church, 28, 66, 79,
98–99, 130–31, 170–71, 189.
See also Ryan, Kathryn (research
informant); Treadwell, Chuck
(research informant)

Evangelicals, 40, 63, 78, 137, 167, 169–70, 172–73, 192, 205. *See also* Arla (research informant); Baptists
excess deaths, 3–4
Exodus, Book of, 116

Facebook, 133, 184–85, and funerary professionals, 39; and invented ritual, 53–56; and mourners, 94–98, 139; and polarization, 103; and religious professionals, 32–33; and research, 15, 198, 200, 204–5. *See also* community, virtual; COVID-19 Loss Support for Family & Friends (Facebook group); social media
FaceTime, 67
Feltmate, David, 73
Filipino Americans, 138, 156. *See also* Julia (research informant)
Florida, 40, 51, 120
Floyd, George, 102
France, 61
Freud, Sigmund, 17
Friedman, Elisha (rabbi), 132
funeral, 65, 180–181; and Hinduism, 1–3; and Islam, 42–44; and Judaism, 45–46; and liturgy of death, 7–8; as ritual, 19–23; and strengthening community ties, 65, 72; unsatisfying, 35–36, 39–45; virtual, 3, 24–25, 35–37, 39, 42, 80
funeral home, 21–22, 24–25, 33, 39, 42, 45

funerary professionals, 23–24, 39, 41, 204, 206. *See also* Chafetz, Mitzi (research informant); Davis, Richard (research informant); Neuhaus, Eric (research informant)

Geertz, Clifford, 203
Genesis, Book of, 109, 114
Georgia, 64, 141, 215n44
ghusl, 42–43
Giani, Ajit (research informant), 70, 129–30, 214n19
grief counselors, 4
Growling, The (bar), 1, 198
Gurpreet (research informant), 34, 142–43, 178
Guru Granth Sahib, 34

hadith, 7, 113, 129
Halacha, 84
Hayword, David, 173
Hebrew Bible, 127–28, 132, 195
Henry, Andrew Mark, 18, 25
hermeneutics of suspicion, 187. *See also* religion: academic study of
Hervieu-Léger, Danièle, 125
Heymann, Martha B. (research informant), 52–53, 153
Hinduism, 2–3, 38, 54, 142, 190
HIV/AIDS epidemic, 24, 165
hospice, 49–50, 156, 159, 163, 166, 201
hospital, 8, 21, 71, 154–56, 174, 190–91

Houston, 3, 23, 35, 69–70, 75–76, 83, 100, 115–16, 126, 137, 147, 154, 164
Hurricane Katrina, 104, 161, 193
hydrodynamic flows, 138. *See also* Tweed, Thomas

identity, religious, 10, 19, 107, 111–15, 144, 149, 205; rejecting, 134–37,
immigration, 2, 22, 37, 63–64, 70, 88
In America: We Remember (Firstenberg), 162
India, 38, 82, 87, 95, 106, 142
Indigenous, 21, 37, 61–62
Instagram, 15, 94, 127, 204. *See also* social media
intensive care unit (ICU), 48–49
interdependence, 117–18
intubation, 121, 154, 156, 161
Isaiah (prophet), 129
Islam, 7, 11, 113–14, 128–29; funerary traditions of, 42–45; good death in, 160; and moral integration, 74–75; and narrative, 113–14, 128–29; and religious trauma, 182. See also *ghusl*; hadith; Muhammad; Omara, Sheikh Attia (research informant); Quran; Ramadan; Sabila (research informant); *shari'a*
Israelites, 116, 139
Ivermectin, 57. *See also* Trump, Donald

James, William, 10, 179
Japan, 191, 193

Jennifer (research informant), 63, 72–74, 160, 176
Jesus of Nazareth, 102; as Muslim prophet, 129; narratives of, 94, 112, 189; presence of, 32, 82, 99; protection from COVID-19, 91, 174–175, 185; as radical, 172–173, 191.
Job, Book of, 195–196, 199
Job (prophet), 129
John the Baptist, 112
Judaism, 80–81, 151, 157; difficulties shifting to virtual, 83–85; and doctors, 109–10; and funerary practice, 45–46; and narrative, 127–29, 131–33; and prayer; and religious trauma, 182; and theodicy, 179–80. *See also* Blumofe, Neil (research informant); Chafetz, Mitzi (research informant); *Chevra Kadisha*; Halacha; Hebrew Bible; kiddush; *midrash*; *minyan*; *mitzvoth*; Passover; *pikuach nefesh*; Purim; Salanter, Israel (rabbi); *shomrim*; *shradda*; Talmud; Torah; Tikkun Olam; *yahrzeit*; Yom Kippur
Ji, Jue (research informant), 22, 2–29, 34, 87, 117–19
Julia (research informant), 41, 90, 123, 138, 156, 158, 161, 183

karma, 35, 118–19
Kay (research informant), 24–25, 33, 65, 111–12

kiddush, 133
Knights of Columbus, 80
Koenig, Harold, 193
Korea, 64
Korean Americans, 63. *See also* Yoon Tae (research informant)
Korean War, 127
Kravitz, Jack (research informant), 109, 110, 156, 158, 163–64
Kravitz, Larry (research informant), 109–10, 158, 168–69, 190
Kübler-Ross, Elisabeth, 173
Kuhlman, Chuck (research informant), 66, 99, 192

Laderman, Gary, 21
Laitinen, Arlo, 110
Lao Tzu, 129
Last Rites, 28, 67
Laycock, Joseph, x, 59
Lazarus, 112
LDS. *See* Church of Latter-day Saints
Lepore, Jill, 206
Leviticus, Book of, 139
Lithuania, 132
liturgy, 6, 18, 28
liturgy of death, 6–8
Longest Night Mass, 189

MacGyver, Angus, 120
Mama Lola, 59
Manpreet (research informant), 38, 87, 90, 97, 122–23, 134–35, 148, 183
Maria (research informant), 141

McElroy, Lou (research informant), 75–76, 100, 115–16, 126–27, 146–47, 154
martyrdom, 113
Martyrs of Memphis, 131
Mary (research informant), 47, 50, 92, 155–56, 169, 190
Mass, 6, 19, 32–33, 64, 66–67, 80–82, 99–100
medical professionals, 88, 201, 205–6; and anger at Trump, 168–69; care for families, 156, 159–60, 190–91; distrust in, 145, 148–49; and duty, 108–9; and invented ritual, 47–51; and stress, 92, 158, 175–76; as warriors, 163–67. *See also* nurses; doctors
Mexican Americans, 92, 114, 155
miasma theory, 21
midrash, 127–28
milagros, 115
minyan, 83
missionaries, 99, 116
mitzvoth, 45, 128, 132–33
moral community, 10, 104; and America, 85–89; and conversion, 63; definition of, 62; failure of, 78–81, 91–94, 100; and grief, 64–65, 81; intersection with other communities, 63, 77–78, 97; in virtual space, 66–69, 96–98. *See also* Durkheim, Émile; moral integration; social integration
moral integration, 65, 68–78

Mormons, 73. *See also* Church of Latter-day Saints
Moses, 109
Muhammad, 7, 43, 113, 128, 129

Native Americans, 88
Near Death Experiences, 144. See also *Surviving Death* (docuseries)
Nelson, Russell M., 148
networked community, 98
Neuberger, Greg (research informant), 125, 127
Neuhaus, Eric (research informant), 23
New England, 141
New Jersey, 2, 42, 134, 162
New Orleans, 104, 193
New Testament, 112
New York, 100, 118, 127
New York City, 38, 51, 80, 120, 140, 157
nurses, 9, 159–60, 164–66, 201; distrust in, 92–93, 148–49, 155–56; and duty, 108; and invented ritual, 49–50. *See also* Christine (research informant); Mary (research informant); medical professionals

offering, 11, 26–27, 54, 82–83, 115
Old Testament, 115, 195
Olivia (research informant), 91–92, 112, 154, 170, 174–75, 178–79, 185, 191–92
Omara, Sheikh Attia (research informant), 42–44, 74, 128–30

Orsi, Robert, 187–88, 199, 203

Panchuk, Michelle, 181
Passover, 84, 116
Paul (research informant), 80–81, 85, 97, 157
people of color, 87, 196
Persia, 82
Personal Protective Equipment, 23, 48, 159
Pflugerville, 24
phenomenological time, 108, 115–16, 119–20, 134, 144, 150. *See also* emplotment
phenomenology of disgust, 186–88, 199
phenomenology of humanness, 199–200, 204
pikuach nefesh, 133
post-traumatic stress disorder, 124
postmortem contact, 120–125, 135
prayer, 11, 83, 133; as comfort, 70, 130, 191; funerary, 4, 34, 44; unanswered, 135, 138–39, 156, 177–79, 183–85; virtual, 32–33, 47
Primiano, Leonard, 138. *See also* vernacular religion
Prosperity Gospel, 192
prostrations, 27
Prothero, Stephen, 105
psychedelic drugs, 138, 143
Puerto Rico, 24, 34, 64. *See also* Kay (research informant)
Purim, 179

QAnon, 192
Quran, 43, 113, 129

racism, 79, 86–87, 102, 215n44
Ramadan, 114
rebirth, 2
Reddit, 15, 94, 204–5. *See also* social media
religion: academic study of, 5, 10, 74, 78, 152, 182, 186, 198, 200–201; definition of, 10, 12
religious professionals, 4, 14, 85, 190, 204, 206; changing funerary rituals, 41, 43–46, 57; future of religious communities, 101–2; and narrative, 115–19, 125–30; and social integration, 66–69. *See also* Andre, Rich R. (research informant); Baillio, Bruce (research informant); Blumofe, Neil (research informant); Clayville, Kristel (research informant); Dastur, Khursheed (research informant); Ji, Jue (research informant); Kuhlman, Chuck (research informant); McElroy, Lou (research informant); Neuberger, Greg (research informant); Omara, Sheikh Attia (research informant); Ryan, Kathryn (research informant); Swami Nikhilanand (research informant); Taylor, Craig (research informant); Treadwell, Chuck (research informant)
religious trauma, definition of, 181–82. *See also* spiritual wounding

ren, 199
Republican Party, 102, 169–70, 188
Ricoeur, Paul, 106–8, 119, 134
ritual: definition of, 18, 20, 25, 26; invented, 9, 38, 46–55, 96
Roman Catholic Church, 51, 97; difficulty shifting to virtual practice, 80–82, 85, 99; and a good death, 160; inadequacy of, 138–39, 143–44, 183; and Latinix practice, 51, 114–15; and Mass, 32, 66, 80–82, 99; and a phenomenology of disgust, 186–87; sacraments in, 28–29, 81–82, 99. *See also* Andre, Rich R. (research informant); Julia (research informant); Kuhlman, Chuck (research informant); Mass; Paul (research informant); transubstantiation
Ruth, Kibbie, 185
Ryan, Kathryn (research informant), 66, 79, 99, 131, 170, 189

Sabila (research informant), 42, 53, 90, 95, 113–114, 123, 154, 161, 200
Salanter, Israel (rabbi), 132–133
San Antonio, 39, 72, 99, 116, 125, 147
Satan, 59, 179, 195
Satanic Temple, 59
Seligman, Adam, 26–27
shari'a, 43–44
Sheila-ism, 138
shomrim, 45–46
shradda, 54

Sikhism, 4, 34, 38, 87, 110, 134–135, 143, 178, 183, 142. *See also* Manpreet (research informant); Gurpreet (research informant); Guru Granth Sahib
Skype, 39
Smith, Jonathan Z., 30–31
social integration, 65–69
social media, 5, 15, 133, 157, 184, 198; and ableism, 89; and invented ritual, 53–56; and moral communities, 93–98, 161; and narratives of postmortem contact, 121–122; and social isolation, 89–90, 176; and spirit mediums, 139. *See also* Facebook; Instagram; Reddit; TikTok; YouTube
social problems paradigm, 73–74
Sofia (research informant), 143–144
South Africa, 100
Spanish flu, 127, 197
Spinoza, Baruch, 151
spirit mediums, 4, 77, 138–141, 145–146, 200, 205. *See also* Susan (research informant); Maria (research informant); Carla (research informant)
spiritual innovators, 137–145
spiritual wounding, definition of, 181–184. *See also* religious trauma,
spirituality, definition of, 11
Stone, Alyson, 181
suicide, 104, 141
Sunstein, Cass, 103
Super Bowl, 2021, 163

Surviving Death (docuseries), 121–122
Susan (research informant), 140, 145, 200
Swami Nikhilanand (research informant), 190
swine flu, 127
Szijártó, István, 206

tahara, 45
Taiwan, 87, 117
Talmud, 45, 128
Taoism, 11
Tatum, Paul E. (research informant), 159, 166, 168, 201
Taves, Ann, 18
Taylor, Charles, 106
Taylor, Craig (research informant), 35, 40, 67–68, 101, 137
Terror management theory, 151
Texas, 3, 162; African American community in, 75, 126–27, 147; distrust of government, 79, 171; and Greg Abbott, 169; Jewish community in, 75; Muslim community in, 42–43, 74–75; nurses in, 47, 49; racism in, 87; research in, 14, 204–5; social integration in, 66, 71–72; and Winter Storm Uri, 71–72; Zoroastrians in, 83. *See also* Austin; Houston; San Antonio
theodicy, 140, 179–80
Thing, The (1982 film), 149–50
Thomas (apostle), 189
Tikkum Olam, 110
TikTok, 15, 94. *See also* social media

Torah, 131
totem, 62–63
transubstantiation, 81–82, 99
trauma, definition, 152
Treadwell, Chuck (research informant), 28–29, 36–37, 98–99, 130, 131
Trump, Donald, 57, 102, 167–71, 186, 188
Tveten, Jason (research informant), 99, 116–17
Tweed, Thomas, 9, 138

vaccine, 57, 76, 84, 195–196; denial, 94, 107, 145–148, 196
vegetarianism, 118
ventilator, 3, 47, 50, 54–55, 88, 154, 163–164
vernacular religion, 138
Washington, D.C., 162
Wessinger, Catherine, 193
White, Hayden, 108
Wiesel, Elie, 179, 195–96
Winnell, Marlene, 181
Winter Storm Uri, 71

women's suffrage movement, 127
World Health Organization (WHO), 3, 23, 169
World War I, 127
World War II, 103, 127, 179, 195
Wuhan, 79, 145
Wuthnow, Robert, 103

yahrzeit, 54
yellow fever, 131
yellow heart, as COVID death symbol, 55–56
Yom Kippur, 132
Yoon Tae (research informant), 40, 63–64, 81, 95, 102, 141–43, 158, 176–77, 184
YouTube, 15, 18. *See also* social media

Zoom, 24–25, 35, 37, 39, 46, 66–67, 99, 102, 203
Zoroastrianism, 69, 82–83, 85. *See also* Dastur, Khursheed (research informant)

GPSR Authorized Representative: Easy Access System Europe, Mustamäe tee 50, 10621 Tallinn, Estonia, gpsr.requests@easproject.com

www.ingramcontent.com/pod-product-compliance
Lightning Source LLC
Chambersburg PA
CBHW031239290426
44109CB00012B/365